C000221472

# Victory on the Western Front

*For*

*Jenny, Jane, Richard, Simon and Edward*

# VICTORY ON THE WESTERN FRONT

## THE DEVELOPMENT OF THE BRITISH ARMY 1914-1918

MICHAEL SENIOR

Pen & Sword
MILITARY

First published in Great Britain in 2016 by
Pen & Sword Military
an imprint of
Pen & Sword Books Ltd
47 Church Street
Barnsley
South Yorkshire
S70 2AS

Copyright © Michael Senior 2016

ISBN 978 1 78340 065 2

The right of Michael Senior to be identified as the Author of this Work has been asserted by him in accordance with the Copyright, Designs and Patents Act 1988.

A CIP catalogue record for this book is available from the British Library

All rights reserved. No part of this book may be reproduced or transmitted in any form or by any means, electronic or mechanical including photocopying, recording or by any information storage and retrieval system, without permission from the Publisher in writing.

Typeset in Ehrhardt by
Mac Style Ltd, Bridlington, East Yorkshire
Printed and bound in the UK by CPI Group (UK) Ltd,
Croydon, CRO 4YY

Pen & Sword Books Ltd incorporates the imprints of Pen & Sword Archaeology, Atlas, Aviation, Battleground, Discovery, Family History, History, Maritime, Military, Naval, Politics, Railways, Select, Transport, True Crime, and Fiction, Frontline Books, Leo Cooper, Praetorian Press, Seaforth Publishing and Wharncliffe.

For a complete list of Pen & Sword titles please contact
PEN & SWORD BOOKS LIMITED
47 Church Street, Barnsley, South Yorkshire, S70 2AS, England
E-mail: enquiries@pen-and-sword.co.uk
Website: www.pen-and-sword.co.uk

# Contents

# List of Maps

# List of Plates



Photographs courtesy of the Taylor Library.

WAR PLANS 1914
Dover
Ostend
Antwerp
Calais
Ypres
BELGIUM
Brussels
FIRST
Aachen
Mons
Liège
SECOND
Arras
Namur
Maubeuge
B.E.F.
Rhine
Somme
THIRD
le Cateau
Amiens
5th
LUX.
FOURTH
Sedan
Trier
Oise
Aisne
4th
FIFTH
3rd
SIXTH
Marne
Verdun
Paris
Metz
SEVENTH
FRANCE
Nancy
2nd
Seine
Meuse
Strasbourg
1st
ALSACE GROUP
Alsace Group 1st Army

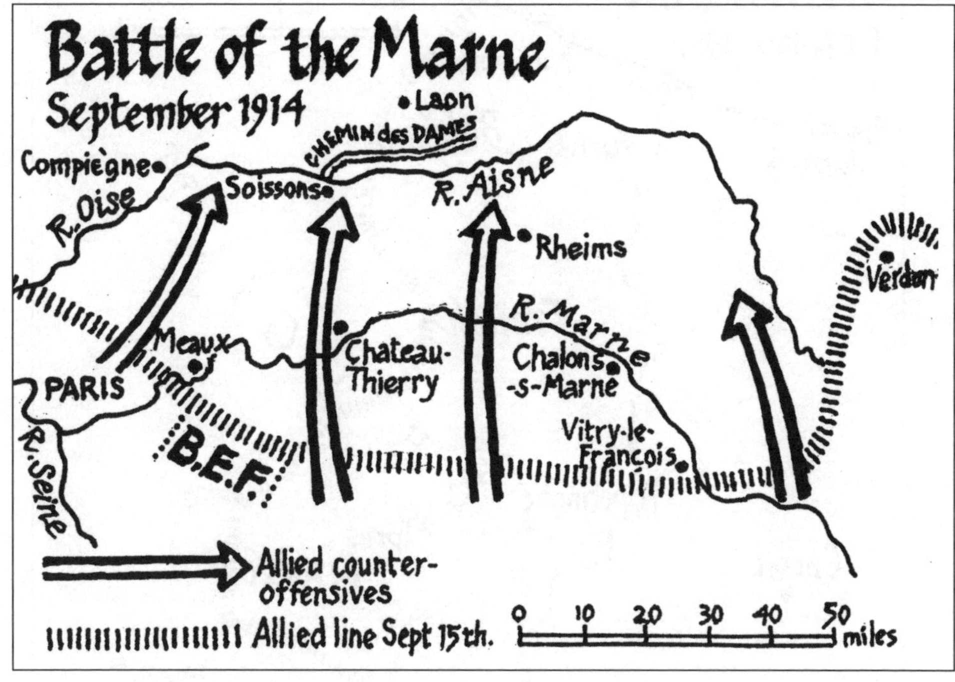
Battle of the Marne
September 1914
Laon
CHEMIN des DAMES
Compiègne
R. Oise
Soissons
R. Aisne
Rheims
Verdun
R. Marne
Meaux
Chateau-Thierry
Chalons-s-Marne
PARIS
R. Seine
B.E.F.
Vitry-le-François
Allied counter-offensives
Allied line Sept 15th.
0 10 20 30 40 50 miles

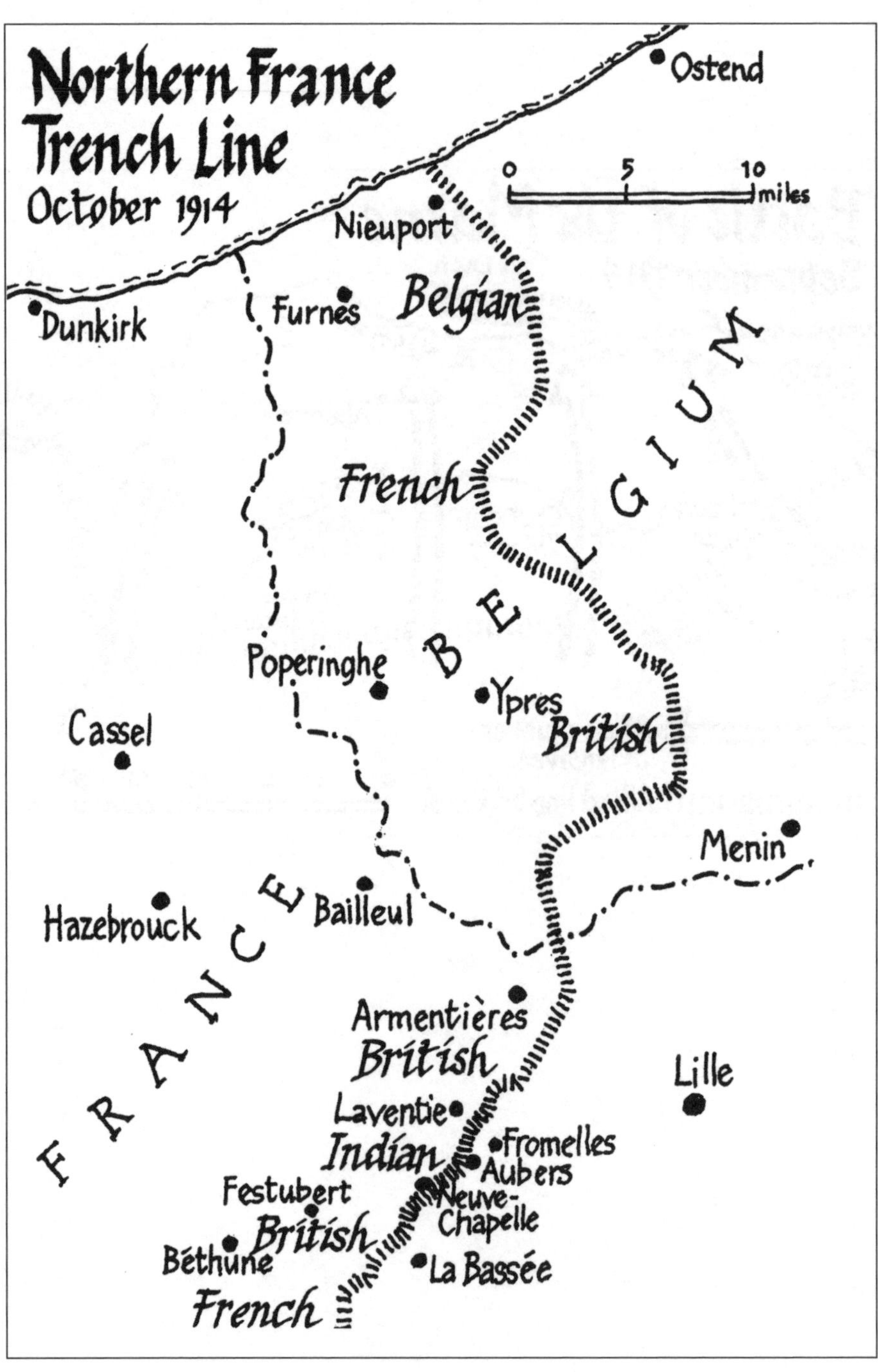
Northern France
Trench Line
October 1914
Ostend
0
5
10
miles
Nieuport
Dunkirk
Furnes
Belgian
BELGIUM
French
Poperinghe
Ypres
British
Cassel
Menin
Hazebrouck
Bailleul
FRANCE
Armentières
British
Lille
Laventie
Indian
Fromelles
Aubers
Festubert
Neuve-
Chapelle
British
Béthune
La Bassée
French

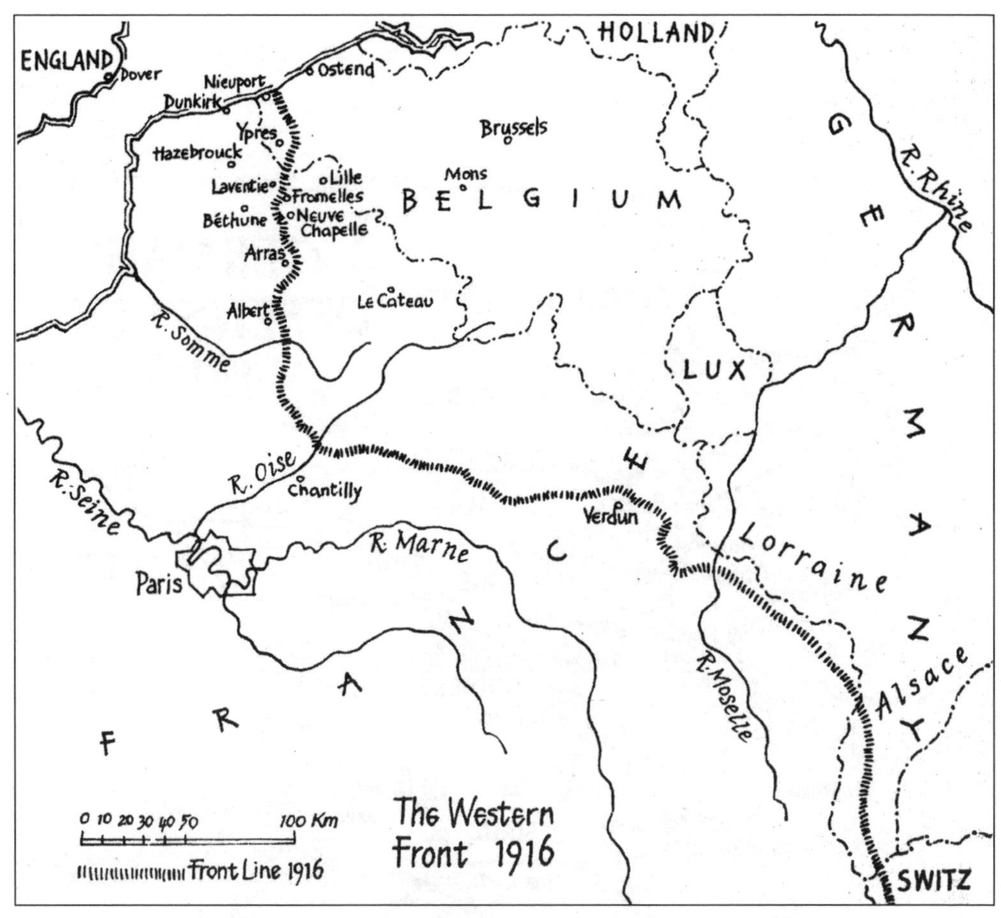

The Western Front 1916

GERMAN OFFENSIVES 1918
Zeebrugge
Ostend
Calais
Ghent
Lys
GEORGE II
4th Army
Ypres
Passchendaele
Boulogne
Hazebrouck
GEORGE I
Brussels
Armentières
Messines
Montreuil
GEORGETTE
Lille
Liège
1st Army
la Bassée
Mons
Namur
Meuse
Lens
Douai
BELGIUM
Vimy
MARS/
VALKYRIE
Sambre
Arras
Doullens
Cambrai
Maubeuge
Somme
3rd Army
Bapaume
MICHAEL III
le Cateau
Amiens
Albert
MICHAEL II
Villers-Bretonneux
Péronne
MICHAEL I
St Quentin
FRANCE
Ham
5th Army
Montdidier
Laon
BLÜCHER
Mézières
Sedan
GNEISENAU
Compiègne
REIMS-
MARNESCHUTZ
Soissons
Aisne
Longwy
Oise
Rheims
Vesle
Verdun
Château Thierry
Seine
Meaux
Marne
Paris
St. Mihiel

Battle of the Lys
April 1918
Ypres
Poperinghe
APRIL 30
APRIL 16
BRITISH
SECOND ARMY
GERMAN
FOURTH
ARMY
19
DIV
Mt. Kemmel
R. Lys
Hazebrouck
Bailleul
APRIL 16
APRIL 12
25
DIV
APRIL 8
Armentières
34
DIV
APRIL 9 NIGHT
40
DIV
Merville
Estaires
Lille
R. Lys
2 Port
DIV
GERMAN
SIXTH ARMY
Lestrem
La
Couture
Neuve
Chapelle
Richebourg
0
5
miles
55
DIV
Locon
Béthune
Festubert
La Bassée
Givenchy
La Bassée Canal

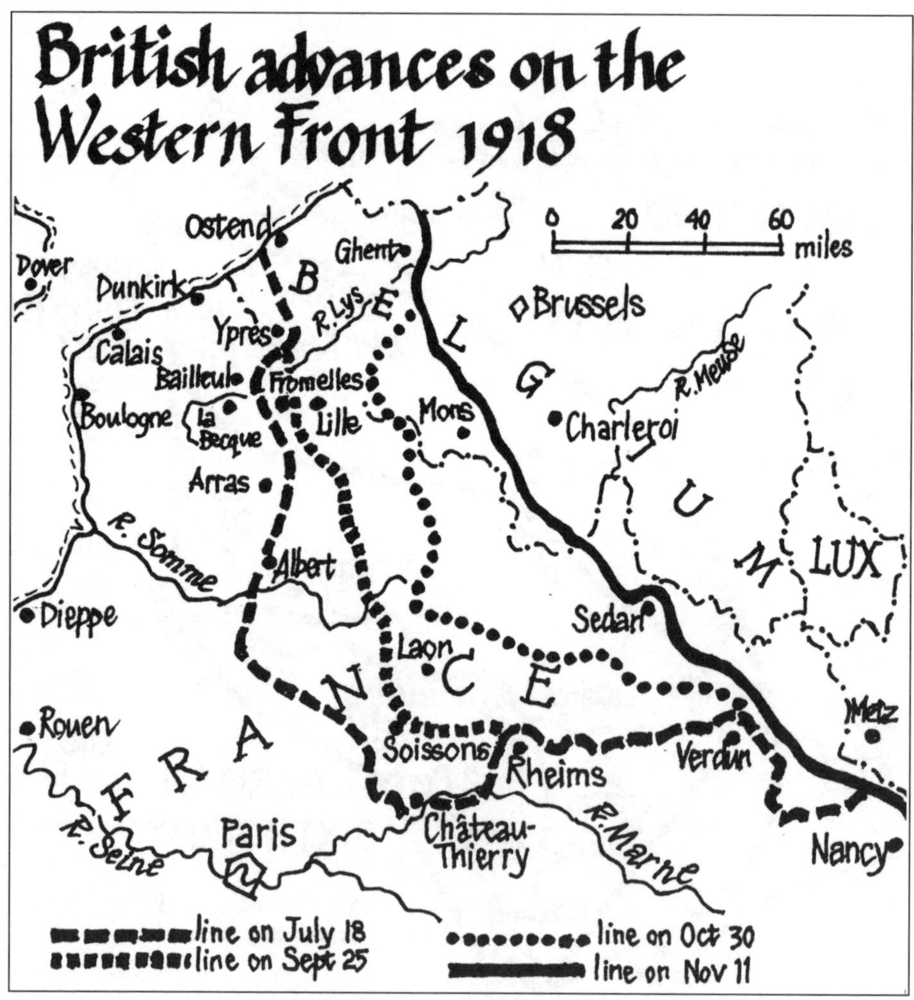
British advances on the Western Front 1918
0
20
40
60
miles
Ostend
Ghent
Dover
Dunkirk
B
E
L
G
I
U
M
Brussels
Calais
Yprès
R. Lys
Bailleul
Fromelles
Boulogne
La Becque
Lille
Mons
Charleroi
R. Meuse
Arras
R. Somme
Albert
LUX
Dieppe
Sedan
Laon
F
R
A
N
C
E
Metz
Rouen
Soissons
Rheims
Verdun
Paris
Château-Thierry
R. Seine
R. Marne
Nancy
line on July 18
line on Sept 25
line on Oct 30
line on Nov 11

# Acknowledgements

The chapter endnotes and the Bibliography in this book indicate quite clearly the huge debt I owe to the many writers who have specialised in the First World War and who, over several decades, have stimulated my interest in this complex subject. Throughout the book I have quoted from and made references to numerous monographs and articles and I have endeavoured to make the appropriate acknowledgements. My sincere thanks go to all the authors concerned.

In addition I would like to thank the staff of The National Archives, the Imperial War Museum, the Hendon Air Museum and the Western Front Association for their courteous and efficient support. I have also received considerable help from Professor Ian Beckett, Chris Carleton-Smith, Tim Halstead, Francis Hanford, Dr Emily Mayhew, John Newton, Jane Perkin, Professor Andrew Rice, Air Marshal Sir Michael Simmons, Jim Spence and Geoff Spring. I would particularly like to thank my wife, Jenny, who has contributed in so many ways to this book.

It has been a pleasure to work with my editors Rupert Harding and Matilda Richards and also with other members of the Pen & Sword Books Ltd team – Lisa Hooson, Dave Hemingway, Jon Wilkinson and Roni Wilkinson. I am grateful to them for their encouragement and practical advice.

Any errors that might be found in this book are entirely mine and I offer my apologies in advance.

# Abbreviations

| | |
|---|---|
| AEF | American Expeditionary Force |
| ANZAC | Australia New Zealand Army Corps |
| BE | Bleriot Experimental |
| BEF | British Expeditionary Force |
| BOH | British Official History |
| CFS | Central Flying School |
| C-in-C | Commander-in-Chief |
| CIGS | Chief of the Imperial General Staff |
| CO | Commanding Officer |
| CWC | Clyde Workers Committee |
| DH | De Havilland |
| DMO | Director of Military Operations |
| DMT | Director of Military Training |
| DSD | Director of Staff Duties |
| DSO | Distinguished Service Cross |
| FE | Farman Experimental |
| FM | Field Marshal |
| GHQ | General Headquarters |
| GPO | General Post Office |
| GSO | General Staff Officer |
| HE | High Explosives |
| HM | His Majesty |
| HQ | Headquarters |
| IWM | Imperial War Museum |
| LI | Light Infantry |
| MC | Military Cross |
| MGRA | Major General Royal Artillery |
| NCO | Non-Commissioned Officer |

| | |
|---|---|
| OHL | Oberste Heeresleitung |
| OTC | Officer Training Corps |
| PM | Prime Minister |
| psc | passed Staff College |
| RAF | Royal Air Force |
| RAMC | Royal Army Medical Corps |
| RE | Reconnaissance Experimental |
| RFA | Royal Field Artillery |
| RFC | Royal Flying Corps |
| RNAS | Royal Naval Air Service |
| RQMS | Regimental Quarter Master Sergeant |
| SE | Santos or Scouting Experimental |
| SS | Stationery Stores (War Office) |
| SWB | South Wales Borderers |
| TF | Territorial Force |
| TNA | The National Archives |
| TNT | Trinitrotoluene |
| VC | Victoria Cross |

# Introduction

On 8 April 1919 the *London Gazette* carried Field Marshal Sir Douglas Haig's final despatch which summarized his views on the course of the war on the Western Front. Early in this document Haig commented on the state of the British army in August 1914:

> we were unprepared for war, or at any rate, for a war of such magnitude. We were deficient in both trained men and military material, and, what was more important, had no machinery ready by which either men or material could be produced in anything approaching the requisite quantities.

Towards the end of the despatch Haig wrote:

> To have built up successfully in the very midst of war a great new army on a more than continental scale, capable of beating the best troops of the strongest military nation of pre-war days, is an achievement of which the whole Empire may be proud.

While much of Haig's final despatch can be read as a *post hoc* justification of his own command, neither his contemporaries nor historians have disagreed with the substance of these two statements. The development of the British Expeditionary Force (BEF) from the original 125,000 relatively ill-equipped men who crossed the Channel in 1914 to the army of 1.8 million with an abundance of armaments in 1918 is one of the remarkable phenomena of the First World War. It is equally remarkable that the BEF, a small appendage to the massive French army in 1914, became a war-winning force that, during the last three months of 1918, was able to make a singular contribution to the defeat of the German army on the Western Front. The BEF had clearly undergone a massive transformation.

This book is about that transformation. It is concerned not only with the growth of the BEF in terms of manpower and equipment, but also with its technical and tactical development. The main theme is change – the changes that occurred and the underlying factors that caused them to take place. These developments are discussed in relation to various important issues of the war and to the role of the BEF on the Western Front.

Not least among these issues is the contribution of the commanders of the BEF – the generals. BEF generals have long been the subject of controversy and even demonization. They have been described as donkeys, boneheads, butchers and bunglers.[1] Criticism of the way in which they fought the war on the Western Front has been relentless. It began in earnest towards the end of the 1920s and into the 1930s when both Lloyd George and Winston Churchill published their memoirs roundly condemning the conduct of the war. In 1927 Churchill criticized the BEF attritional offensives on the Somme (1916) and at Passchendaele (1917) and was particularly scathing about the large casualty lists: 'What is the sense in attacking only to be defeated: or of "wearing down the enemy" by being worn down more than twice as fast oneself?'.[2] This criticism of the BEF senior commanders has continued to the present day. In August 1983, for example, a contributor to the Western Front Association publication *Stand To!* expressed his opinion of BEF commanders with some feeling: 'inefficient, incapable, inconsiderate, callous gang of morons called Generals'.[3] An article in the *Daily Telegraph* of 29 July 2009 complained of the 'terrible and futile sacrifice' of the war and of the 'incompetent generalship'. Of all the BEF generals, the one that has attracted most negative comment and, indeed, outright hatred, has been Sir Douglas Haig who commanded the BEF from December 1915 until the Armistice in November 1918. In 1936 Lloyd George wrote of Haig: 'He did not possess the necessary breadth of vision or imagination to plan a great campaign against some of the ablest Generals in the War. I never met any man in a high position who seemed to me so utterly devoid of imagination'.[4] Such has been the venom directed against Haig that a campaign was launched in November 1998, eighty years after the end of the war, for his statue in Whitehall to be removed. The work of 'revisionist' historians to give a more balanced account of the war in the West has done little to adjust the jaundiced views of much of the British public. The distorted but powerful impression of BEF generals as portrayed in *Oh! What a Lovely War* and *Black Adder Goes Forth* has had more influence on public opinion than the efforts of academia.

The changing requirements of the BEF in terms of weaponry, manpower and strategy meant that the working relationship between the generals and the politicians was frequently placed under considerable strain and this resulted in a number of contentious issues. In 1914 Lord Kitchener, as Secretary of State for War, snubbed the Territorial Force by rejecting their framework as the basis for the development of the New Armies. In 1915 Field Marshal French initiated the shell shortage 'scandal' and pointed the finger of blame in the direction of Kitchener and the War Office. In 1918, the animosity and mutual mistrust between Haig and Lloyd George was particularly evident in the controversies surrounding casualty figures and the allocation of manpower. At the most critical point of the war, spring 1918, Lloyd George, not for the first time, agreed to subordinate Haig and the British army to a French commander-in-chief and at the same time engineered the removal of a number of Haig's trusted advisors.

One of the most important issues of the war was also the cause of a further serious disagreement between the generals and the politicians: whether the Western Front should dominate British strategy or whether, since the Western Front had by 1915 become a trench-bound stalemate, manpower and armaments should be diverted elsewhere to defeat the Germans. The generals – Field Marshal French, Haig and the French commanders, Joffre and Foch – were convinced, along with other 'Westerners', that the war could only be won where the bulk of the German army was positioned, i.e. in France and Belgium. The 'Easteners', led by Churchill and Lloyd George, held that defeating Germany's Allies through aggressive action in, for example, Turkey, Mesopotamia and Salonica, would end the deadlock and bring victory. This debate, which continued for the greater part of the war, had a direct effect on the operating strength of the BEF in France and Belgium. The following chapters discuss the contributions of both the generals and the politicians to the war effort: how they dealt with the many challenges that confronted them and how they managed the changes that were required.

The success of the BEF on the Western Front rested largely on the development of the infantry and the artillery. The tactics and technology employed by these two arms in autumn 1918 were substantially different in both character and effect from those used in the early years of the war. They altered the way in which battles were fought and the nature of the BEF offensives in the final stages of the war. The two War Office publications SS 109 (*Divisions for Offensive Action*, May 1916) and SS 135 (*The Division in Attack*, November 1918) illustrate the changes in operational thinking. The first was concerned primarily with infantry matters while the second emphasized that infantry 'must be practised in cooperation with the artillery, trench mortars, tanks, machine guns and contact patrol aeroplanes'. After years of stultifying trench warfare, the 'all-arms' approach, which had been anticipated in the 1914 *Field Service Regulations*, was actively followed by the BEF during the summer and autumn of 1918.

While in an historical context the development of the infantry and the artillery, the pillars of the British army for generations, can be regarded as evolutionary, the contribution of new weapons added a different dimension to the performance of the BEF. The tank and the aeroplane were used for the first time in the 1914–1918 war, as was poisonous gas. It is interesting that gas, which was used widely in the First World War, was hardly used at all in the Second World War, largely because forms of protection had become more effective. It was the tank and the aeroplane that became, at least by 1918, significant BEF weapons. Churchill described the tank as 'a military fact of the first order'[5] and considered it a war-winning weapon. The aeroplane was described by Lloyd George as 'one of the essentials of victory'.[6] Just how these two new weapons originated and how they were developed and used on the Western Front and whether their performance justified the accolades of Churchill and Lloyd George are important factors in the evolution of the BEF. Their use also throws considerable light on the attitudes of BEF commanders towards technological development.

A further issue is the timing of the BEF's improved operating performance during the war. There was certainly a great difference between the failures of the BEF in 1915 and its overwhelming successes of the second half of 1918.

Much has been written about the 'learning curve' of the BEF. This concept has been used to describe the changes that came to fruition during the last year of the war and which resulted in the victories of August-November 1918 – a period commonly referred to as the Hundred Days.[7] Generally the proponents of the 'learning curve' have identified the Battle of the Somme in 1916 as the starting point for new and superior developments in tactics and technology. These developments have been described in various ways: 'the really decisive moment in infantry-artillery cooperation appears to have come at some point during the Somme battle itself';[8] 'The British army had by July 1918 tamed the new technology and worked out effective ways of harnessing it';[9] and, similarly, 'In the Hundred Days [the BEF] would finally and decisively appear in its full stature and sweep all before it'.[10] It is convenient to take the early days of the Somme, with the lack of territorial gain and the vast number of casualties, as the low starting point of a 'learning curve' and, two years later, the Hundred Days as the eventual successful high point. Not all historians agree with this version of BEF success.[11] As will be argued in the following pages, the learning experience of the BEF was a far more complex process than has been generally recognized.

Of course, none of the developments that took place in the BEF during the four years of the war occurred in isolation. They were the outcome of the necessities of war where the aims of survival and victory were paramount. The British, the French and the Germans each had their own particular learning experience and any advance in technology or tactics, by either side, had to be countered with as little delay as possible to avoid adverse consequences. Examples of how the opposing armies dealt with various threatening initiatives will be described in the relevant chapters.

The critical need for increased quantities of equipment, guns and munitions at the front meant that the civilian populations of the belligerent countries, working in factories, offices and laboratories, became an essential part of the total war effort. The way that Britain organized and controlled its home front was a crucial factor in achieving the successes of 1918.

That the British and French were able to turn near defeat into victory in 1918 was a considerable achievement. A number of powerful reasons have been put forward as to why Germany surrendered in November 1918. These include the new-found cohesion of the BEF; the unified command of the

Allies under General Foch; the entry of the United States into the war in 1917; the effects of the blockade by the Royal Navy; and the failed strategy of the German army in the first half of 1918. These and other reasons have been the subject of much debate, particularly their relative importance, and they will be discussed in the conclusion to this book.

That the BEF developed into a formidable and victorious fighting force on the Western Front is a tribute not only to the work of the generals and the politicians, but also to the courage and dedication of ordinary service personnel and members of the civilian population. The narrative and discussion that follows will show that their combined contribution was not without tragedy, disappointment, failure and serious disagreement, but they will also show that the eventual successful outcome was a triumph of continuous experimentation, innovation, improvization and tenacity.

*Chapter 1*

# The Development of the British Expeditionary Force

*'amateurs and professionals, they are all very much alike'*

*Mr Punch*[1]

The development of the British Expeditionary Force (BEF) between 1914 and 1918 was extraordinary. Its growth was rapid and largely unplanned and its composition and character evolved piecemeal through the course of the war. Altogether, it was an outstanding, and eventually successful, masterpiece of improvization.

Compared with the armies of the major powers in Europe, the BEF in 1914 was insignificant. Germany, with a population of 60 million, had a conscript army with a peacetime strength of some 800,000. All able-bodied men aged 20–22 underwent two years of military service and for the following sixteen years were liable for re-call as Reservists. When mobilization was ordered, Germany could call on 4.3 million trained soldiers. France also had a conscript army, but it was drawn from a smaller population (38 million) than that of Germany. In order to match Germany's military strength, France, in 1911, extended its period of military service from two to three years with a further period of twenty-four years in Reserve. As a result, France's peacetime army numbered 670,000 and, at mobilization, the size of its army was similar to that of Germany.[2]

Britain, on the other hand, had an army that was entirely voluntary and was developed for colonial rather than continental service. It was made up of Regulars who served for seven years with the colours and then a further five years in Reserve.[3] One such Reservist was Private Bernard Smith who joined the 2nd Battalion of the Leicester Regiment in 1905. After six years in India Private Smith returned to England and completed his time with the colours. He then worked in the local GPO. In 1914, as a Reservist, he was re-called to the 1st Battalion of the Leicesters and went with them to the Western Front.[4]

In 1914 half the army was stationed abroad – spread around the British Empire with the great majority based in India. In addition, there were two other military groups which had been formed in 1908 by the then Secretary of State for War, Richard Haldane. The first group was the Special Reserve made up of the disbanded County Militia and the second group, formed from the old Volunteers and Yeomanry (cavalry), was the Territorial Force. The role of the Special Reserve was to reenforce the Regular units in a time of war, whereas the Territorials were primarily established for home defence. These changes were not without considerable opposition. The Militia, the Volunteers and the Yeomanry were all firmly embedded in county life and in some cases had been since medieval times. Haldane, however, considered them ill-prepared for modern war – their performance in the Boer War had been generally unspectacular – and with great political courage he persisted with his programme of reforms.

In 1914 the strengths of the three military forces were: Regulars – 247,400; Reserves – 224,200; and Territorials – 268,800. The total British military force, home and abroad, therefore numbered around 740,400 – about one-sixth the size of either the German or French armies. Since the Territorials and many Reservists required a period of training before being sent abroad, only 125,000 home-based Regulars and Reservists were immediately available for active service in France. They constituted the original BEF. Comparatively speaking, it was a pitifully small force – even 'gallant little Belgium', invaded by Germany on 3 August 1914, possessed an army of some 117,000.

The foundation of the British army was its regimental structure. It provided both a mechanism for recruitment and a military tradition. In 1881 Edward Cardwell, Gladstone's Secretary of State for War, had abolished the then existing regiments of foot and, instead, linked regiments with the regions and counties of Britain. Hence, for example, the 43rd and 52nd Regiments of Foot were amalgamated to become the Oxfordshire and Buckinghamshire Light Infantry. Similarly, the 37th and 67th Regiments of Foot became the Hampshire Regiment. In 1914 a regiment was made up of two battalions each having a nominal strength of around 1,000 men. One battalion was stationed at the home depot and was responsible for recruitment and training and for maintaining the strength of the second battalion which was serving abroad.

This system had a number of important advantages. Strong links were developed with county and regional communities and this local identity aided recruitment. The regimental structure was such that it could be expanded as required simply by forming additional battalions. In addition, the links with the regiments of foot provided a ready-made military tradition. When Lieutenant Colonel Eric Stephenson of the 3rd Battalion the Middlesex Regiment was killed at Ypres on 23 April 1915 his dying words exhorted his fellow soldiers to 'Die hard, boys, die hard'. These words were not only the motto of the regiment, they echoed the words of William Inglis of the 57th Foot, a precursor of the Middlesex Regiment, at Albuhera in 1811.[5]

If the regiment was the 'home' of the serving soldier, the division was his main fighting unit. Regimental battalions generally did not serve together but were spread across divisions. Each division was made up of three infantry brigades each with four battalions. Apart from infantry battalions, a division also included artillery, engineers, medical personnel, military police and veterinary and postal services. It was a complete fighting unit of around 20,000 men. Divisions were grouped together to form corps and one or more corps constituted an army. The cavalry was made up of two main sections – the household cavalry and the cavalry of the line – and they totalled thirty-one regiments each of about 500 men. The artillery element of the BEF consisted of five Royal Horse Artillery 13-pounder batteries with the cavalry, and each infantry division had four Royal Field Artillery brigades of 18-pounders and 4.5-inch howitzers, and one Royal Garrison Artillery heavy battery of 60-pounders.[6] When war was declared on 4 August 1914 six infantry divisions and one cavalry brigade (about 125,000 men) were available for action. However, two divisions of this small force were retained in Britain because of the fear of invasion.

* * *

At the beginning of August 1914 it was by no means certain that Britain would go to war. The Liberal Prime Minister, Herbert Asquith, was having problems within his own party, many of whom wanted Britain to remain neutral, and the Cabinet was split. Peace rallies were taking place in London. On 31 July the French Ambassador, Paul Cambon, asked the British Foreign Secretary, Sir Edward Grey, if Britain would enter the war. Grey gave a non-committal answer, pointing out that Britain had no formal commitment to France. Even on 1 August King George V noted in his diary that it was unlikely that Britain would send an expeditionary force to the continent. But Germany's declaration of war on France on 3 August convinced the British Cabinet that war was inevitable and that Britain would have to take part. Germany possessed the largest army in Europe and the second largest fleet. If Germany defeated France then Britain's economic interests and political status would be at risk not only in Europe, but around the world. Now that war was a certainty, Britain and France needed to act together if Germany's military strength was to be defeated. Britain had been party to a treaty in 1839 (as had Prussia) to safeguard Belgium's neutrality and it was Germany's demand for an unrestricted passage through Belgium into France that provided the British government and the British people with a *casus belli* – a moral basis for a 'just' war.

Such was Britain's lack of preparedness for a European conflict that, even after finally declaring war on Germany, the British government was by no means clear as to how and where the BEF might be employed. There was an assumption that, in the event of a war, Britain's role would be essentially maritime. The Royal Navy was expected to destroy or at least contain the German battle-fleet; safeguard Britain against possible invasion; and blockade and therefore weaken Germany. In this scenario, Britain's Allies, France and Russia, would overcome the forces of Germany and Austria-Hungary and Britain's small though well-trained army would be required to play only a limited supporting role. Circumstances, however, were to dictate otherwise.

Although Grey was correct in saying to the French ambassador that there was no binding agreement that would oblige Britain to support France against Germany, he was being somewhat disingenuous. There had been, since 1905, numerous 'conversations' between the British and French army staffs about possible co-operation should such a war take place. Both Asquith and Grey were fully aware of these talks, though information about their content and progress was not made available to the full Cabinet, some of whom were against any definite political alignment.[7] Despite their covert nature, the eventual outcome of these discussions was a detailed arrangement for mutual support and common action. In August 1914 it was the only plan available and, as a consequence, it had considerable weight.

This plan was largely the work of Brigadier General Henry Wilson. In 1909, Wilson, an extreme Francophile, had been the Commandant of the Staff College at Camberley and had formed a close working relationship with Ferdinand Foch, his opposite number in Paris as head of the *École Supérieur de Guerre*. Following Wilson's appointment as Director of Military Operations in 1910, he and Foch and their staffs had drawn up and agreed a scheme for co-operation between their two armies. The plan was referred to as the 'W.F. Scheme', not standing for 'Wilson-Foch', but for 'With France', though such was Wilson's influence that in French staff papers the BEF was alluded to as 'l'armee W' which did stand for 'Wilson'.[8] A key feature of this scheme was that the BEF would, on the declaration of war, assemble at Maubeuge near the Belgium border. The choice of Maubeuge was not unreasonable. It placed the BEF on the extreme left of the French forces and within 80 miles of the strategically important Channel ports.

During his time as Director of Military Operations, Wilson placed great emphasis on making detailed plans for the mobilization of the BEF and for transporting it to the ports of embarkation. By the end of 1912, an arrangement had been agreed with France that the BEF would be ready for action fifteen days after mobilization. While Wilson was working on these issues, the then Chief Secretary to the Cabinet, Maurice Hankey, had been compiling a War Book – a list of the actions to be taken by every government department when war was declared. Among many other things, the War Book covered such details as the proclamations needing the King's signature, the procedure for contacting the Reservists and the Territorials, the requisitioning of trains and horses, and the measures for dealing with spies. It was a remarkable document that proved invaluable in early August 1914. It had, however, a major defect of great concern to Wilson in particular. While it covered in vast detail events relating to mobilization there was no mention of actual embarkation. It was an omission that put Wilson's semi-secret plan and timetable for the positioning of the BEF in serious jeopardy.[9]

Given the somewhat veiled nature of the British-French 'conversations' it was hardly surprising that, at the meeting of the War Council on 5 and 6 August, there was an element of confusion. During the discussion on the assembly point for the BEF, Antwerp was suggested and so was Amiens. General Sir Douglas Haig suggested that the BEF should be held back for three or four months until 'the immense resources of the Empire could be developed'.[10] As regards the timing of embarkation, the view of the appointed Commander of the BEF, Sir John French, was adopted – cross to France immediately and decide the destination later.

On 5 August the army was mobilized. During the next few days, 1,800 special trains carried troops from all parts of Britain to ports on the south coast and on 8 August 80,000 troops together with 30,000 horses sailed from Southampton and Portsmouth to Boulogne, Rouen and Le Havre. It was not until 12 August that the War Council finally agreed, to the immense relief of Wilson, that the BEF should be positioned at Maubeuge. Given the circumstances it was, for all practical purposes, the only decision that could have been taken. However, the choice of Maubeuge had the effect of placing the BEF directly in front of von Kluck's advancing German First Army. The retreat from Mons (12 miles north of Maubeuge) and the Battle of Le Cateau resulted in Britain's first major casualty lists of the war.

* * *

Two days after Britain's entry into the war, Prime Minister Asquith appointed Field Marshal Lord Kitchener as Secretary of State for War and a member of the Cabinet. Asquith himself thought that this appointment was 'a hazardous experiment'.[11] Kitchener was neither a politician nor an administrator. Nevertheless, his service in Egypt, South Africa and India had gained him an immense reputation with the British public to whom he was a national symbol of strength and reliability.

Kitchener's great attributes were breadth of vision and extraordinary foresight. He was among the very few who thought that the war would be both long and bloody. His view was that the coming conflict could not be won at sea by the British Navy and that Britain's contribution could not be limited to a small Regular army: 'We must be prepared to put armies of millions in the field and maintain them for several years'.[12]

Supported by the House of Commons, Kitchener set about his task with great energy. On 7 August he appealed for the first 100,000 volunteers. They were to be in the age group 19–30 and they signed on for a period of three years or the duration of the war. On 28 August Kitchener called for a second 100,000 and this was followed by four more appeals each for 100,000 men. The response to Kitchener's personal appeals was astonishing. His call for 200,000 men in August resulted in 300,000 volunteers. In one week, 30 August–5 September, 174,900 men enlisted. The daily rate of enlistment rose to a peak of 33,000 on 3 September. In the first eight weeks of the war 761,000 men joined the army. Such was the response by the young men of Britain that on 11 September the minimum acceptable height was increased from 5ft 3in to 5ft 6in in an effort to slow down the flood of volunteers. By the end of the year a total of 1,186,337 men had enlisted and by September 1915 the number had grown to 2,257,521. In all, some 2.4 million men joined the British army voluntarily.

Kitchener's batches of 100,000 men were labelled K1, K2, etc. and each batch was divided into battalions and divisions. The divisions were numbered sequentially so that, while the Regular Divisions were numbered 1–8 (the original six plus two from abroad), the K1 divisions were numbered 9–14: K2 divisions were 15–20, and so on. Each group of six Kitchener divisions was known as a New Army. In August 1914, the BEF was made up of the original six divisions organized in one army and two corps. By December 1914 more divisions had arrived from various parts of the Empire and the BEF was then organized into two armies made up of five corps and ten divisions. As additional volunteer divisions became available, new armies were formed and, by the middle of 1916, the BEF had grown to a force of five armies.[13]

While the overall level of recruitment was encouragingly high, there were variations across the country in terms of the speed of enlistment. In some rural areas recruitment was slow, generally because men were needed to bring in the harvest. The recruiting officer for Haddenham in Buckinghamshire, for example, reported on 28 August: 'The Bucks yokels are terribly slow to move – we are trying to wake them up'. There was also variation in the numbers of recruits from area to area. Of the 250 battalions in K1, K2 and K3, Scotland and Yorkshire provided over eighty while Devon, Dorset, Cornwall and Somerset contributed only eleven. By the end of 1915 the number of recruits from Scotland represented 26 per cent of their eligible population. For England and Wales the proportion was 24 per cent and for Ireland 11 per cent.[14] There were also discrepancies between occupational groups. A Board of Trade Survey in February 1916 showed that 40 per cent of recruits came from professional jobs – commerce and finance – while 30 per cent had previously been employed in agriculture, transport and industry.[15] Within these figures, certain trade groups were over-represented. In the first month of the war 115,000 miners enlisted and by June 1915 the figure had reached 230,000.

Ireland presented a complex political problem to the British government. In August 1914 the Home Rule Bill was on the Statute Book, but, by agreement, its progress was suspended for the duration of the war. This inevitably set up tensions within Ireland and affected the attitude of Irishmen towards enlistment – hence the relatively low proportion of recruits compared to Scotland, Wales and England. Nevertheless, the 36th (Ulster) Division and the Irish Nationalist Divisions, the 10th and the 16th, were formed early in the war and by the end of April 1915 some 75,000 Irishmen had volunteered. However, the Irish divisions were not allowed to have their own artillery (field batteries were loaned by Britain) since the government did not want either the UVF or the Nationalists to possess such weapons after the war. In any event, and despite the Easter 1916 uprising, the Irish divisions showed great tenacity and bravery as part of the BEF on the Western Front and the Protestant and Catholic soldiers fought side by side at Messines and during the Passchendaele offensive of 1917. The Irish Peace Park, near Ploegsteert Wood, was opened on 11 November 1998. It commemorates all Irishmen who died in the First World War, regardless of their political or religious beliefs.

* * *

The reasons behind an individual's decision to volunteer in the early months of the war varied widely – the wish to escape monotonous work; the pressure from womenfolk; the encouragement of employers; the powerful effect of peer-pressure and sheer impulsiveness. As Donald Hankey of the 1st Royal Warwickshire Regiment put it: 'Some of us enlisted for glory, some for fun, and a few for fear of starvation.'[16] Certainly the fall in economic activity that immediately followed the start of the war and the consequent increase in unemployment was an important factor. By the end of August 1914 480,000 men had lost their jobs and many more were on short time.[17] The reason for enlistment given by Harry Fellows, who lived in Nottingham, probably applied to many other young men who joined up in 1914:

> For me to say that a surge of patriotism or urge to kill some Germans caused me to join the army in 1914 would not be the truth ... I was now finding it difficult to pay for my board and lodgings ... I and two other lads in my department decided to join the army ... It would certainly ease our financial problems, we would be assured of food and clothing and, in any case, didn't everyone say it would be all over by Christmas.[18]

Some men volunteered looking for excitement. William Maslin of Bristol wrote; 'my young blood soon began to call for fresh excitement and after my younger brother had joined the 6th Gloucesters ... I joined the 4th Gloucesters'.[19] Feelings of patriotism and duty also played their part. When Joe Beard together with five of his friends enlisted in August 1914 he noted that: 'A wave of intense patriotism swelled throughout the nation with recruiting offices opened in every town. Mansfield Town Hall near where I worked as a teacher was besieged by applicants'.[20] Patriotic feelings were encouraged by a concerted propaganda campaign organized by the Parliamentary Recruiting Committee who produced 160 different posters encouraging enlistment. The success of the Kitchener slogan 'Your Country Needs You' was followed by posters with messages such as: 'Go, It's Your Duty Lad', and 'Take Up the Sword of Justice'. Long-retired generals toured the counties of Britain making impassioned appeals. In Buckinghamshire, for example, Major General Swann declared:

> If we cannot obtain [volunteers] in Bucks, we shall have to obtain men from elsewhere. We don't want our County Regiment filled with men

> from Birmingham or the East End of London. We don't want these men to fight in the name of Bucks. We want Bucks men to fight for Bucks and the King.[21]

* * *

When Kitchener formed his New Armies, he deliberately disregarded the Territorial Force (TF) which had been specifically structured by Haldane in 1908 in such a way that it could be expanded in wartime. Territorials were part-time, unpaid soldiers who attended weekly training sessions in their local Drill Hall and took part in an annual two-week camp. By 1910 some 250,000 men had joined the TF. The Territorial units were organized by County Associations, and were integrated into the County Regimental system, as were the Reserve and New Army battalions. As a result of Kitchener's decision to use his New Armies as the basis for military expansion a volunteer might choose to join a Territorial battalion, a New Army battalion or, indeed, a battalion of the existing Regular army. It was an arrangement that caused much unnecessary duplication of effort and needless competition, particularly between the Territorial and New Army recruits. In Sheffield only one New Army battalion was formed because the TF Hallamshires were considered a more appealing option.[22] Overall, 1,741,000 men joined the Kitchener armies while 726,000 joined the Territorials.

The problem was that Kitchener had formed an unfavourable view of the Territorials. Just before the war the TF numbers were some 30 per cent under complement. He had witnessed examples of poor performance by French Territorials in the Franco-German war of 1870 and had not been impressed by the British Volunteers (the precursors of the TF) during the Boer War. In addition, since the TF had been primarily formed for home defence, they could not be sent abroad in times of war, unless they voluntarily signed an Imperial Service Obligation. Since many Territorials were family men in their thirties they were understandably reluctant to do this and at the beginning of 1914 only 7 per cent had done so.

Kitchener's view that the Territorials were simply amateurs, 'Saturday Night Soldiers', 'Dog-Shooters' and 'Featherbed Heroes' proved to be misplaced. When war came, over 90 per cent of Territorials signed up to serve abroad. Six weeks after the declaration of war, the 42nd (East Lancs) TF Division was on its way to Egypt to release Regular battalions for France. The Territorials of the London Scottish went to France in September 1914 and took part in the fierce fighting at Messines. By the end of December 1914 twenty-two Territorial battalions were in France as part of the BEF. By February 1915 twenty-six other battalions had joined them. Field Marshal Sir John French was later to write: 'I say without hesitation that without the assistance which the Territorials afforded between October 1914 and June 1915, it would have been impossible to have held the line in France and Belgium, or to have prevented the enemy from reaching his goal, the Channel seaboard'.[23] The battalions of the TF in France in 1914 and early 1915 may not have been trained or equipped to the standards of the old Regular army, but they played an important supporting role. The Territorials became increasingly proficient and continued to give valuable service throughout the war. It was, notably, the 46th Territorial Division that broke the German defences on the Hindenburg Line at Riqueval in September 1918.

Kitchener's recruitment policy meant that the County Regiments across Britain were made up of a complex mixture of Regular army, New Army and Territorial battalions. The Oxfordshire and Buckinghamshire Light Infantry, for example, was, by mid-1915, composed of the following battalions: the 1st and 2nd were the original Regular battalions; the 3rd was formed from the Special Reserve (ex-Militia); the 4th was a Territorial battalion based in Oxford; the Bucks Battalion, also Territorial, was based in Aylesbury and was unnumbered; the 5th, 6th, 7th and 8th were New Army (Service) battalions and the 9th was a New Army Reserve battalion. During the war the Ox and Bucks Light Infantry expanded further as new battalions were formed. By 1918 the regiment was made up of, in total, eighteen battalions spread among the brigades, divisions and corps of the British army. Of these eighteen battalions, ten saw active service.

Generally, Regular battalions served in Regular divisions, New Army battalions served in New Army divisions and TF battalions served in TF divisions and once a battalion was placed in a division, it was rarely transferred out. The range of battalions in a division can be illustrated by examining the composition of three divisions that fought on the first day of the Battle of the Somme, 1 July 1916. The 8th Division (Regular) included battalions from the Devons, the West Yorks, the Middlesex, the Scottish Rifles, and the Royal Berks. The 32nd Division (New Army) included the Lancs Fusiliers, the Northumberland Fusiliers, the Border Regiment and the Highland Light Infantry, and the 49th Division (Territorial) included battalions from the West Yorks, the Duke of Wellingtons, the Yorks and Lancs and the King's Own Yorkshire Light Infantry.[24]

Among the New Army units that saw action for the first time on the Somme in July 1916 were the 'Pals' battalions. The concept of friends from civilian life – fellow workers, neighbours, members of the same sports club – forming a local battalion and serving alongside one another was, in 1914, a powerful recruitment tool. Promoted by Lord Derby in Liverpool and seized on by local authorities, particularly in the North and London, the Pals battalions were characterized by their outstanding morale. They were local men officered by local gentry.

Lord Derby put the concept of the 'Pals' to Kitchener who readily supported this novel means of recruitment. The scheme was particularly attractive to Kitchener since the local authorities agreed to relieve the British army of the responsibility for feeding, housing and clothing thousands of Pals volunteers for several months until the army was ready to absorb them. Only weapons for training purposes were provided by the army. Gradually, the Pals battalions were transferred to New Army units – a process that began in mid-1915.

Pals battalions were identified not only by their local name, but also by their official Regimental titles. The first Pals unit, formed in the City of London in August 1914, became the 10th (Stockbrokers) Battalion, Royal Fusiliers. Various sportsmen grouped together and became the 17th and 23rd Battalions of the Middlesex Regiment and a London bankers' battalion was designated as the 26th Royal Fusiliers. Examples from the North are the St Helens Pals (11th South Lancs Regiment), the Oldham Pals (24th Manchesters) and the Durham Pals (18th Durham Light Infantry). The Tyneside Scottish raised four battalions to become a brigade in the Northumberland Fusiliers with the third battalion setting a record by recruiting 1,169 men in just over twenty-four hours.[25] As might be expected, some Pals battalions were made up of several groups of volunteers. So, the Accrington Pals (11th East

Lancs) came not only from Accrington but also from the nearby towns of Burnley, Chorley and Blackburn. About three-quarters of one Tyneside Scottish battalion were in fact not Scots but Geordies. Even so, all these Pals battalions had local or personal links and all had a great spirit of camaraderie. Altogether, 145 infantry battalions were formed in this way and, in addition, there were forty-eight engineering companies, twenty-eight brigades of artillery and eleven divisional ammunition columns.[26]

The Pals battalions were placed into divisions on a regional basis. Hence the 30th Division was made up of eight Manchester and four Liverpool Pals battalions, while the soldiers of the 31st Division came mainly from Yorkshire and included Pals from Hull, Leeds, Bradford, Barnsley, Sheffield and Halifax. In total, there were twelve Pals divisions (numbered 30–41) and they made up K4 and K5 of Kitchener's New Armies. These divisions, following several months of training, were sent to the Western Front between October 1915 and June 1916 and they all took part in the Battle of the Somme. During the course of that battle, which lasted from July to November 1916, it became clear that the strength of the Pals battalions was also their weakness. When those battalions suffered heavy casualties, as they did particularly on the first day of the Somme battle, the effect both on those who survived and on their home communities was devastating. On 1 July the Accrington Pals lost 584 men – more than half their number. The Pals from Hull, Leeds, Bradford, Barnsley, Sheffield and Halifax, who attacked alongside the men from Accrington, all suffered heavy casualties. After the experience of the Somme, such concentrations of men from the same localities and social groups were purposely avoided by the army authorities.

* * *

The rapid growth of the BEF brought significant problems. There was initially a chronic shortage of uniforms, weapons and accommodation. Many recruits began their army life wearing civilian clothes, living in tented camps and drilling with wooden rifles. A 1915 photograph of a group of seven recruits who had recently joined the 11th Battalion, the Welsh Regiment, shows three in uniform, but without headwear; four in three-piece civilian suits of whom three wore collar and tie while the fourth wore a bow-tie;

and, of those in civilian clothes, two wore trilbies and one a flat cap. Lack of suitable footwear was a particular problem. In one division, the 18th (Eastern), men whose boots were in need of repair were given permission to march on grass – slowly.[27] The Sheffield City battalion (12th Yorks and Lancs) only received its full quota of rifles one week before it went abroad.[28] During the winter of 1914, thousands were billeted with local families and this often caused some resentment. The 2nd Bucks Battalion had followed the 1st Bucks Battalion into billets in the Springfield area of Chelmsford and they were to be followed by a Scottish Lowland battalion. But the locals had by that time had quite enough of soldiers in their homes and placed signs in their windows saying, 'Not available for Billets' and locked their doors against the army authorities anxious to find accommodation.[29]

An even greater problem was the lack of officers and newly commissioned officers (NCOs) to train and lead the eager, but green, volunteers. The problem in the early months of the war was that the BEF was geared to a pre-war force of some 200,000 and it now had to deal with multiples of that number. Most officers, Staff officers and NCOs of the Regular army had gone to France leaving a vacuum of experience. A number of Regular NCOs were subsequently commissioned and proved to be outstanding officers. RQMS P.B. Welton of the 2nd Royal Welsh Fusiliers, for example, was commissioned in autumn 1914, won the MC, and in 1918 commanded a battalion of the South Wales Borderers. Harry Carter was in 1914 a signalling sergeant in the South Staffordshire Regiment. He was commissioned in 1915 and by the end of the war he had been awarded the DSO and Bar and the MC and was in command of the 7th South Staffs.[30]

The shortage of officers for the New Armies was particularly acute. Kitchener's first army, K1, alone required 18 brigadiers, 72 battalion commanders, 288 company commanders and some 1,500 junior officers.[31] These numbers increased dramatically as other New Armies were formed and, in addition, officers and NCOs were required for the expanding Territorial Force. Early in the war Kitchener announced that he required 30,000 new officers and he gathered them from wherever he could find them. In August 1914 around 500 Regular officers were in Britain on leave from their units in India and these were immediately posted to the New Armies. There were also some 5,500 Special Reserve officers and officers who had recently retired, but the great majority of newly commissioned officers was recruited from the leading schools and the universities. In 1908 Haldane had encouraged the public schools and universities to establish Officer Training Corps (OTCs) at the army's expense. This initiative led to the formation of twenty-three university and 166 public school OTCs who, between them, provided 20,577 junior officers for Kitchener's armies. The creation of OTCs had a significant effect on the ethos of public schools, one of duty and service to King and Country, and when war was declared men from these schools enlisted in their thousands. They also died in their thousands. Eton provided 5,650 of whom 1,157 were killed. One in three Haileybury boys who had entered the school between 1905 and 1912 died in the war. Charterhouse lost 686, Wellington 699, Dulwich 518, Marlborough 733 and so on. Overall, the death rate of officers from public schools was almost twice the national average.[32] While most of the officer recruits from the leading schools were spread around the various units of the army, a significant proportion chose to enlist together. A Public Schools Battalion was formed and became the 16th Middlesex Battalion. Four battalions of the Royal Fusiliers (18th–21st) were composed of men from the universities and public schools. Grammar schools also played their part. The Grimsby Chums, for example, were formed around a company of 250 Old Boys of the Grammar school who had been recruited by the headmaster.[33] It became clear to the authorities that for these well-educated and committed young men to serve in the ranks was a misuse of scarce talent and it was not long before these and similar battalions were used as a source of officers. A further 120,000 'suitable young gentlemen' were commissioned as a result of personal recommendation. Robert Graves, who had just left Charterhouse, obtained a commission in the Royal Welsh Fusiliers thanks to a recommendation from the Secretary of the Harlech Golf Club.[34]

The pre-war (first-line) Territorials already had their full complement of officers, but when the second-line battalions were raised they too had to search for officers. The formation of the 2nd Bucks Battalion in September 1914 is an example of how the dearth of officers was met. The CO, Lieutenant Colonel H.M. Williams, a manager at the Wolverton railway depot, had retired from being the CO of the 1st Bucks Battalion earlier in 1914. He was recalled to lead the 2nd Battalion and set about selecting his complement of thirty officers. They were drawn from local professional men – solicitors and businessmen – and most of them were known to one another. Local ex-public schoolboys were also offered commissions. Charles Phipps, who was 19 and who had recently left Winchester, became a Second Lieutenant as did G.L. Stevens, who had been a Sergeant in the Eton College OTC. Harold Church, a local solicitor, had been in his school OTC and had also received some officer training at the Inns of Court. Ashley Cummings and Ivor Stewart-Liberty, both barristers and both ex-Winchester, were given immediate commissions. Geoffry Christie-Miller, who had been a member of both the Bucks Militia and the pre-war Territorials, was passed over by the 1st Bucks because, as a child, he had lost the use of one eye. Nevertheless, his experience was quickly welcomed in the 2nd Battalion with whom he served with distinction through most of the war.[35]

Lieutenant Colonel Williams was an example of those officers called out of retirement and who became known, half affectionately and half disparagingly, as 'dug-outs'. Williams did earn the respect of his soldiers as did Brigadier General Lord George Baillie-Hamilton-Billing. Billing had retired from the army in 1907, but was 'dug out' aged 60 to command the 41st Brigade, which he did until August 1916. Another 'dug-out' who served with distinction was Lieutenant Colonel Angus Douglas-Hamilton who commanded the 6th Cameron Highlanders at Loos in September 1915 aged 52. He rallied his battalion four times during that battle before being killed. But many 'dug-outs' proved either incompetent or ill-suited to military life. The comments of Lieutenant Colonel Gibson of the 24th Division, a New Army division that fought at the Battle of Loos, were probably extreme, but gave an idea of the calibre of some of the hastily appointed officers:

> Of ex-regular officers there was a paucity, and of these, the older ones had been dug out of the musty reading rooms of clubs in Cheltenham, Bath or Bournemouth. The younger ones were mostly the cast-offs from the Old Army owing to mental or physical disabilities. In one battalion, and it was typical of many, three ex regular officers were given command of companies. The fourth was a militiaman. But of the three ex-regulars, one had to be left behind when the battalion embarked for France. He was too mad to be trusted with a Company in the field.

> The second was gallant and sensible, but stone deaf. The third had the thickest head that ever grew on a man's shoulders.[36]

Dealing with the problem of incapable officers was an important issue within the BEF throughout the war.[37] In 1914 General Sir Aylmer Haldane removed three of his four battalion commanders in 10 Brigade and Major General E.C. Ingouville-Williams sent home three battalion commanders of 16 Brigade. Haig himself claimed to have dismissed over a hundred brigadiers. In 1917 a bizarre situation arose when Lieutenant Colonel F. Rayner of the 59th Division was 'degummed' (dismissed) by his brigadier, E.W.S.K. Maconchy. Maconchy was then sent home by his Division commander, Major General A.E. Sandbach, who, in turn, was also dismissed. They all travelled back to England on the same cross-Channel steamer. These three 'degummed' officers were considered too old to perform their duties effectively and they were among many older commanders who were sent home. As younger officers were promoted the average age of senior officers at army, corps and divisional levels fell during the war. Most affected were divisional commanders whose average age fell from 55 at the beginning of the war to 49 at the end.[38]

The problem of 'degumming' incapable officers gave rise to the consequent problem of finding suitable replacements. This issue was also approached with some vigour. In July 1915 Prime Minister Asquith visited Sir Douglas Haig, who was then commanding the First Army in France. Haig noted in his diary that they discussed,

> the necessity for promoting young officers to high command … We went through the list of major generals, etc. on the Army List. I said it was important to go down low on the list and get young, capable officers. He agreed. I said in reply to urgent questions that the best to command Corps seemed to be as follows, in order of seniority – Major Generals Morland, Horne, Gough and Haking. Mr Asquith wrote the names down.[39]

Within a year, all four of the named generals had become corps commanders. By the end of the war, as a result of the weeding out process and the promotion of more able officers, the BEF was commanded by senior officers who were generally considered as competent and energetic leaders. A list of several outstanding corps commanders in 1918 would include Cavan (XIV Corps), Jacob (II Corps), de Lisle (XV Corps), Morland (XIII Corps), Watts (XIX Corps) and there were many more.

* * *

The shortage of experienced officers and staff officers, both at home and in France, meant that the training of NCOs in the New Armies had to be carried out with great speed. Heavy casualties, particularly among young subalterns, aggravated the situation. Field Marshal French had commented towards the end of 1914 that: 'Our losses in officers in the campaign up to then had been prodigious, and I was trying to devise some means to fill up their ranks'.[40] Several initiatives were employed. The length of courses at Sandhurst (infantry) and Woolwich (artillery) were reduced to process an increased number of officer cadets. Building on the work of Lord Haldane before the war, various battalions were selected to be officer training units. These included the Inns of Court and the Artists' Rifles. By mid-1915 the Inns of Court was providing training for eighty officers per week – a valuable contribution, but one that could satisfy only a small proportion of the demand.[41] The Honourable Artillery Company (HAC) was also called upon to produce officers. In January 1915, for example, twenty-three HAC privates were commissioned into the Worcesters, the Wiltshires, the South Lancs and the Royal Irish Rifles.[42] The establishment of Schools of Instruction at various levels in the BEF was a significant step forward. What was probably the first school was set up towards the end of 1914 under Major H.N.R. Crowe who was attached to the Artists' Rifles. It was officially called the Cadet School and the officer course, which lasted four weeks, included a forty-eight-hour attachment to a battalion in the trenches. By 1916 there were schools for officers and NCOs in each army, corps and division and a GHQ order of that year instructed every battalion to have permanent instruction staff who were not permitted to go into battle. Somewhat belatedly, in early 1917, GHQ appointed Brigadier General Solly-Flood to lead a Training Directorate. Solly-Flood had already made a significant contribution to training by running courses on instruction techniques for Lieutenant Colonels and Majors through 1916. He now used his new position to prepare and issue a series of 'good practice' pamphlets for the use of corps and divisional officers. Hence, SS 152 was on the subject of 'Instruction for Training Within Schools'; SS 159 outlined schemes for the training of junior officers and NCOs; SS 204 dealt with infantry and tank cooperation, and so on. In mid-1918 the whole subject of training was placed on a higher level when Lieutenant General Sir Ivor Maxse was appointed Inspector General of Training. Nevertheless, training in general was somewhat spasmodic and most was in the form of 'learning on the job'. Major General Stephens of the 5th Division commented in October 1917 that 'most troubles have come from our lack of training' and in September 1918 Lieutenant General G.M. Harper of IV Corps gave his opinion that 'British troops had not reached a sufficiently high standard of training'.[43]

The training of Other Ranks was as ad hoc and uneven as that of officers and NCOs. Kitchener had refused to intersperse the Regular divisions with New Army battalions which would have helped the inexperienced troops to acclimatise to the rigours of trench warfare. It was a situation that contrasted with the German and French armies in which, thanks to their pre-war conscription policy, had the benefit, at least in the early years of the war, of many trained NCOs and junior officers.

As with the training of officers and NCOs, GHQ lagged behind the armies and corps in organizing training for Other Ranks. In July 1915 it became Third Army practice for all infantry battalions, when out of the line, to have daily sessions of rapid loading and rapid firing. Some divisions set up firing ranges and insisted that frequent use was made of them. During 1915–17 trench raids became a feature of the Western Front and increasingly sophisticated forms of pre-raid training were developed. It became normal procedure to practice a forthcoming raid in mock-up trenches behind the lines.

While basic training was given immediately after recruitment, the job of instructing green troops mainly fell to young platoon officers. They carried out that role generally with commendable dedication, but the fact remained that these subalterns were themselves often half-trained. Most training was done 'on the job' by NCOs and more experienced comrades – a system that had built-in limitations. When, in April 1916, Major Christie-Miller was sent to the front line in advance of his TF unit he was assigned to a battalion of the South Wales Borderers (SWB). Although he gathered much valuable information he was not particularly impressed by some of the SWB practices.[44]

* * *

Efforts to develop an efficient fighting force were seriously hampered by the constant loss of men. By the end of 1914, following the fighting at Mons, Le Cateau, the Marne, the Aisne and the First Battle of Ypres, the original BEF had been almost totally destroyed. Around 85,000 of the 120,000 men sent to France in August and September 1914 were gone – wounded, missing or killed. Individual units had suffered catastrophic casualty levels. By late September the 4th Division, for example, had lost eleven of its twelve battalion commanders. By 1 November, of the BEF's eighty-four infantry battalions, seventy-five had fewer than 300 men. Eighteen battalions had been reduced to fewer than 100 soldiers.[45] The BEF had begun its fighting in France as a small but highly trained professional army. By the end of 1914 it was no longer able to call on the experience of the original Regular and Reserve troops. Henceforth, the BEF relied on amateur soldiers – the Territorials, the New Armies and the Dominion troops.

Strictly, the Dominion troops were not part of the BEF, but when Britain declared war on Germany it did so on behalf of the entire British Empire. This general commitment risked some adverse reaction – after all, Australia, Canada and New Zealand had their own governments each with independent status. South Africa had been in conflict with Britain only fourteen years earlier and the shadow of the Mutiny was still present in India. But this assumed involvement in the war was not only accepted without particular protest – there was a marked degree of enthusiasm and this showed itself at the recruiting stations. In Australia and Canada it would no doubt have helped that 18 per cent and 42 per cent respectively of those who enlisted were British-born.[46]

Contingents from the Indian army were the first of the Empire troops to arrive in Europe. They fought alongside the BEF Regulars at Ypres in

October 1914 and also took part in the battles of 1915 before leaving France to fight against the Turks. The Canadians formed a division in England in late 1914 and went to France in February 1915. A new acronym was coined to identify the Australian and New Zealand troops – ANZAC – who formed divisions in the Middle East, fought in Gallipoli and arrived in France in June 1916. By November 1918 some 1.3 million troops from these countries had enlisted and fought in the various theatres of the war. On the Western Front Australia provided five divisions, Canada four, New Zealand one and South Africa one brigade. Although the Dominion divisions were independent in some respects, for example the Australians refused to accept the death penalty as part of their disciplinary code, they were subject to GHQ orders and they were integrated into the armies and corps of the BEF. They had arrived on the Western Front when they were most needed and their contribution was immense.

By mid-1915 it had become clear that Britain's voluntary system of recruitment could not sustain the army's incessant and increasing demands for manpower. Casualties at the front had to be replaced and the flow of volunteers at home was slowing. Wages in Britain had risen as industry geared itself to meet wartime demands and there was no longer a pool of unemployed eager to join the army. In the month of February 1915 the number of those enlisting fell to 87,900 – the first time that a monthly figure had dropped below six figures. In October 1915 Kitchener estimated that it was necessary to recruit 35,000 men per week to maintain the strength of the armed forces, but in the month of September only 71,600 had enlisted – half the rate required by Kitchener.

It had also become clear that voluntarism was neither fair nor efficient. The willing men enlisted and the reluctant men did not – a situation that caused much resentment. Moreover, the government had no control over the number of key workers who volunteered and left their jobs in critically important industries such as mining and munitions. This particular weakness in the voluntary system was highlighted in early 1915 when the munitions industry was unable to keep pace with the ever-increasing requirement for shells. British guns were rationed to a few rounds per day and Field Marshal French blamed the failure of the attack at Neuve Chapelle on the lack of ammunition for the artillery. In order to replace the casualties at the front and to manage the manpower requirements at home it became painfully clear that national conscription had to be introduced.

The government had delayed the decision on conscription as long as it could. Lloyd George was reluctant because of the 'violent prejudices which would be excited'.[47] And, indeed, serious prejudices did exist. The parish church in the village of Chipperfield in Hertfordshire, for example, has on its walls two quite separate marble plaques commemorating the local men who fought in the war. One lists those who 'risked their lives voluntarily' and the other pointedly lists those who, simply, 'risked their lives', i.e. were conscripted. Churchill, almost alone in the Cabinet, argued for compulsory service, but his colleagues rejected his proposal on the grounds that Britain had traditionally raised a voluntary army and to do otherwise would be contrary to the concept of individual freedom.

It was a major political problem and the government approached the issue cautiously. First, in August 1915, it introduced a National Register whereby all men and women aged 16–65 declared their age, sex and occupation. It was a national census which gave valuable information and, later, was useful for conscription purposes. In October 1915 the Derby Scheme[48], using information from the National Register, invited men between the ages of 18 and 41 to 'attest', i.e. affirm their willingness to enter military service when called upon. An undertaking was given that married men would not be called up before eligible bachelors. The immediate short-term outcome was a rush to the recruitment centres by single men who realized that if they volunteered quickly they would at least avoid any stigma of conscription. But the Derby Scheme did not have its desired effect. Of the 2.2 million eligible single men who registered, only 1.15 million attested and of these, only 318,500 were actually available for service. The remainder were either medically unfit or in essential ('starred') occupations. The response to attestation among married men was little better. The last effort to continue with voluntarism had failed.[49]

The first Military Service Act was introduced on 27 January 1916 and applied to single men and widowers without children in the age group 18–41. However, the numbers fell short of requirements and on 3 May the Act was extended, on the basis of equal sacrifice, to cover all men aged 18-41 regardless of marital status. There were to be exemptions – skilled men in 'starred' occupations and conscientious objectors – and military tribunals were set up across the country to rule on claims for exemption. For political reasons, Ireland was also exempt. In general, universal conscription had arrived and, despite the fears of the politicians, it was accepted by the British public with scarcely a murmur. Between August 1914 and December 1915, 2.4 million men enlisted voluntarily. From January 1916 to November 1918, 2.6 million men were conscripted. The major battles of Loos, the Somme, Arras and Passchendaele together with the daily losses in the trenches had progressively reduced the number of volunteer soldiers who had originally made up the Territorials and the New Armies. A list of BEF casualties for each full year of the war makes sombre reading: 297,000 in 1915; 642,000 in 1916; 818,000 in 1917 and 853,000 in 1918. Of these numbers, totalling some 2.7 million, about one in five were killed. It therefore came about that, by 1918, the majority of British soldiers on the Western Front were conscripts.

Despite conscription, the BEF continued to be short of men. The casualties of 1917 together with the government manpower policy, which gave priority to industries such as shipbuilding, tank and aircraft production, timber and iron ore as well as merchant shipping, caused the generals much concern. In February and March 1918 the BEF was obliged to reduce the number of infantry battalions from twelve to nine in forty-eight of its divisions. Regular, first-line Territorial and Dominion divisions were not affected by this reorganization, but the New Armies lost 30 per cent and second-line Territorials lost 60 per cent of their battalions. The troops from the redundant battalions were redistributed to make up battalions below strength. It was significant that among the conscripts arriving from Britain there were, for the first time in the war, young men of 18. Such was the need for men that, in April 1918, a further Military Service Act raised the age limit for conscription to 50 with provision for a further increase to 56 if required.

There was some effort to keep new recruits together in their local regiments, but generally the traditional regimental ties with regions and counties had become much weaker. By the summer of 1917 the 16th Highland Light Infantry, originally composed of Glaswegians, contained men from Nottinghamshire, Derbyshire and Yorkshire. Similarly, by 1918, almost half of a Cheshire Territorial battalion came from outside that county.[50] English reinforcements were allocated, for the first time, to Scottish, Irish and Welsh units – a development that caused much resentment. The same process blurred the lines between Regular, New Army and Territorial units. Direct recruitment into the Territorials ended with the Military Service Act and Territorial units, once discrete formations, were increasingly interspersed among New Army divisions. In the same way, volunteers and conscripts found themselves serving side by side. The composition of the BEF had changed out of all recognition since the beginning of the war. From being originally composed of professional Regular soldiers in 1914 it became, by 1918, an integrated army of volunteers and conscripts.

Also between 1914 and 1918 the effects of rapid expansion together with technological and tactical developments had caused considerable internal change within the BEF. The proportion of combatants (those directly involved in the fighting) to non-combatants (the support units) had reduced from 83 per cent/17 per cent in 1914 to 65 per cent/35 per cent in 1918.[51] In 1914 the infantry had accounted for some 65 per cent of BEF manpower. In 1918 it was 57 per cent. The proportion of Royal Engineers had increased from 6 per cent to 11 per cent and the Artillery had increased from 20 per cent to 27 per cent. It should be noted that the cavalry had reduced from 5 per cent to 2 per cent of the BEF during the course of the war whereas the Royal Flying Corps had grown from small beginnings to 3 per cent by 1918. Both in size and composition the small colonial army of 1914 had developed, by 1918, into a complex continental fighting force.

* * *

The size, composition and character of the BEF between 1914 and 1918 was determined by a handful of powerful personalities reacting with pragmatism, determination, forethought and great energy to the threat and demands of war.

The architect of the British army of 1914 was the politician Richard Haldane. Haldane had been educated at the universities of Edinburgh and Göttingen where he studied mainly classics and philosophy. He became a successful barrister but he was persuaded by his friend, Herbert Asquith, to enter politics, which he did in 1885. When Asquith's Liberal Party came to power in 1905 Haldane accepted the post of Secretary of State for War. His achievements in that role were far-reaching and central to his many reforms was his belief that Britain should prepare itself for any possible war in Europe.

This so-called 'continental strategy' became, from 1906, the focus of military planning in Britain. A direct outcome of this policy was the creation of the BEF and the Territorial Force. The BEF Regulars were equipped and ready for foreign service. As regards the Territorials, Haldane wrote in February 1906: 'The basis of our whole military fabric must be the development of the idea of a real national army, formed by the people. It might be styled the Territorial Army'.[52] The formation of the Territorial Force, supported publicly by Edward VII, took place with marked success and within a year it had attracted 9,313 officers and 259,463 Other Ranks. Anticipating the expansion of both the Regular forces and the Territorials, Haldane, with great foresight, set up the OTCs to provide the necessary officers.

Haldane's reforms were also directed at the War Office. The Esher Report of 1904 had recommended that certain changes should take place in the War Office, so had the Hartingdon Committee of 1890, but it was not until Haldane took office fifteen years later that major change actually took place. A General Staff was established for the first time with the task of advising the Secretary of State on 'the strategic distribution of the army … the education of officers, and the training and preparation of the army for war'.[53] The War Office was organized into three main branches – Operations and Intelligence; Administration and Personnel; and Supplies. A new post, that of Chief of the Imperial General Staff (CIGS), was created and reporting to him were the Directors of Military Operations (DMO), Staff Duties (DSD), and Military Training (DMT).

Between 1906 and 1912 Haldane made a unique contribution to the development of the British army. However, he became the victim of allegations, made by sections of the Press and his political opponents, that he was pro-German. The *Daily Express* referred to 'elderly lawyers with German sympathies'.[54] It was known that he had attended a German university, that he could speak German fluently, that he had a high regard for German philosophers and that he had, in 1912, attempted to negotiate with Germany a reduction of naval armaments. These insinuations against Haldane may have been unfair, but they left their mark and he was obliged to leave the War Ministry. Asquith appointed him Lord Chancellor, but when the Coalition government was formed in May 1915, Haldane's enemies triumphed and he was omitted from the new Cabinet.

If Haldane was the architect of the BEF, Brigadier General Sir Henry Wilson was the man who set it on its course for France and Maubeuge. Wilson, having failed the entrance examinations to both Sandhurst (three times) and Woolwich (twice), entered the army via the Militia and was commissioned into the Rifle Brigade. He was unusually tall at 6ft 4in, lean, angular and had a wound above the eye, gained in Burma in 1887. A fellow officer described him as 'the ugliest officer in the army'.[55] His other characteristics, which showed themselves throughout his career, were a sharp wit, high intelligence, considerable organizing skills and, in addition, a marked penchant for political intrigue.

His progress in the pre-war army included attendance at the Staff College (1891–93); service in South Africa where he came to the attention of Lord Roberts; an Assistant Military Secretary in the War Office and Commandant of the Staff College (1907–10). After the Staff College, Wilson was appointed Director of Military Operations and it was in that role that he made his greatest contribution to the future of the BEF.

The vague 'conversations' concerning military cooperation with the French became substantial plans with definite aims and detailed timetables. Previous DMOs had achieved little, but Wilson took on the task with vigour. He wrote that he 'conceived it to be my most important duty to continue this work and so far as human foresight was possible to complete a scheme which would be at once useful and practical'.[56] Wilson had two objectives; to prepare the BEF for rapid mobilization in the event of war and, critically, to ensure that the destination of the BEF was as agreed with the French authorities, i.e. on the left of the French near Maubeuge. It should be noted that Wilson, as a Brigadier and DMO, was not especially high in the military hierarchy – there were four military ranks above his and, at the War Office, he, among others, was on the third level of authority. Given his rank and position, it was an amazing achievement of conviction and self-confidence that enabled Wilson to conduct discussions and arrive at serious decisions not only with Foch, but also with French politicians and members of their General Staff. It was these discussions that shaped and controlled the movements of the BEF in 1914. In his diary entry for 4 December 1914, Wilson recounted a conversation with Lord Stanfordham, the Secretary to King George V, in which Stanfordham had remarked that Wilson was 'more responsible for England joining the war than any other man'. Wilson added with his customary lack of modesty, 'I think that is true'.[57]

After the war, Wilson wrote to Churchill: 'the [1914] Expeditionary Force of 6 Divisions had no relation to any wars that could be conceived – it was too big for some and it was too small for others'.[58] The man who was quite clear as to the required size of the BEF was FM Lord Kitchener. The development of the BEF in 1914 and 1915 and the nature of the army that fought on the Somme was primarily the work of Kitchener. His contribution as a symbol of reliability to the British public and as the recruiting sergeant of the K Divisions was a personal triumph of foresight and single-minded determination. As Lloyd George later wrote: 'from farm and village and City streets young men thronged to the recruiting offices at the sound of Lord Kitchener's call to arms … In the magnitude and grandeur of the response it has no parallel in history'.[59]

Nevertheless, Kitchener's actions were not without criticism from his contemporaries, particularly the way in which he dealt with the Territorials. Sir Douglas Haig, as Director of Training at the War Office, had worked closely with Haldane to create the TF and remarked in his diary (5 August 1914) that he was 'struck' by 'Kitchener's ignorance of the progress of the Territorial army towards efficiency'.[60] Churchill considered that Kitchener should have used the TF to expand the army: 'It would have been better to have formed the new volunteers upon the cadres of the Territorial Army, each of which could have been duplicated or quadrupled in successive stages'.[61]

Whether Kitchener's high-handed treatment of Haldane's Territorial Force was ultimately advantageous or disadvantageous to the development of the army is problematic. To have used the TF framework would have certainly been neat and convenient and this was the view of the Kirke Committee when it published its *Lessons of the Great War* in 1932.[62] The Territorials had an established structure, were reasonably well-trained and had a complement of staff, officers and NCOs. It was also clothed and fed by the County

Associations. But with the influx of Kitchener's volunteers it is quite likely that the Territorial organization would have been swamped. As with the New Armies, uniforms, provisions, billets, training facilities as well as officers and NCOs would quickly have become rare commodities. Kitchener's fears regarding the commitment of the Territorials may have been ill-founded, but he could not have known that with certainty in August 1914. On balance, it is likely that nothing much was either gained or lost by Kitchener's insistence on raising his K Divisions as part of the Regular army.

Kitchener may have disregarded Haldane's plans for the Territorials, but he was soon to find that his own views were not treated as sacrosanct. During the War Council discussions of 5/6 August 1914 on the proposed destination of the BEF, Kitchener suggested Amiens – a view that he clung to, much to Wilson's chagrin, for a further week before eventually accepting Maubeuge. Kitchener's plan for his New Armies was that they should be held back until 1917. By that time the forces of the other belligerents, argued Kitchener, would be exhausted and Britain could then proceed to win both the war and the peace. But the casualties of 1915, at Festubert, Neuve Chapelle, Aubers Ridge, Loos and Gallipoli, rendered such a plan unrealistic and inappropriate and the New Armies were sent to the Western Front a year earlier than Kitchener would have wished.

As Secretary of State, Kitchener's dictatorial style coupled with his lack of administrative skills and reluctance to delegate brought criticism from his Parliamentary colleagues and from within the Cabinet. He took little note of the General Staff, which, despite his immense workload, he chose not to enlarge. His reputation, although still high among the general public, began to suffer at Westminster – a process not helped by the military failures of 1915. What Asquith had described as a 'hazardous experiment' was becoming a reality and Kitchener's immense influence diminished. In May 1915 Kitchener's responsibility for munitions was transferred to Lloyd George. When Sir William Robertson was appointed CIGS, Asquith ensured that the post reported to the War Council, not to the Secretary of State for War as it had done previously. Only Kitchener's death at sea, in June 1916 when on a mission to Russia, prevented any further ignominy and erosion of his powers. One biographer has commented that Kitchener was 'not much regretted in government and by no friends, for he never had any'.[63] And yet, despite Kitchener's various weaknesses, nothing can detract from his outstanding work in the early months of the war. None of his contemporaries had his breadth of vision and only Kitchener could have created the vast volunteer army of 1914.

The decisions of the two wartime Prime Ministers were also important in the development of the BEF. Asquith, who led both the Liberal and the Coalition governments, was instrumental in guiding the country towards conscription in January 1916 even though he himself was a reluctant convert to compulsion. While the necessity for more troops and effective manpower planning made conscription inevitable, Asquith nevertheless faced strong opposition. Sir John Simon, the Home Secretary resigned. But Asquith persevered. As Clementine Churchill noted in a letter dated 29 December 1915: 'The PM appeared at the Cabinet yesterday and did all the talking for compulsion'.[64] When the Military Service Bill was given its first reading it was passed by 403 votes to 105, but there were 160 abstentions, mainly from Asquith's own party. An important clause included in the final Act, and supported by Asquith, allowed conscientious objection to military service and it eased the way for many Liberals to support the legislation. The effect of conscription on the size and character of the BEF was profound.

David Lloyd George became Prime Minister in December 1916 and throughout 1917 and into 1918 he faced a series of conflicting manpower issues. The requirements of the Royal Navy, industry and agriculture together with the constant demands of the generals for more troops in Palestine, Italy and on the Western Front all constituted an ongoing manpower crisis. As far as the BEF was concerned, the February 1918 reduction in the number of battalions and the consequent redistribution of troops may have increased the strength of under-complement units, but it failed to add a single man to the overall headcount.

The shortage of manpower in the BEF became a critical issue for the government and when it was discussed in Parliament, Lloyd George claimed that there were more troops in France in January 1918 than there had been a year earlier – an increase from 1,591,745 to 1,828,616. These numbers were quite correct, but Lloyd George failed to point out that the additional men were largely non-combatants rather than Category A soldiers suitable for front-line service. The issue was brought to a head when Sir Frederick

Maurice, who had held the post of Director of Military Operations in the War Office, wrote to the Press accusing Lloyd George of misrepresenting the figures and adversely affecting morale among the senior officers in the BEF. The matter was further inflamed when revised manpower figures were published showing that the 1918 numbers originally quoted by Lloyd George had been overstated by some 86,000. The outcome of this unsatisfactory episode was that Lloyd George, with his plausible oratory and parliamentary skills, survived the attack and Maurice was obliged to resign his commission. Though not directly connected to these events, Lloyd George introduced the Military Service Act of April 1918 which extended the age range of those who became eligible for enlistment. The net effects on the BEF of these Lloyd George measures were a reduction in the number of battalions, considerable disruption as thousands of soldiers were transferred from one unit to another other, and a marked increase in the number of 18 year olds serving in France.

The development of the BEF, its size, composition and character, was therefore largely brought about by the determination and actions of five men – Haldane, Wilson, Kitchener, Asquith and Lloyd George. All of these men contributed in their different ways with the first three providing the major impetus. The BEF increased in size from just four infantry divisions and one cavalry brigade at the beginning of August 1914 to a peak of 1.8 million men in fifty-six divisions in 1917. The composition and character of the BEF evolved as the Regular army was replaced by the Territorials, the Dominion troops and the New Armies, in which the Pals divisions were a remarkable phenomenon. Conscription brought about further major change in both the composition and character of the BEF. Writing in 1919, Lieutenant General Sir John Keir commented on the social structure of the army and noted that, for the first time, Britain had a 'real National Army … Hitherto, the Regular Army consisted of two main groups, the patricians and the proletarians. The officers were the patricians and the men almost entirely proletarian. Between these two extreme poles of the social system there was no shading off.'[65] This transformation from a small professional army to an army of volunteers, to a truly national force capable of playing a decisive part in the defeat of the German army on the Western Front was nothing short of amazing. It was a triumph of improvization led by a handful of dedicated and single-minded men and occasioned by the sombre demands of war.

*Chapter 2*

# The British Expeditionary Force Generals on the Western Front

*Our God and Soldiers we alike adore,*
*Ev'n at the brink of danger, not before.*
*After deliverance, both alike requited:*
*Our God's forgotten and our Soldier slighted.*

*Francis Quarles*[1]

In 1914 the British Expeditionary Force was unprepared for a vast continental war. In particular, the generals who commanded the BEF were lacking in relevant experience and were far from ready to meet the ferocious challenges that confronted them. That they eventually did meet those challenges, despite serious setbacks, is a tribute to their tenacity of purpose and ability to adapt to a new and terrible form of warfare.

The success of the BEF in 1918 was not the result of wholesale changes among the senior generals of 1914. Indeed, there was a remarkable continuity of command throughout the war. Sir Douglas Haig, the commander-in-chief of the BEF (1915–18), served with nine army commanders during the course of the war. Of these, Sir Edmund Allenby was transferred to Palestine and became a Field Marshal; Sir Charles Monro was appointed commander-in-chief, India; Sir Horace Smith-Dorrien was sent back to England by Field Marshal French (and later judged to have been unfairly treated) before Haig took over as commander of the BEF; and Sir Hubert Gough, generally regarded as a scapegoat, was dismissed following the collapse of the Fourth Army in spring 1918. The remaining five generals who, together with Haig, led the BEF to victory in 1918, were all senior generals at the beginning of the war. In October 1914, Haig and Sir Herbert Plumer were Lieutenant Generals while Sir William Birdwood, Sir Julian Byng, Sir Henry Horne and Sir Henry Rawlinson all held the rank of Major

General.[2] Moreover, the pre-war army, despite the influx of Territorial and New Army officers, maintained a firm grip on senior appointments in the BEF. During the course of the war over 80 per cent of the generals at corps and divisional levels were serving Regular officers in 1914.[3]

The senior generals of the BEF had several characteristics in common. Their social backgrounds were similar. Of the field marshals, full generals and lieutenant generals who served in the war – totalling 122 – fifty came from military families, eleven from landed gentry, eleven from the clergy and most of the remainder from the higher professional classes.[4] There was a sprinkling from the aristocracy, notably Viscount Byng and Lord Rawlinson. The majority had attended a public school and the Royal Military Academy at either Sandhurst (Cavalry and Infantry) or Woolwich (Artillery and Engineers). Given this background, it is not surprising that being a 'gentleman' was considered an important characteristic. Early in the war, Rawlinson criticized the officers of the 51st Highland Division complaining that there were 'too few gentlemen amongst them'.[5] At one point, Plumer was saved from being removed from his command of the Second Army because Haig considered him to be 'an honest, straight-forward gentleman'. Byng was described as 'a perfect old courtier and gentleman'. Being a good horseman or games player was also thought to be a worthwhile attribute.[6]

The senior generals also had similar educational and professional backgrounds. Of the army generals who served with Haig during the war, four were educated at Eton (Byng, Gough, Plumer and Rawlinson), two at Harrow (Smith-Dorrien and Horne), and one each at Clifton (Birdwood), Haileybury (Allenby), and Sherborne (Monro). Five of these generals attended Sandhurst and one was trained at Woolwich. Six, by attending Staff College, were able to put the coveted initials 'psc' (passed Staff College) after their names. Seven of these generals had served in South Africa, five in India and four in the Sudan. Smith-Dorrien had the distinction of having served in all of these theatres.

These common characteristics of the army commanders were also evident amongst their immediate subordinates – the corps and divisional generals. Of these officers, some 75 per cent attended public school, mainly at Eton, Wellington, Harrow, Marlborough, Charterhouse and Winchester. Over 80 per cent were the sons of army officers, landed gentry, clergymen or the aristocracy. More than half had attended Staff College. In 1914, over 80 per cent had previous battle experience in some part or other of the British Empire.[7]

This shared background of the BEF generals has been criticized as being narrow and inward-looking – a 'custom-bound clique'[8] – and certainly it was a world where personal contacts and patronage played an important part in career progression. Haig had strong connections with the Royal Family – his wife Dorothy had been one of Queen Alexandra's ladies-in-waiting – and other senior generals, including Allenby and Rawlinson, were invited by George V to correspond on military matters. Sir John French had received the personal support of General Sir Redvers Buller; Haig's career owed much to both French and Kitchener; and Rawlinson and Horne, among others, had benefitted from Haig's patronage.

The first commander-in-chief of the BEF, Sir John French (1914–15), despite being an excellent horseman, was, in many ways, an exception to this general pattern. Although born on a small estate in Kent, French's family fortunes were slender. He strenuously resisted the efforts of his family to send him to Harrow and instead entered the navy at the age of 14. After six years, French changed his allegiance and joined the army. He gained his commission in the 19th Hussars through the 'side door' having served in the Militia. As regards being a 'gentleman', French's weakness for the opposite sex and his continuing lack of cash caused him serious embarrassment and almost cost him his career. He had numerous extra-marital affairs, one with the wife of a brother officer. He also borrowed money, some £2,000, from one of his subordinates, a certain Major Douglas Haig. There is no evidence that the loan was repaid. Nevertheless, because of his innate leadership ability, his courage and his professional competence – shown in Egypt and South Africa and in a series of War Office appointments – he gained rapid promotion. From 1906 onwards French was recognized as commander-in-chief designate of the BEF.

Sir Douglas Haig, the second commander-in-chief of the BEF, had a considerably more conformist background than that of Sir John French. Haig was a member of a wealthy whisky family. He had attended Clifton College, Oxford University and Sandhurst. He also attended Staff College and so impressed his professors that the teacher of Strategy and Tactics,

G.F.R. Henderson, marked him out as a future leader of the British Army.[9] Thereafter, Haig's career blossomed both in the field and at the War Office and, by 1914, he was the commander of I Corps reporting to French.

The interwoven backgrounds of the BEF generals provided them with values and interests that characterized them as a unique institution having its own particular ethos of obedience, duty and service. Such a common culture, however, did not prevent rivalries or, indeed, outright feuds. When General Sir Horace Smith-Dorrien followed Sir John French as commander at Aldershot in 1907, French resented many of Smith-Dorrien's new procedures and changes of policy. This resentment was not helped when Kitchener insisted on Smith-Dorrien becoming II Corps commander in August 1914 instead of French's own choice, Sir Herbert Plumer. Even more hostility developed later that same month when Smith-Dorrien acted contrary to French's orders and made a stand at Le Cateau during the Mons retreat. Things came to a head in May 1915 when French received from Smith-Dorrien a somewhat pessimistic assessment of the BEF position during the Second Battle of Ypres. French took this opportunity to send Smith-Dorrien back to England and appoint Plumer in his place.

Sir John French was himself eventually removed from his post as commander-in-chief following the intrigues of his subordinates, among them Haig and Gough. French had been losing the support of HM the King, Asquith and Kitchener for some time. Haig noted in his diary on 14 July 1915: 'He [the King] referred to the friction between Sir John French and Lord K and hoped that I [Haig] would do all I could to make matters run smoothly … he [the King] had lost confidence in Field Marshal French'.[10] And on 17 October 1915, Haig remarked to General Robertson, French's chief of staff, that he 'had come to the conclusion that it was not fair to the Empire to retain French in command' and added that 'none of my officers commanding Corps had any opinion of Sir John French's military ability or military views …'.[11] The failures of the 1915 battles – Neuve Chapelle, Aubers Ridge and Festubert – had been bitterly disappointing, but it was the mismanagement of the Reserves at Loos in September 1915 that brought French's downfall. He was obliged to resign on 6 December 1915 and was replaced by Haig – once French's favoured subordinate and now his arch rival.

French was not particularly popular – Sir James Edmonds, later the British official historian, regarded him as 'a vain, ignorant and vindictive old man' and Gough described him as an 'ignorant little fool'[12] – but the main charge against him was military incompetence. He had been unable to demonstrate either to his superiors in London or to his subordinates in France that he had any clear idea as to how best to conduct the war. As commander-in-chief of the BEF French was just not equipped mentally, physically or by experience to deal with the problems of modern warfare. Moreover, he had shown no signs of adapting to the new situation.

French was not the only British general who was unprepared for the type of war that had developed on the Western Front. They all lacked relevant operational experience. Only some ten years earlier the traditional Square formation had been used in Africa against the natives of Nigeria and Somaliland. As Smith-Dorrien remarked: 'One could never become an up to date soldier in the prehistoric warfare to be met with against the Dervishes'.[13] Even Britain's most recent war, the Boer War (1899–1902), could not be described as a military success. The British army, frequently outmanoeuvred, had needed to raise a force of over 448,000 to subdue no more than 60,000 mounted farmers.[14] In addition, the generals lacked experience in handling large formations. Only three serving generals (French, Haig and Smith-Dorrien) had commanded the peacetime corps at Aldershot – the only establishment of its kind in Britain. By contrast the French had twenty-five such commands and Germany thirty-five.[15]

* * *

The generals of the BEF faced not only the problem of organizing a rapidly expanding army – already by 1915 larger and more complicated than at any other time in its history – but also a form of warfare characterized by trenches and barbed wire and by weaponry that possessed great accuracy and destructive power. During the thirty years or so before the war – the period that coincided with the military careers of the BEF generals – a revolution had taken place in the development of weapons which had massive implications for the conduct of any future war.

In the 1880s all the European armies began to use small-bore bolt-action rifles which fired multi-rounds from spring-loaded clips inserted into a magazine. The French Lebel rifle was developed in 1886. It was followed in 1887 by the German Mauser-Gewehr, and the British introduced the Lee-Enfield in 1907. All these rifles were able to fire 10–15 rounds per minute with a range of up to a 1,000 yards. Never had the infantryman been so well armed. The development of the rifle was accompanied by the invention of smokeless explosives. In 1887 Alfred Nobel produced cordite and thereafter the rifleman could, for the first time, deliver devastating fire without giving away his position.

The design of the machine gun was improved in 1885 by Hiram Maxim who made the first water-cooled portable automatic version – a design taken over by the British Company, Vickers, in 1889. The Maxim could fire at twice the speed of the old Gatling gun and with greater accuracy. Other European countries produced their own machine guns based on the Maxim principles – the Maschinengewehr in Germany (1908) and the Hotchkiss in France. By 1911 lighter machine guns such as the British Lewis gun were being manufactured in increasingly large numbers. All these weapons were able to fire at 500 rounds per minute. The fire power of a single machine gun was estimated to be the equivalent of eighty riflemen.

The design of artillery pieces was also revolutionized. Field guns were developed with recoil systems that required only small adjustments before the next round could be fired. The principle German field gun was the 15-pounder with a range of 11,000 yards, while the British standard field gun was the Mark I 18-pounder with a range of 7,000 yards. In 1897 the French introduced the most celebrated field gun of the war – their 75mm model, which could fire at 15–30 rounds per minute over a distance of up to 9,000 yards. Such was the superiority of these field guns over previous models that they collectively became known as 'Quick Firers'.

The Howitzer, designed to lob heavy shells using a high trajectory, was also improved in the 1890s with the French 155mm Schneider, the German 10.5cm Howber and the British 60-pounder. In addition, heavy, long-range guns were developed, notably the German Big Bertha which could fire a 2,000lb shell 15,000 yards and the 'Paris' gun (264-pounder), also German, that had a range of over 80 miles. All these artillery weapons were able to fire either high explosive rounds that detonated on impact or shrapnel shells with a time fuse that caused an explosion in flight.

During the period 1880–1914 the military authorities of all countries were therefore grappling not only with the problems associated with testing and commissioning these significantly improved weapons, they were also having to assess how battle tactics would be affected by them. Traditionally, the assumption was that the advantage was always with the attacker and not the defender. In 1880, just four years before Haig went to Sandhurst, a handbook on tactics asserted that:

> the great advantage that an assailant has is his power of choosing his own time and point of attack. It is this, and the knowledge that the defenders have that the assailants are doing something…they know nothing of, which gives such moral power to the offensive and is so demoralising to the defence.[16]

However, with the rapid improvements in infantry and artillery fire power, assumptions about the superiority of the attacker over the defender were starting to be questioned. Even in 1878, at the time of the Russo-Turkish War, the correspondent of the *Daily News* commented: 'The whole system of attack upon even the simplest of trenches will have to be completely changed in future. Assault, properly speaking, will have to be abandoned'.[17] In 1894 a cadet at Sandhurst, H.C. Potter, wrote in his notebook under the heading 'The Effect of More Recent Improvements in Firearms on Tactics': 'a purely frontal attack is futile … the position of defenders, lying motionless behind cover, would be very difficult to discover, while their view of the attacker is much improved by the absence of smoke'.[18]

Professor G.F.R. Henderson of the Staff College had been on Lord Roberts's staff for a period during the Boer War. Henderson summed up the lessons from that campaign:

> Nowadays the ground in front of a strong line of [defending] infantry, provided that the rifles are held a few inches above the level, is so closely swept by the sheet of lead as to be practically impassable by [attacking] men standing upright or even crouching. The long deadly zone of this

> horizontal fire, which every improvement in firearms tends to increase, is the most potent factor in modern battle.[19]

The British Army *Field Service Regulations* of 1905 similarly reflected the lessons of the Boer War. Section 106 recognized the advantages inherent in defence: 'It should be generally comparatively easy for the defender to hide his dispositions and to effect a surprise. Entrenchments, moreover, are more easily employed by the defence, and by their aid a position may sometimes be rendered sometimes impregnable'.[20]

The general mood, immediately after the Boer War, was that the offensive, although essential to victory, had become an extremely hazardous undertaking. Success could only come from superior fire power and by attacks carried out by large formations out-flanking the enemy and concentrating on weak spots. Section 107 of the British Army *Field Service Regulations* of 1905 read: 'The strength of the assailant has always lain … in his power of manoeuvring, and of concentrating unexpectedly against some weak or ill-defended point'.

By 1909, however, this guarded approach to the offensive had undergone a radical change. A significant factor in this change was the interpretation, by the majority of the European observers, of the lessons of the Russo-Japanese War of 1904–5. Both the Russians and the Japanese were equipped with the most modern weapons – rifles with magazines, quick-firing artillery pieces and machine guns – equipment that was, in fact, to change little before the beginning of the 1914 war. The Russians were defending their territories in Southern Manchuria and the Japanese, by means of a series of offensives, gradually drove them out. The cost to the Japanese was high. They lost 50,000 men at Port Arthur and 70,000 men at the Battle of Mukden. The campaign clearly showed that the rifle and artillery fire of entrenched defenders could inflict heavy casualties on massed infantry, but it also showed that carefully prepared attacks by committed troops could lead to victory over the enemy. The main lesson absorbed by the European observers was that, even against defenders possessing modern weapons, barbed wire and elaborate trench systems, a determined offensive could be successful. The military observers concluded that the Japanese had won their battles because they were infused by the offensive spirit and that well-trained infantry with courage and willingness to take heavy casualties could achieve victory. As a consequence of these lessons taken from the Russo-Japanese War, the Boer War experience came to be regarded as unrepresentative and could not be taken as an example of modern warfare. The point was made forcibly by a British commentator in 1914:

> There were those who deduced from the experience in South Africa that the assault, or at least the assault with the bayonet, was a thing of the past, a scrap heap manoeuvre, … the Manchurian campaign showed over and over again that the bayonet was in no sense an obsolete weapon … the assault is even more important than the attainment of fire-mastery that antecedes it. It is the supreme moment of the fight. Upon it the final issue rests.[21]

Lieutenant General Kiggell, later to become Haig's chief of staff, expressed the same view at a Conference for General Staff Officers held in 1910: 'Victory is won actually by the bayonet or by the fear of it, which amounts to the same thing so far as the conduct of the attack is concerned. The fact was proved beyond doubt in the last [Manchurian] war'.[22]

By 1914 it was the offensive, not the defensive, that determined the mindset of British generals. The 1909 *Field Service Regulations*, in contrast to those of 1905, stated that:

> Decisive success in battle can be gained only by vigorous offensive … Half-hearted measures never attain success in war and lack of determination is the most fruitful source of defeat … if victory is to be won the defensive attitude must be assumed only in order to obtain or create a favourable opportunity for **decisive offensive action** … the advance … must be characterised by **the determination to press forward at all costs**'.[23]

It should be noted that the 1909 *Regulations* were formulated by Haig when he was Director of Staff Duties at the War Office 1907–9. It should also be noted that in the 1909 *Regulations* the phrase 'at all costs' appeared for the first time. The offensive had become an established imperative. A widely read training manual, published in 1913, stated that: 'There is only one rule that can never be departed from and which will always lead to success, and that is always to push forward, always to attack.'[24] The 1914 edition of the *Regulations* emphasized the point further: 'The paramount duty of all leaders in the firing line is to get their troops forward ... he must be imbued with the determination to close with the enemy'.[25]

However, not all senior officers in the British army followed the doctrine of the offensive without question. Major General May, writing in the *Army Review* of 1913, gave his opinion that the emphasis on the attack 'threatens to be a stereo-typed phrase...a tribute to the prevailing fashion'.[26] General Sir Ian Hamilton, who was to command the Gallipoli campaign in 1915, at one time held the view that: 'Sheer numbers of infantrymen regardless of the elan that might have infused them, could not break a resolute defence'.[27] On a later occasion, however, Hamilton had a change of mind and argued that: 'New weapons could be overcome by new men'.[28]

Despite some dissidents, the doctrine of the offensive had, by 1914, become firmly accepted by the generals of the BEF. Haig's Staff College notes indicate a basic belief in the offensive – 'only the decisive offensive could influence war'.[29] It was a view that Haig and the great majority of generals were to hold throughout the war. And it should be noted that the doctrine of the offensive was not simply a British phenomenon. Through a similar process of reasoning and discussion all the main contestants in the war followed the same general approach. The German military strategist, General Friederich von Bernhardi, wrote: 'those troops will prove superior who can bear the greatest losses and advance more vigorously than others'.[30] Similarly, Marshal Joffre, who was Chief of the General Staff of the French Army in 1911 and commanded the French Army in 1914, spoke of 'the eternal principles underlying the necessity of the offensive'.[31] It was these principles that gave rise to the German Schlieffen Plan and the French Plan XVII in 1914 and the thousands of attacks, great and small, that characterized the Western Front throughout the war.

The doctrine of the offensive had not been arrived at hastily. It had been the subject of discussion and debate at General Staff Conferences and in military literature in the years leading up to the war and it was enshrined in the *Field Service Regulations*. The accepted argument was straightforward:

the defender certainly had some advantages over the attacker, but only the attacker could overwhelm a strongpoint, destroy the enemy, gain territory or win a victory. And the cult of the offensive had not been adopted without a clear understanding of its implications in terms of suffering and casualties. Colonel F.N. Maude put the matter starkly:

> The chances of victory turn entirely on the spirit of self-sacrifice of those who have to be offered up to gain opportunity for the remainder... Success in the assault is all a case of how you train beforehand – to know how to die or to avoid dying. If the latter then nothing can help you, and it would be wiser not to go to war.[32]

At a General Staff Officers' Conference in 1909 it was estimated that casualty figures following an attack would be in the order of 25–30 per cent. These figures were discussed and accepted without question[33] and casualties around that level and greater became evident during the early months of the war – at Mons, Le Cateau, the Marne and the Aisne.

* * *

By October 1914 it had become clear that the German Schlieffen Plan to take Paris and force the French out of the war had failed. British and French troops had pushed the Germans northwards from the Marne to the Aisne, but at that point the Germans had dug in and could not be moved. The traditional tactic when faced by an unmoveable enemy was to outflank him. Both sides employed this tactic, but neither was able to make significant headway. Each stage of the outflanking process resulted in both sides digging entrenchments and over a period of weeks these entrenchments extended north-westerly towards the Channel coast and south-easterly towards Switzerland. There were concerted efforts to make a break-through at certain points of the front. At Ypres, for example, the Germans attacked for six weeks during October-November 1914. The British and French were able to halt the German attacks, but at a cost of some 100,000 casualties. The Germans lost around 130,000.

The series of entrenchments were strengthened with barbed-wire entanglements and by December the Western Front had been formed – 480 miles of parallel trenches stretching from the North Sea in to the Alps. Overall, the opposing forces were evenly matched in terms of courage, numbers, weaponry and defensive systems. The situation was stalemate and it largely remained so for the next three and a half years.

The German army in France had some considerable ground advantages. In the early days of the war it had advanced into Northern France and was in possession of, and exploited, more than half of France's most productive coal, iron and steel works as well as a large proportion of its best farmland. In addition the Germans controlled the rail network around Lille, thus facilitating the movement of their troops and supplies. Equally important from a tactical point of view was the German practice of falling back where appropriate to take command of the higher ground. In 1914, for example, German troops had overrun the French town of Merville. But Merville was in the low-lying and marshy area of the River Lys and the Germans were quite prepared to withdraw some 10 miles to the tactically more advantageous higher ground of the Aubers Ridge. By 1916 the BEF occupied the line from Ypres down to the Somme – about 80 miles – and for much of that front the Germans held the high ground – the ridges east of Ypres; the Messines Ridge; the Gheluvelt Plateau; Aubers Ridge; Vimy Ridge; and so on. From these vantage points, which were often not more than 40 or 50 feet above the surrounding area, the Germans could observe clearly the front lines and register their artillery with accuracy on the British trenches.

Between 1914 and 1917 the British generals also had to contend with a complex and often restrictive relationship with their major ally, France. The French army was the dominant force and for most of the war the BEF was obliged to play a supporting role. Under the circumstances, such a role was quite understandable. The French were numerically superior. Moreover, the fighting was taking place on French soil and a significant amount of French territory had fallen into enemy hands. The politicians in London accepted this situation and when the BEF went to France in August 1914 the formal instructions received by Sir John French read: 'The special motive of the force under your control is to support and cooperate with the French army'.[34] When Haig became the commander of the BEF in December 1915 he received essentially the same instructions.

The practical nature of the Anglo-French military relationship soon became clear. During the retreat from Mons in late August 1914, Field Marshal French proposed to protect the BEF by withdrawing it from the Allied line and placing it at a safe distance behind Paris. Both the British Cabinet and the French commander-in-chief, Joffre, were dumbfounded by this proposal which effectively meant that the British would be abandoning its ally. Kitchener, in full Field Marshal's uniform, was immediately despatched by the Cabinet to France with the instruction that the BEF should remain in the fighting line 'conforming to the movements of the French army'.[35]

It was not helpful to either Field Marshal French or Haig that the original written orders from the British Cabinet as to the relationship with the French were somewhat conflicting. On the one hand, the BEF was to support the French in repelling the Germans in France and Belgium. On the other hand, the Cabinet stressed that the BEF was an independent force; that the commander-in-chief was responsible for its survival; and that the BEF was not to undertake offensives that were not supported by the French.[36]

These instructions determined the sequence and character of BEF military operations for much of the period 1914–17. As a consequence, the BEF fought in support of French offensives in sectors of the front that were not of its choosing. Both Field Marshal French and Haig would have preferred to carry out attacks to the north in French Flanders to protect the Channel ports and ensure that their main lines of supply were kept open. In March 1915, however, the BEF were obliged to attack at Neuve Chapelle in support of a French offensive towards the Vimy Ridge. In the event, the French changed their plan, but the British IV and Indian Corps nevertheless continued with their attack and Neuve Chapelle was taken. Two months later, in May, the BEF attacked at Aubers Ridge and at Festubert, both in support of a Joffre offensive in the Artois area. The two British attacks were failures and the French offensive petered out inconclusively after six weeks. This same pattern of the BEF supporting the French was repeated at Loos in September 1915 and, on a much larger scale, on the Somme in July 1916. In neither case was the attack area selected by the commander-in-chief of the

BEF. On both occasions the British would have preferred to attack further north in the Ypres area.

The casualties incurred in these attacks were high: 15,000 at Neuve Chapelle; 26,000 at Aubers Ridge and Festubert; 48,000 at Loos; and a staggering 480,000 during the five months of the Somme offensive. During all these operations, the Germans had the advantage of the defender against the attacker and of holding well-positioned and heavily defended trenches. It was in these circumstances that the mindset of the British and French generals, and their basic approach to the war on the Western Front, showed itself to be quite different from that of the Germans. The Germans carried out only two major offensive operations in the years 1915–17. The first, against the British at Ypres in February 1915 and the second, against the French, at Verdun in February 1916. Neither was successful and both were exceptions to the overall German strategy in the West.

Germany's thinking was influenced by two major considerations: its geographical position in the centre of Europe and its main ally, Austria-Hungary. The first, while giving the advantages of centralised communications, also committed it to a war on two fronts – in the West against France and Britain, and, in the East, against Russia. The second was a source of military concern. Germany needed Austria-Hungary for support against Russia, yet the Austro-Hungarian forces were unpredictable in their reliability and frequently needed to be bolstered by German troops. Germany could not apply its full power on the Western Front because its generals and soldiers were being diverted to the East. In any event, the Western Front had become a stalemate, while the vast extent of the Eastern Front offered scope for possible victories. It was these considerations that led Falkenhayn, the German Chief of the General Staff, to abandon the offensive in the West. German troops were ordered to go on the defensive for the foreseeable future. In February 1915 the German army in the West was restructured with every division reduced from four to three infantry regiments, thus creating a reserve for use elsewhere.[37]

The Germans in the West, therefore, focused on holding the valuable territory that they had already won and they allowed the Allies to batter themselves against their constantly improving defences. By contrast, the French and British mindset was strongly inclined to the offensive. The

Germans had to be driven from French soil. This imperative was at the root of French strategy throughout the war and the role of the BEF, as the subordinate force for most of that time, was to act in support.

The character of the opposing trenches reflected these two different mindsets. The German trenches in front of the BEF were generally deep and defended by concrete pillboxes. Even in the low-lying marshy sectors of French Flanders the German trenches were kept reasonably dry by means of powerful pumps:

> all the material and mechanical advantages of Lille were exploited for the purposes of war by the Germans. The electric tram system was extended, electric power was diverted to the front line and used for many purposes, amongst which may be cited universal electric lighting of dug-outs and the installation of powerful pumps for the drainage of the primeval swamp that the front line resembled.[38]

A light railway was constructed south of Armentières and in the 6th Bavarian Reserve Division sector 'shell-proof shelters were installed on average every 25 metres'.[39] Further south, in the chalk of the Somme region, German dug-outs were often 40 feet below ground and equipped with electric lighting, beds with mattresses, and wood-panelled walls. The Germans took the view that they were sitting-tenants and they were there to stay.

The British trenches, although constructed with sandbags, parados and parapets, and having barbed-wire defences and dug-outs, were relatively flimsy. They were not built for long-term occupation, but as temporary shelters from which attacks could be launched. The aim was to push the enemy back, not to consolidate a defensive position. It was in this context that the BEF generals pursued a policy of active aggression. Anything less would only have condoned an unacceptable stalemate.

* * *

It is not surprising, given the lack of forward movement by the BEF and the heavy casualties it had sustained, that the politicians were attracted to alternative strategies other than the bludgeoning on the Western Front. The battles of 1915 had proved unsuccessful and, as the British official historian Sir James Edmonds wrote: 'In view of the situation on the Western Front and the subsequent failures of the French and British offensives in 1915, the wisdom of the decision to make trial elsewhere – provided that surprise was ensured – can hardly be questioned'.[40] Both Churchill and Kitchener shared this logic. Churchill's opinion was: 'From first to last it is contended that once the main armies were in deadlock in France the true strategy … was to attack the weaker partners … with the utmost speed and ample force'.[41] Kitchener wrote to Field Marshal French in January 1915: 'The German lines in France may be looked upon as a fortress that cannot be carried by assault and also that cannot be completely invested, with the result that the lines may be held by an investing force while operations proceed elsewhere'.[42] Lloyd George entered the discussion and went even further, suggesting that the BEF should be removed from France and sent to some other theatre of war.[43]

It was this thinking, supported by Asquith and the British War Council[44], that led to Gallipoli, Salonika, Mesopotamia and the other 'side-shows'. The concept of disabling Germany and its allies by what amounted to traditional out-flanking movements on a grand scale was seductive. If an attack on Gallipoli was successful and Constantinople taken, then not only would Germany's ally, Turkey, be forced out of the war, but a much-needed supply route to Russia through the Dardanelles would be opened. A leading article in *The Times* of 22 February 1915 put the case for attacking Gallipoli forcibly:

> The way to the Black Sea is closed by the Dardanelles and the Bosphorous. Vladivostock is too far away to be of much use. Russia is in bonds, and it is the duty of the Allies to burst them open if they can. Immeasurable advantages would flow from the opening of a clear way to Odessa. Ships laden with wheat would stream outwards and ships laden with equipment and stores which Russia so greatly needs would stream inwards … The effect upon the hesitancy of the Balkan kingdoms and other neutrals would be instant … The fall of Constantinople, should it be brought about, would probably mean the collapse of the Turkish offensive.

Lloyd George, who despaired at breaking the stalemate on the Western Front, pleaded for 'a definite victory somewhere', proposing several schemes to defeat Germany by 'knocking the props under her'.[45] At the War Council meeting of 24 February 1915 he put forward the view that 'if we failed at the Dardanelles we ought to be ready immediately to try something else'.[46]

The reaction of the French and BEF generals to these proposals was predictable. Both General Joffre and Field Marshal French were opposed to the idea of sending British troops to any theatre of war other than the Western Front. When, towards the end of 1914, the Germans withdrew eight infantry and six cavalry divisions from France to strengthen their position on the Eastern Front, Field Marshal French wrote to the War Council: 'in view of numbers and German commitments in Russia, it seems of the utmost importance that we should strike at the earliest possible moment with all our available strength'. He added that, until the impossibility of a breakthrough on the Western Front was proved, there could be no question of making an attempt elsewhere.[47]

The outcome of these conflicting discussions between the 'Easterners' and the 'Westerners' was unsatisfactory. The government decided that the main theatre of war should continue to be the Western Front, but if offensives in France proved unsuccessful, then British troops would be moved elsewhere. Given the overall shortage of both men and material this arrangement was unlikely to be of benefit either in the West or in the East. By the end of 1915 Gallipoli had been abandoned with the loss of 260,000 men; in Mesopotamia 9,000 British and Indian troops were under siege at Kut; and Salonika had absorbed 500,000 men for no real purpose. Both Field Marshal French and General Haig were quite clear as to where the manpower and resources of the British Empire should be placed and where the war would be won – or lost. In January 1915 French wrote: 'There are no theatres, other than those in which operations are now in progress, in which decisive results can be achieved'.[48] When it was suggested by Kitchener that the New Armies might be used elsewhere than the Western Front, Haig's reaction was: 'we ought not to divide our Military Force, but concentrate on the decisive point which is on this frontier against the German main Army'. Haig was convinced that any diversion of troops away from the Western Front was 'a violation of sound strategic principle ... we cannot hope to win until we have defeated the German Army. The easiest place to do this is in France, because our lines of communication are the shortest to this theatre of war'.[49] Haig held to this view and repeated it many times throughout the war. Both Haig and French were supported by Lieutenant General Robertson who had been appointed Chief of the Imperial General Staff. In December 1915 Robertson wrote to Haig:

> I am doing all right on the War Committee but it is difficult to keep one's temper. At the last meeting Balfour weighed in with a proposal that as the Western Front was so strong we should transfer all possible troops to cooperate with Russia on the Eastern front! Words failed me and I lost my temper.[50]

However, despite the firm advice of the senior generals in the BEF, British troops were employed 'elsewhere'. Even in October 1917, at a critical stage of the Passchendaele offensive, Lloyd George, then Prime Minister, insisted on sending General Plumer and four divisions from France to support the Italians following their defeat at Caporetto. Haig had not even been consulted about the transfer. He wrote in his diary: 'Was ever an Army Commander and his Staff sent off to another theatre of war in the middle of a battle?'.[51]

* * *

It was against this background of uncertain support from the British government that Haig doggedly pursued his policy of 'wearing down' the enemy. The war on the Western Front had developed into one of grim attrition and the succession of British offensives from Neuve Chapelle in 1915 to Passchendaele in 1917 had produced horrendous casualty figures. In every month of the years 1915, 1916 and 1917 the French and British losses exceeded those of the Germans.[52] This caused, understandably, great concern and adverse comment. In 1916 Churchill questioned in the House of Commons the issue of Haig's policy of attrition, pointing out the imbalance in the number of casualties suffered by the British compared to those of the enemy. Moreover, said Churchill, the 'wearing down' policy was producing no worthwhile territorial gain and was therefore pointless.[53]

Lloyd George also criticised Haig's policy of attrition and later wrote in his *Memoirs*:

> To concentrate almost exclusively on the Western Front, where your enemy had exercised his utmost engineering skills to construct considerable entrenchments, where the transport system was perfect, where he had more cannons and machine guns than we had; and where, consequently, we lost three men in fruitless attacks for every two he lost in successful defence – suited the foe … the idea of a war of attrition was the refuge of stupidity and it was stupidly operated …[54]

Despite these bitter comments there was evidence that the policy of attrition, although costly, was having its effects. Haig identified the Somme offensive as 'the opening of the wearing-out battle'[55] and Field Marshal Hindenburg, the German commander on the Western Front from August 1916, later commented: 'There we passed from one crisis to another. Our lines were permanently in a condition of the highest tension'[56] The German *Reichsarchiv's* post-war assessment of the battle stated that: 'the grave loss of blood affected Germany more heavily than the Entente'.[57] The Germans had lost irreplaceable experienced NCOs and junior officers and their morale had been seriously dented. The Somme had brought about a shift of emphasis. At the end of 1916 General Falkenhayn wrote that Germany 'was now engaged in a struggle in which the very existence of our nation, and not only military glory, or the conquest of territories, was at stake'.[58] Captain von Hentog, a German officer with the Guard Reserve Division, described the Somme as the 'muddy grave of the German field army'.[59] A German soldier, Friedrich Steinbrecher, wrote on 12 August: 'Somme. The whole history of the world cannot contain a more ghastly word'.[60] The Battle of Verdun, which lasted for nine months from February 1916, was another blow to Germany. This German offensive was aimed at 'bleeding the French army white' but it ended in stalemate with some 350,000 casualties on each side. The BEF offensive at Passchendaele in 1917, like that on the Somme in 1916, was intended to be a breakthrough, but, again as the Somme, it ended as yet another battle of attrition. At Passchendaele both sides lost around 250,000 men and the British lines had advanced only 5 miles.

How long could the belligerents on the Western Front carry on losing so many men and using up such quantities of materials? Could the reserves of Britain and France last longer than the reserves of Germany?[61] The answers to these questions were, to say the least, problematic and certainly in early 1917 nobody could even hazard a guess. However, by late 1917 it became painfully clear to Germany that the balance of power on the Western Front would, at some point in 1918, move heavily against them. America had entered the war against Germany in April 1917. The manpower and resources potentially available to the Allies were immense, but it would take some time before they could be put to use. Meanwhile the outcome of the war was far from clear. There was still much fighting to be done.

* * *

BEF generals have been criticised harshly over the years. It is true that they came from a narrow social and educational background; that their military experience was limited to small colonial wars; that they were often over-optimistic in their planning; and that their adherence to the doctrine of the offensive was inflexible. On the other hand, it is also true that these generals had to deal with a completely new form of warfare using weapons that could kill as never before; that they were obliged to act for much of the war as a component of the French army; that they faced a determined, skilled and well-entrenched enemy; and that they had to face the efforts of politicians to direct manpower and resources away from the theatre where the enemy had the bulk of its troops and where the war was eventually won – the Western Front. It was the combination of professionalism, common purpose and determination that enabled Haig and his senior BEF generals to stick to their task for four gruelling years. Their common social, educational and military backgrounds, far from being a disadvantage, served to provide a useful framework of understanding and an operational ethos of discipline, duty and service. It says much for their tenacity of purpose that they were able to adapt to the changing circumstances of the war and it is significant that the group of generals who suffered the setbacks of 1914 and 1915; the grinding offensives of 1916 and 1917 and the German onslaught of spring 1918 were essentially the same generals who brought the BEF to victory in November 1918.

Following the failure of the Schlieffen Plan in September 1914 and the German occupation of much of Northern France the war on the Western Front became a stalemate. The BEF generals together with the generals of

France were controlled by the circumstances that confronted them. The British were concerned with the need to support their main ally, France, and safeguard the Channel ports; the French, still suffering from the humiliation of their defeat by Prussia in 1870 and the loss of Alsace-Lorraine, were obsessed with their aim to drive the Germans out of their country; and the Germans were content, at least for the time being, to defend their new and extended frontier in the West. The opposing forces were evenly matched and neither side was able to gain any particular territorial advantage. The static trench system across Europe hardly changed for three and a half years and even the withdrawal of the Germans to their Hindenburg line in March 1917 was simply a tactical move to a stronger defensive position. It was the Germans who determined the shape and character of the Western Front.

The devotion of the British and French generals to the offensive was not only mainstream military thinking of the time, it was the only way that the German army could be defeated and that defeat had to take place where the main German army was positioned – the Western Front. The Germans themselves were well aware of this. When they released divisions from the Eastern Front in late 1917, they were sent to France, not to some other theatre of war. The efforts of the British War Council to cripple Germany and its allies by means of operations in the East were ineffective. The military leaders from all the Allied countries – Britain, France, Russia, Italy, Belgium and Serbia – never did have much faith in 'side-shows'. At their Chantilly Conference in December 1915 they agreed that: 'the decision of the war can only be obtained in the principle theatres, that is to say in those areas in which the enemy has maintained the greater part of his forces … only minimum forces should be employed in the secondary theatres'.[62] Nevertheless, a total of some 3.6 million British Empire troops served in theatres other than the Western Front during the war.[63] A proportion of these were positioned in areas of strategic importance – Palestine and Mesopotamia for example – but others were not. Even an extra one million men on the Western Front would have done much to prevent the crisis of March-April 1918 when the German offensives almost brought them victory.

Relationships between the BEF generals and the politicians in London were severely strained by the issue of employing scarce troops other than in France. They were also strained by the view, held strongly by Lloyd George and Churchill, that Haig and his generals were callous and profligate in the use of their troops. Lloyd George openly and cynically criticised the cost of 'great victories' in France. The casualty lists were certainly horrific and both Lloyd George and Churchill were doubtless sincere in their wish to reduce what Churchill called 'the Blood Count'.[64] It is nevertheless a fact that the British suffered losses that were proportionately fewer than those of other countries. The total killed during the war in all theatres as a percentage of those mobilized was 8.8 per cent for the British Empire (excluding Britain and Ireland) and 11.8 per cent for Britain and Ireland. For France it was 16.8 per cent; for Italy 10.3 per cent; for Russia 11.5 per cent; for Germany 15.4 per cent; and for Austria-Hungary 12.2 per cent.[65] It is against these figures that the 'profligacy' of the British generals should be judged.

Lloyd George did what he could to restrict the number of troops that could be sent to France. Haig demanded 600,000 men for 1918 and this number was reduced to 150,000 on the grounds that other activities such as munitions, shipbuilding and aeroplane manufacture were also of vital importance. There may have been sound grounds for this decision, but it left the BEF seriously under-complement when it faced the major German offensives in the first half of 1918.

These issues brought Haig and Lloyd George into sharp conflict. Lloyd George believed that Haig was 'intellectually and temperamentally unequal to the command of an Army'.[66] Haig told his wife that he 'had no great opinion of L.G. as a man or a leader'.[67] There was little hope for a constructive meeting of the minds and Lloyd George was determined to remove as much authority from Haig as possible. At the Calais Conference of February 1917 Lloyd George, without any prior discussion, attempted to subordinate Haig and the BEF to the French General Nivelle who was about to lead his disastrous offensive in Champagne. The CIGS, Robertson, was utterly taken aback and Haig threatened to resign in the knowledge that HM the King would support him. Lloyd George was obliged to accept that Haig's role as 'chief of staff' to Nivelle would only be temporary. Haig wrote to Robertson: 'Will History ever forgive the members of the War Cabinet for declining in January 1917 to have any confidence in the power of the British Army to play its part with credit on the Western Front'.[68] Lloyd George eventually succeeded in engineering the removal of General

Charteris, Haig's Intelligence Chief, and also Robertson, Haig's greatest military supporter, who resigned rather than accept a lesser role. There is no doubt that Lloyd George would have replaced Haig if he possibly could, but he faced an insuperable problem which he reluctantly admitted in his *Memoirs*: 'the British Army did not bring into prominence any Commander who, taking him all round, was more conspicuously fitted for this post'.[69] Lloyd George's aim of reducing Haig's power by making him subordinate to a supreme commander was eventually realized in March 1918 at the height of the German Spring Offensive. But this was not Lloyd George's doing: it was Haig himself, realizing the benefits of unified command at that critical juncture, who suggested during the Doullens Conference that Foch should take on the role of co-ordinating all Allied armies on the Western Front. The relationship between Haig and Foch was not always harmonious, but they had a mutual trust and understanding and their joint efforts were key to the Anglo-French successes during the second half of 1918.

Lloyd George, Churchill and the War Council were ready to see more of the weaknesses and mistakes of the BEF generals than they were to recognize their achievements. But weaknesses and mistakes there certainly were. The battles of 1915 provided valuable lessons for the future, but there were also serious errors. At Neuve Chapelle on 10 March the battle effectively ended after the first hour. German reinforcements were quickly positioned to prevent any likelihood of a further advance, but the fighting was allowed to continue without further gains until the night of 12 March. During the attack at Aubers Ridge on 8 May, there was a needless repetition of assaults over the same stretch of ground which resulted in 11,500 casualties. The handling of the Reserves at Loos in September was sheer mismanagement by both Field Marshal French and Haig. The prolonged battles on the Somme in 1916 and at Passchendaele in 1917 gave diminishing returns. Although Generals Gough and Plumer had both recommended to Haig that the Passchendaele campaign should be called off on 5 October, it was allowed to grind on until 20 November. These and other setbacks, together with their consequent heavy casualties, can only be explained in the overall context of the war. Haig and his generals considered that a policy of aggression and attrition was the only available way forward on the Western Front.

It should also be remembered that it was not only the British generals who attempted and failed to make a war-winning breakthrough during the three and a half years of trench fighting. The French and German generals were equally unsuccessful. The French failed in 1917 in Champagne and the Germans failed both at Ypres in 1914 and 1915 and at Verdun in 1916 – all with massive casualty lists. The generals were obliged to conduct this new form of warfare as best they could, taking opportunities as they presented themselves and sticking to their task. Taking all the circumstances into account – the occupation of much of northern France by the Germans, the trench stalemate, the mindset and technology of the time and the evenly matched forces – there was an inevitability about the way the war was conducted on the Western Front. The chilling conclusion is that the generals had no alternative.

## *Chapter 3*

# The Royal Flying Corps on the Western Front

*'Supremacy in the air has become one of the essentials of victory'.*
*Lloyd George*[1]

That the number of personnel in the Royal Air Force (RAF) at the end of the war exceeded that of the entire British Expeditionary Force at the beginning is a significant indicator of the rate of development of British air power between 1914 and 1918.[2] However, official acceptance of the potential of the aeroplane for war purposes had been slow in coming. The Wright brothers, who had made the first heavier-than-air powered flight in North Carolina in December 1903, offered to sell the rights of their invention. This offer, having been turned down by the United States government, was then made to Britain. On three occasions between 1906 and 1908 the British War Office and the Admiralty dismissed this opportunity to gain a lead in aircraft development.[3] The rights of the Wright brothers' invention, and several of their machines, were eventually acquired by the French.

In Britain it was left to enthusiastic individuals to deal with the problems presented by heavier-than-air flight. Such pioneers included A.V. Roe, Robert Blackburn, Geoffrey de Havilland, F. Handley Page, T.O.M. Sopwith and Horace and Oswald Short – names that became famous as designers and builders of aircraft during the course of the First World War. The authorities provided scant support. In 1908 A.V. Roe produced a powered aircraft that flew 60 yards at a height of 2 feet, but the War Office refused him facilities for further development. Also in 1908, John Dunne designed a bi-plane, but was obliged to abandon his efforts when the War Office dismissed his request for a £2,500 grant. Expenditure by the British government on military aeronautics averaged some £18,000 per annum for the years 1904–9. These figures can be compared with the German budget for military aircraft in 1908–9 of £400,000.[4] The highly sceptical attitude of the War Office towards aircraft development was summed up in the 1910 statement of the CIGS Sir William Nicholson. He considered that the whole thing was 'a useless and expensive fad, advocated by a few individuals whose ideas are unworthy of attention'.[5] The First Sea Lord, Admiral Sir Arthur Wilson, was of a similar opinion. When asked about the naval requirement for aircraft his answer was – two. The War Office at least made the major concession of allowing serving army officers to learn to fly, but at their own expense. They would be reimbursed only if they successfully gained their 'ticket' – the Royal Aero Club certificate of competence.

However, events from 1909 began to make the obstructive and unhelpful attitude of the War Office untenable. In July 1909 Bleriot's monoplane crossed the Channel in forty minutes and landed near Dover Castle. The effect of this achievement was to shatter the belief that Britain could continue to rest under the protection of its navy. Direct attack from the continent was now clearly possible – a threat underlined by Germany's development of the Zeppelin airship. In 1912–13 three Zeppelins had between them made 880 flights covering 65,000 miles without mishap.

That Germany was a likely aggressor was also becoming clear. The appearance of the gunboat *Panther* off Agadir in July 1911 alerted Europe to the war-like intensions of Kaiser Wilhelm II. In 1912 the Conservative politician Balfour wrote a well-publicised article on Anglo-German relations in which he accused Germany of planning a war of aggression to extend its territories both in Europe and overseas.[6] Popular novels such as Erskine Childers' *The Riddle of the Sands* (1903) and H.G. Wells' *The War in the Air* (1908) and *The World Set Free* (1914), fuelled a fear of a German invasion of Britain and of attack from the air.[7]

It was against this background that, in November 1911, Prime Minister Herbert Asquith, 'requested the standing sub-committee of the Committee of Imperial Defence … to consider the future development of aerial navigation for naval and military purposes, and the measures that might be taken to secure to this country an efficient aerial force'.[8] One of the submissions considered by the standing committee was a prescient memorandum from a pioneer flyer, Captain Bertram Dixon:

> In the case of a European war between two countries, both sides would be equipped with large corps of aeroplanes … the effect that each would exert in order to hinder or prevent the enemy from obtaining information would lead to the inevitable result of a war in the air, for the supremacy of the air, by armed aeroplanes against each other. This fight for the supremacy of the air in future wars will be of the first and greatest importance.[9]

That Britain was far from ready for a 'war in the air' was put starkly by the chairman of the standing sub-committee, Colonel J.E.B. Seeley: 'At the present time in this country we have, as far as I know, of actual flying men in the Army, about eleven and of actual flying men in the Navy about eight, and France has about 263, so we are what you might call behind'.[10]

The recommendation of the sub-committee was that an aerial service should be formed, designated 'The Flying Corps'. This corps would consist of a Naval Wing, a Military Wing and a Central Flying School that was to train pilots for both Wings. The interests of the Services would be co-ordinated by an Air Committee. The balloon factory at Farnborough would become the Royal Aircraft factory for the development and production of future aircraft. Asquith approved the recommendations and, without a parliamentary vote, established the Royal Flying Corps (RFC) by Royal Warrant on 13 April 1912.

* * *

The origins of the RFC were not, therefore, based on well-considered and forward-looking policies led by the War Office. The RFC largely came into being through the persistent efforts of enthusiasts and despite official negative attitudes and parsimonious government support. The outcome was that, in 1914, Britain lagged behind other major countries in the field of aeronautics. It was without a significant aircraft industry and was lamentably short of airframes, engines and key components. Magnetos, for example, were, before the war, almost entirely supplied from Germany as were ballbearings.[11] As a member of the RFC HQ later wrote: 'It is a great mercy we have a flying corps at all and the nation owes an eternal debt of gratitude … to those who fought the battle for the adoption of the aeroplane as a military weapon before the war.'[12]

Fortunately, Britain's main ally in the war, France, was at the forefront of aircraft development. It was significant that in 1909, the year in which Bleriot flew the Channel, the words 'aileron', 'fuselage' and 'nacelle', clearly of French origin, were for the first time included in the Oxford Dictionary.[13] British observers at the French army manoeuvres in 1911 noted that there were some 200 French aircraft in service. The British army at that time had twelve.[14] In 1913 France held flying records for speed, for distance and for altitude.[15]

It was also fortunate that Britain was able to develop a strong practical cooperation with its French ally. Maurice Baring, attached to the RFC HQ, recorded many examples of Anglo-French liaison. On 24 August 1914 he visited Bleriot's factory and bought a machine and on the same day he went to the Gnome [engine] works.[16] On 30 November 1916 Baring noted: 'We went to Paris to discuss questions of guns, machines, and engines with the French … also visited Nieuport's works'.[17] Similar visits and discussions took place frequently throughout the war and were largely to the benefit of the British.

Such close liaison with the French was essential not only to exchange information on new developments, but also because most of the RFC equipment, particularly at the beginning of the war, was of French origin. When the RFC arrived in France 13–15 August 1914 the four squadrons had a mixture of French and British aircraft. Hence No. 2 squadron had BE 2a's (Bleriot Experimental); No. 3 Squadron had Bleriot XI's, a Bleriot Parasol and Henri Farman F20's; No. 4 Squadron had BE 2a's and No. 5 Squadron had Henri Farman F20's and Avro 504's. There was also a great reliance on French engines. The BE 2a was powered by a Renault engine and the Bleriot, Henri Farman and Avro all had a Gnome engine.

During the war, the RFC flew no fewer that seventy different aircraft with engines from twenty-three different manufacturers. Of the seventy models, sixty-six were biplanes and forty-three were two-seaters. Eight were 'Pushers' with the engine and propeller behind the cockpit and the remainder were 'Tractors' with the engine and propeller in front.[18] To complicate the situation even further, each engine manufacturer produced several different specifications. For example, the French Gnome engine had 80hp and 100hp variants; the Le Rhone engine range was 80hp, 100hp and 120hp; and the Royal Aircraft Factory produced engines of 90hp and 150hp.

Such a proliferation of aircraft types and engine variants arose simply because of the pre-war insistence by the War Office that aircraft production should be left largely in the hands of private organizations who vied with each other to improve aircraft capability. Alongside machines developed at Farnborough by the Royal Aircraft Factory – the BE (Bleriot Experimental), the FE (Farman Experimental), the SE (Santos or Scouting Experimental) and the RE (Reconnaissance Experimental) – were those from famous private companies – Avro, Handley Page, de Havilland and Sopwith, as well as aircraft from French manufacturers such as Morane and Nieuport.

As far as the RFC was concerned, this wide range of aircraft and engines had both advantages and disadvantages. The flow of new and better models was quicker with a large number of manufacturers, but, on the other hand, the problem of having spares in the right places was a major logistical challenge. Lieutenant Y.E.S. Kirkpatrick records in his diary for 19 May 1918 that he was ferrying a Sopwith Camel to Guisnes when he was forced to land at an aerodrome on the way because of a problem with the landing gear. The aerodrome turned out to be the base for a Bristol Fighter Squadron and no Sopwith parts were available. Spares were eventually brought from a Camel squadron, but many hours were lost.[19] A similar point was made in 1915 by Corporal P.E. Butcher of No. 2 Squadron: 'lack of standardisation made it very difficult to get spares for engines so that we had to rob Peter to pay Paul. This went on day after day, causing delays in getting machines repaired'.[20]

Having a large range of aircraft had significant implications for the training of pilots. The Central Flying School was based at Upavon, Wiltshire and the first course began on 12 August 1912. Trainees were given tuition on a Maurice Farman, an Avro and a BE 2. After a period of solo flying the final test was a cross-country flight of 30 miles at 3,000ft and a spiral landing with the engine stopped. The average time in the air for a trainee before the final test was around 25 hours. However, the capacity of the CFS was only 20 per course and each course lasted three months. When war started the demand for pilots increased dramatically and it became necessary to set up eleven additional training centres.

The personal papers of various pilots show a range of training experiences. Captain C.A. Brown flew solo after 3 hours 25 minutes of dual instruction. He was trained in a Maurice Farman, a BE 2c, and a DH2. For his first offensive patrol, Brown flew an FE8. During his time with the RFC Brown flew twenty-five different types of aircraft.[21]

Most initial instruction took place in Maurice Farmans and BE2's. Captain F.C. Ransley of No. 48 squadron noted: 'My first dual instruction was in a 70hp Maurice Farman Shorthorn.[22] The "Rumpety", as we called it, was a good machine on which to learn for it was so solidly built that a bad landing seldom caused any damage to the undercarriage'. Ransley went to France after 71 hours 40 minutes solo flying. He was there for two years and during that time he piloted twenty different types of aircraft.[23] Lieutenant C.A. Box flew solo after 5 hours 40 minutes instruction and when he went to France in October 1918 he had completed 76 hours 30 minutes solo flying. Box piloted seven different types of aircraft during his training and recorded the flying times in each. They varied from 28 hours 45 minutes in an Armstrong Whitworth 160 to only 55 minutes in an RE8.[24] Lieutenant A.J. Robinson flew his first solo after 7 hours 20 minutes instruction and went to France after 45 hours 50 minutes solo.[25]

The period of training was certainly variable – it was also exciting and hazardous in the extreme. According to one historian more pilots were killed during their training period (8,000) than in combat with the enemy (6,166).[26] In that context, Lieutenant C.E.Young records a narrow escape during his first solo flight: 'Circuit – bad descent – not as confident as I thought I would be – shaky over turns – throttled down too late – taxiing bad to very bad – spun wheels – turned over – rescued by Lt Kiddie – taken ignominiously home'.[27] Flying instruction was haphazard and trainers often had little more experience than their trainees. Lieutenant Geoffrey Wall went solo after only two hours flying and was immediately appointed an instructor.[28]

It can be seen from the above examples of pilot training that individual experiences varied widely. The degree of proficiency of pilots also varied. Robert Smith-Barry, who in July 1916 commanded No. 60 Squadron in France, was particularly concerned at the incompetence of many of the young pilots sent to the front. In December 1916 Smith-Barry was given command of No. 1 (Reserve) Squadron at Gosport and this gave him the opportunity to put into practice his new theories of flying instruction. Using a dual-control Avro 504 biplane, pupils sat in the front cockpit which was equipped with a full set of controls while the trainer sat behind giving instructions through the specially designed 'Gosport tube'.

A key aspect of the Smith-Barry approach was for trainees to explore the capabilities of an aircraft to its limits and to learn the cause and effect of movements in the air. Instead of avoiding dangerous manoeuvres, they were taught how to get out of them safely. Even after pilots had flown solo, they continued to learn advanced techniques using the dual-control aircraft. The Smith-Barry approach trained pilots quickly and to such a high degree of proficiency that the methods were adopted throughout the RFC. Deaths in training in Britain dropped from one per 90 hours to one per 192 hours.[29] In August 1917 No. 1 (Reserve) Squadron became the School of Special Flying – a unit to teach instructors. The Gosport principles were codified in a manual entitled 'General Methods of Teaching Scout Pilots' – the first ever standardized system of flying instruction in the world.

* * *

The role of the RFC developed dramatically during the war years and while the primary function was always seen as reconnaissance, the *Field Service Regulations* of spring 1914 clearly expected both air-to-air combat and bombing. It was in the reconnaissance role that flights on 22 August 1914 brought the news that German troops (von Kluck's First Army) were advancing westwards on the Brussels-Ninove road while von Bulow's Second Army was marching through Charleroi. There was a great risk that the BEF would be surrounded and, on 24 August, the retreat from Mons began. On 7 September Sir John French, the commander of the BEF, wrote of the RFC: 'Their skill, energy and perseverance have been beyond all praise … They have furnished me with the most complete and accurate information which has been of incalculable value in conducting the operations'.[30] The RFC had therefore justified its existence in the early days of the war as a reconnaissance force and it continued to do so over the next four years. But its role quickly widened.

Trench warfare meant that there was an urgent need to have maps showing militarily significant locations on both sides of the front line such as airfields, artillery positions, trench lines, camps, dumps and railheads. On 15 September 1914 Lieutenant Prettyman of No. 3 Squadron took, on his own initiative, five photographs of German positions on the Aisne. The official history noted: 'most [of the enemy's] batteries located and considerable success was achieved in assisting the ranging of the artillery'.[31] These were the beginnings of what became a comprehensive photographic map of the Western Front. In March 1915 a new box camera, known as 'A' camera, was first used over enemy trenches. The camera was held over the side of the aircraft by the observer. Later, to reduce the problem of vibration, it became fixed to the side of the aircraft. By summer 1915 a semi-automatic plate-changing mechanism, known as 'C' camera, was introduced. This was followed by further advances such as vertical air cameras and cameras of 20-inch focal length and these were fixed to most reconnaissance aircraft.[32]

Official recognition of the importance of aerial photography came with the establishment of an Air Photographic Section in January 1915. This was followed by a School of Photography, Mapping and Reconnaissance set up at Farnborough in 1916. The demand for aerial photographs, accepted as a reliable source of information, increased as the war went on. During the Battle of the Somme (July–November 1916) the RFC took more than 19,000 photos and produced more than 430,000 prints. In 1918 the total number of prints made from photographic maps of the Western Front was some six million.[33] In total, the number of prints made in France during the war was 10.5 million.[34]

During the early days of the war attempts at bombing consisted of dropping grenades and small bombs over the side of the aircraft. During the Second Battle of Ypres in April 1915 several attempts were made to disrupt German troop movements by bombing railway junctions. The first attempts by 7 and 8 Squadrons of Third Wing and by 2 Squadron of First Wing were unsuccessful. However, on 24 April Lieutenant William Rhodes-Moorhouse dropped a 125lb bomb from just 300 feet on the junction at Courtrai, some 35 miles inside the German lines. The bomb caused considerable disruption to the rail system. Field Marshal Sir John French described it as 'the most important bomb dropped in the war so far'.[35] However, Rhodes-Moorhouse was fatally wounded in the process. His bravery earned him the first aerial VC of the war.

During 1915 bombing strategy became increasingly sophisticated. Individual efforts to disrupt railway communications were replaced by sustained attacks co-ordinated by GHQ and, under their orders, French and British aircraft combined to maximise destruction. This policy was put into practice at the Battle of Loos in September 1915 by which time a new sighting device from the CFS had come into use, improving considerably the chances of accurate bombing. The main target was the Lille-Douai-Valenciennes railway triangle. On 23 August, in preparation for the Loos offensive, twenty-three aircraft attacked the Douai-Valenciennes line and eleven aircraft bombed the Lille-Valenciennes line. Despite poor weather, 263 bombs were dropped on these targets over a five-day period causing serious damage to trains, sheds and lines. Only two British aircraft were lost.

This strategy evolved into formation bombing usually carried out by about thirty aircraft. No. 3 Naval Wing, based at Belfort, attacked the Saar industrial area where steel for U-boats was manufactured. Handley Page bombers, which could carry twelve 120lb bombs (compared with two bombs on other RFC planes), were first used in April 1917 when Freiberg was attacked. Bombing was carried out on Cologne, Stuttgart and Mannheim from late 1917. Such was the perceived success and importance of long-range bombing, well into German territory, that the Forty-First Wing at Nancy was, in February 1918, raised to Brigade level. In November 1917 Nancy became the centre for the Independent Air Force and German industrial targets were bombed, subject to weather, day and night until the Armistice in November 1918.

The RFC was increasingly called on to carry out artillery observation. As early as 24 September 1914 General Smith-Dorrien commended the RFC for its efforts in that role over the Aisne: 'Today I watched for a long time an aeroplane observing for the six-inch howitzers of the Third Division … it continued for hours through a wireless installation to observe the fire and indeed to control the Battery with most satisfactory results'.[36]

Air-to-land communication was a major problem. At the beginning of the war only No. 4 Squadron was equipped with wireless which, at that time, was so bulky and heavy (around 75lb) that it took up the whole of the observer's cockpit. However, each squadron was allowed to use one aircraft to experiment with improved artillery observation techniques as well as devices to improve weaponry and bombing.

A significant advance in wireless technology was the Sterling set which weighed less than 20lb. Early wireless signalling certainly had drawbacks: it could be jammed by the enemy or simply by heavy usage of the same wavelength. By mid-1916 this problem had been overcome by the 'clapper-break' which differentiated signals by variations in tone. This immediately made it possible to double the number of aircraft on the same wavelength in any given area. By the end of the war, it was possible to use one wireless aircraft on every 400 yards of the front without fear of jamming.[37]

That the RFC should provide the artillery with accurate information concerning the positions of German targets was clearly of the greatest importance – especially in 1914 and 1915 when shells were in short supply. During the first months of the war, targets were identified simply by reference to a map which proved far from accurate. In October 1914 things improved when Lieutenants B.T. James and D.S. Lewis (two ex-Royal Engineer officers) devised map references based on a grid system and shortly afterwards introduced a 'clock' method. The clock method was so effective that, on one occasion, Captain A.S. Barratt of No. 3 Squadron gave information that enabled No. 19 Signal Battery to score three direct hits on a German long-range gun. In 1916 maps were 'zoned' so that a two-letter call from an aircraft would alert any battery within range and the observer would direct its fire onto the target.[38]

* * *

Having started the war as an observation service, the RFC acquired additional roles that made it an essential part of the BEF. To reconnaissance was added artillery support, a photographic and mapping service, the dropping of spies behind German lines, reporting back on the position of advancing troops ('Contact' patrols) and extensive bombing duties. These different activities required different aircraft. Training was generally carried out in slow but relatively stable Avro, Maurice Farman, BE2 and Bleriot aircraft. Reconnaissance and photographic duties needed aircraft that were stable but also able to climb and these included the BE2, FE2 and 8 and the RE5. Bombing was carried out by heavier and more powerful aircraft such as the Caudron Twin, the RE7 and 8 and various de Havilland and Handley Page models. The trainers and reconnaissance aeroplanes generally had 70–90hp engines while the bombers were fitted with engines that ranged from 110hp to the de Havilland D4 with a 375hp power unit. By the end of the war the Handley Page night bomber had two 275hp Rolls-Royce engines while the de Havilland D10 had two 400hp Liberty engines.

The aircraft used for reconnaissance and photographic duties, though reasonably stable, were also slow. This feature, combined with the need for the pilot and observer to concentrate on their task, made them relatively easy prey for enemy aircraft. The need to protect these vulnerable aircraft, together with the inevitable development of air-to-air combat, led to the introduction of a series of fighters often referred to as Scouts. Fighters had to be fast and manoeuvrable and British fighters included the BE12, the Bristol Scout and Fighter, the DH2 and 5, the FE8, the Martinsyde, the Morane Scout and various models of the SE, the Sopwith and the Nieuport Scout.

As technology developed and as operating experience was acquired the manufacturers made modifications to basic models to adapt them to particular roles or to improve their performance. Sopwith models, for example, included the Tabloid, the Camel, the Dolphin, the One and a Half Strutter, the Snipe and the Pup. De Havilland had models designated DH2, 4, 5, 6, 9, 9a, 10 and 12. These models, apart from being fighters, were also used for reconnaissance and bombing.

The model that flew throughout the war in various forms was the Bleriot Experimental (BE) which was manufactured at the Royal Aircraft Factory at Farnborough. It is worth summarizing the various and somewhat bewildering BE modifications to see the extent and nature of change to this particular aircraft. The BE1 first flew in 1911 and was based on a reconstituted Bleriot Voisin. The BE1 had a 60hp engine and the BE2 was fitted with a 70hp engine. The BE2a had a redesigned undercarriage and fuel system and the BE2b had a modified cockpit separating the pilot from the observer. The BE2c was virtually a new aircraft with ailerons instead of wing warping. It was powered by a 90hp engine. The BE2d had dual controls and the BE2e had newly designed wings. The BE2f was a 2c with 2e wings. The BE2g was a 2d with 2e wings. Finally, in 1918, a BE12 was produced as a single-seater fighter with a 200hp Hispano-Suiza engine. Production of the BE model was so prolific that, during the Battle of the Somme, the BE2c accounted for about a third of the total number of RFC aircraft.

As might be expected, engine capacity, speed and rate of climb all improved during the war years. An analysis of aircraft flying in 1914 compared to those flying in 1918 shows that engine size increased from a range of 70–120hp to a range of 100–375hp. The range of speeds in 1914 was 60–90mph while in 1918 it was 75–143mph. In 1914 the BE2 took nine minutes to climb to 3,000ft while in 1918 the BE12 took 9.5 minutes to reach 6,500ft and 10.2 minutes to reach 10,000ft.[39]

Pilots made no secret of which type of aircraft they preferred. Lieutenant H.G. Holman of No. 20 Squadron wrote: 'Bristol Fighter machines in which we flew were considered "the tops" as, although carrying two people, they had a touch of speed, could fly over 110mph and could climb well. Certainly, the Rolls-Royce "Eagle" and "Falcon" engines were very reliable'.[40] In their history of No. 24 Squadron, Illingworth and Robson noted that: 'On 25 December 1917 the squadron received the best of all Xmas presents – a new machine and both pilots and mechanics heaved a sigh of thankfulness to heaven'. The new machine was the SE5a with a 200hp Hispano-Suiza engine. 'It was a beautiful aeroplane with a splendid performance'.[41] Previously, No. 24 Squadron had flown DH2 and DH5 aircraft with 100hp Gnome and 120hp Le Rhone engines.

On occasions, pilots resorted to verse to express their views, such as the enigmatic 'Pilot's Psalm':

> The BE2c is my bus, therefore shall I want.
> He maketh me to come down in green pastures.
> He leadeth me where I would not go.

Lieutenant Cecil Lewis, of No. 9 Squadron, also commented adversely on the BE2c: 'If there was ever an aeroplane unsuited for active service it was the BE2c'.[42]

Aircraft engines similarly received poetic attention:

I want a Gnome
Give me a Gnome
I don't want a Monosoupe or a Le Rhone
I want a Gnome.[43]

In fact, pilot opinion was at times fickle and tended to reflect pilot experience or lack of it. The DH2 became known in one squadron as the 'spinning incinerator' and fell into disrepute, though when No. 24 Squadron was equipped with the DH2 they thought well of it.[44]

* * *

Air-to-air combat placed a constant pressure on designers and manufacturers to produce aircraft that were not only fast and manoeuvrable but also well-equipped with weaponry. In 1914 observers armed themselves simply with revolvers or .303 rifles. Sergeant Major D.S. Jillings of No. 2 Squadron became the first RFC aerial casualty when, on 22 August 1914, he was hit in the leg by a bullet from a German rifle – though that was fired from the ground. In practice, it was almost impossible for a rifle to be anything like effective when fired from an aircraft.[45] Soon, Lewis machine guns were fitted for use by the observer. 'Pusher' models were initially preferred to 'Tractor' models because the observer had an unobstructed view. The Maurice Farman 'Pushers' of No. 4 Squadron were fitted with Lewis guns as early as September 1914, but 'Pushers' tended to be slower and more cumbersome than 'Tractors'. 'Tractor' aircraft, however, had an inherent problem. The best place to mount a machine gun was where it could fire forward in line with the direction of flight, but this made the propeller of a 'Tractor' aircraft a major obstacle. Lewis guns were therefore mounted on the top wing so that they could be fired above the propeller. This method was not without its problems. Changing the ammunition drum could only be done in flight with great difficulty and the gun oil often froze because of the exposed position.

The problem of firing through the propeller was partially solved by the French pilot Roland Garros in April 1915. Garros had metal deflector plates fitted to the propeller blades of his Morane in line with his Hotchkiss machine gun. This invention had some success and was used experimentally by the British, but it was not entirely reliable. Meanwhile the Dutch engineer Anthony Fokker, working for the Germans, had developed in mid-1915 an interrupter gear that enabled a machine gun to fire through the blades of a propeller. It was not until almost a year later that the RFC was also able to fit an interrupter gear system. The first squadron (No. 70) with synchronized machine guns fitted to Sopwith One and a Half Strutters arrived in France in May 1916.[46]

Supremacy in the air, to make possible the essential work of aerial observation and artillery support, was seen by both sides as crucial and supremacy passed from one side to the other. The pendulum swing of air ascendancy resulted essentially from the relative developments of fighter aircraft. The RFC gained an early supremacy when, in spring 1915, the Vickers FB5 100hp 'Pusher' biplane, armed with a Lewis gun, came into operation on the Western Front. It was known as the 'Gunbus'. But its reign was brief and it was quickly outclassed by Anthony Fokker's 'Eindecker' equipped with the forward firing machine gun. 'Eindecker' pilots worked as individuals patrolling at high levels above their own lines ready to dive on the slower British reconnaissance aircraft. Exponents of this tactic included the German 'aces' Max Immelmann and Oswald Boelcke, both of whom flew Fokker 111 machines. It was Boelcke who first prepared a codified version of air tactics and ensured that his pilots were trained in the principles of aerial combat.

British and French reconnaissance aircraft suffered heavily during the Fokker 'scourge' of late 1915 and early 1916. The heavy Allied casualties were partially contained by the introduction of formation flying. A notable example of successful formation flying took place on 7 February 1916 when four long-range reconnaissance aircraft armed with machine guns and flying in diamond formation were attacked by fifteen German aircraft including two Fokkers. The formation was not broken and no aircraft was lost.[47]

Nevertheless, the 'Eindecker' had the capability of taking complete control of the skies above the Western Front. It was only the timely introduction of the FE2b, the DH2, the Sopwith One and a Half Strutter and a new French Nieuport Scout, all of which in performance could match the Fokker, that restored British ascendancy. Captain Albert Ball of No. 11 Squadron, whose preferred aircraft was a Nieuport, became the first British 'ace'. Between May 1916 and May 1917, Ball shot down forty-three enemy aircraft and was awarded the VC.

British air supremacy during mid-1916 was again shortlived. In September 1916 the German 'Jagdstaffel' squadrons, commanded by Boelcke and having among its pilots Baron von Richthofen, made their appearance. These squadrons were equipped with new and faster fighters – the Halberstadt and the 'D' type Albatros. The Albatros was armed with two machine guns able to fire through the propeller arc. In an early engagement a 'Jagdstaffel' squadron shot down four FE2b's and two BE's without loss. During the period of the Somme battle the RFC had an advantage in numbers of aircraft (380 in the battle area compared with 330 German[48]), but the German aircraft were superior and gradually the control of the air changed hands.

The winter of 1916 and the spring of 1917 were gruelling times for the RFC whose only defence against superior German aircraft was formation flying. British casualties grew at an alarming rate. In March 1917, 120 aircraft were shot down. During the first five days of the Battle of Arras (5–9 April 1917), seventy-five aircraft were lost and a further fifty-six were wrecked in accidents. In the same month, Baron von Richthofen introduced his 'Circus' which became a constant threat to the British reconnaissance aircraft. April 1917 saw the highest number of British losses of the war. It was estimated that the effective service of a pilot or observer in a two-seater reconnaissance squadron was four months; in a fighter/reconnaissance and day bombing squadron, three and a half months; and in a single-seater fighter squadron, two and a half months. In August 1916, at the height of the Somme battle, the effective flying hours of an officer before being killed or wounded was 295. In early 1917 it was ninety-two.[49] The RFC was acutely short of aircrew and the War Office was notified that 1,700 pilots and observers were needed to meet the requirements of the second half of 1917 and 1918. Recruitment and training were given increased emphasis and both the United States and Canada provided aircrew and mechanics.

From mid-1917 the fortunes of the RFC began to improve. New aircraft were introduced – the Bristol Fighter, the SE5 and the Sopwith Camel – and the pendulum of air superiority swung once more. Cecil Lewis described the SE5 as:

> the last word in fighting scouts ... It was fitted with a 140hp Hispano Suiza engine [later 200hp] and two guns; one Vickers firing through the propeller by means of the new Constantinesco gear[50]; and one Lewis gun clamped on to the top plane and firing over the propeller ... Altogether it was a first-class fighting scout – probably the most successful designed during the war.[51]

All these new aircraft together with existing fighters such as the Sopwith Pup were fitted with the Constantinesco synchronized forward-firing equipment. By the time of the Battle of Messines in June 1917, the RFC had regained the initiative and air observation and artillery aircraft were well supported by fighters from a total of eighteen squadrons. Of the 300 aircraft allocated to the battle, one-third were single-seater fighters. The Messines attack was a considerable success and the RFC had made a significant contribution.

When the Third Battle of Ypres began in July 1917 a total of 840 British aircraft were allocated to the area and, of these, 360 were fighters. The German air strength was 600 aeroplanes including 200 fighters. This RFC numerical superiority was despite the diversion of fighters, including twenty-four new Sopwith Camels, for Home defence against German Gotha IV bombing attacks. In terms of aircraft capability, the Camel and the SE5a were well able to hold their own against the German Halberstadt and Albatros D.VII.

During the Battle of Cambrai in October 1917 the RFC, in conjunction with the British infantry and artillery, developed a new tactic. This involved low level formation flying against enemy troops, batteries and rail centres. This tactic continued into 1918 and, although costly in aircraft, caused great damage to enemy installations and morale. During the German advances in spring 1918, for example, British and French pilots attacked Moreil Wood using bombs and machine guns. A German record stated that 'Moreil Wood is a hell'.[52] Just how low the British pilots flew was recorded in the papers of a German soldier of 8 Grenadiers: 'there suddenly appeared before us some twenty British aeroplanes which dived to a height of about 100 to 200 metres, and then, continuing to within 2-3 metres of the ground, attacked us with their machine-guns'.[53] British low flying tactics gave rise to fierce air-to-air fights and it was during one of these, on 21 April, that Baron von Richthofen was shot down and killed. Low flying attacks continued in support of British infantry and artillery until the end of the war.

As far as aircraft developments were concerned, it was fortunate for the British and French that the war did not continue into 1919. The Germans had brought out several new models that might well have caused the pendulum of air supremacy to swing once more in their direction. The new Fokker D VIII could fly at 124mph and had outstanding handling qualities. The Junker J9 and J10 were the first all-metal combat machines. But the appearance of these aircraft in mid-1918 was too late to avert Germany's defeat.

* * *

The RFC went to France in August 1914 with four squadrons and sixty-three aircraft. By the end of the war in November 1918 there were ninety-nine squadrons and 1,800 aircraft on the Western Front.[54] In 1914 there were fewer than 250 officers; in 1918 there were over 30,000. Such an expansion in men and machines could only take place with appropriate and continuous organizational change.

The headquarters of the RFC that accompanied the four squadrons to France in 1914 consisted of ten officers. Left behind in Farnborough was the nucleus of an administrative wing that was to organize further expansion. It amounted to one officer, one clerk and a typewriter.[55] In November 1914 the RFC was organized into two wings and a HQ. As the number of squadrons increased – by mid-1916 there were thirty-one – the structure developed from squadrons to wings to brigades which reported to the RFC HQ. A brigade consisted of two wings – one of fighter squadrons and one for artillery support. A wing had a variable number of squadrons according to operating circumstances and, for the same reason, squadrons had a variable number of aircraft. Responding to the reconnaissance needs of the BEF, each army corps was allocated an artillery squadron.

On 1 April 1918 the RAF was created and the RFC and RNAS merged. This was the result of a report from Lieutenant General Smuts for the War Office which foresaw that aircraft would cease to be ancillary to either the army or the navy and would be used for independent operations. The report was adopted and the RAF henceforth reported directly to the Air Ministry. It was at this point that the Independent Air Force was formed to concentrate on long-distance bombing targets.

Throughout the war the operational development of the RFC was largely in the hands of two men – Sir David Henderson and Sir Hugh Trenchard. Henderson was the commander of the RFC at the beginning of the war and organized its move to France and its early expansion. The Secretary of State for War, Lord Kitchener, regarded Henderson so highly that he rescinded Henderson's promotion to command the BEF First Division in order to keep him with the RFC. Before going to France, Henderson had been the Director General of Military Aeronautics. In that role he was able to exercise considerable influence. He controlled aeronautical contracts and in 1914 the Army Estimates included, for the first time, £1 million for the RFC. Thereafter, with the support of Kitchener, the RFC was able to expand almost regardless of financial constraint. When it was pointed out to Kitchener in early 1915 that the army, then thirty divisions, needed fifty air squadrons to support it, the Secretary of State immediately insisted on doubling that number.

When Henderson went to France, the vacant post of Director General of Military Aeronautics was not filled. It became clear that the RFC needed strong representation in the War Office and in August 1915 Henderson reluctantly agreed to return to London. For the rest of the war he was the political champion of the RFC. In particular, Henderson played a key role in the creation of the RAF and was General Smuts' assistant in effecting the merger of the RFC and the RNAS and easing the birth of the new service.

Even more crucial to the success of the RFC in France was Henderson's successor, Sir Hugh Trenchard. Trenchard had the reputation of being hard-headed, a strict disciplinarian and absolutely dedicated to whatever task he undertook. Before the war he had been second-in-command of the Central Flying School and by the time of his appointment as commander of the RFC (August 1915) he had led both a squadron and a wing in France. What Trenchard brought to the RFC was attention to operational detail; a clear and forceful vision of the role of the RFC; and the ability to motivate his subordinates to a remarkable degree.

It was Trenchard who toured the squadrons questioning officers about their supply problems – no matter how minor – and ensuring that, if at all possible, they were met. This continued throughout the war and Maurice Baring, Trenchard's assistant, noted many examples: 'No. 3 Squadron – end socket for strut tube rear 5408-11 wanted – ordered, further information later; No. 13 Squadron – flexible petrol tubing for extra tank – telegraphed for; No. 11 squadron – 10cwt cable – ordered and hastened'; and so on.[56] Trenchard's eye for detail and insistence that every job should be carried out perfectly was remembered by Edward Bolt, a rigger at the main aircraft repair depot at St Omer: 'Even in such a detail as splicing wire, the great man insisted on four tucks (a tuck being one wire placed under another wire and then drawn through) rather than the more usual three. This, of course, increased the strength and added to safety. It became known as the Trenchard tuck'.[57]

It was Trenchard who advocated a determined policy of the offensive, not the defensive, in the air. Air supremacy meant that British aircraft, unlike those of the Germans, would operate on both sides of the Front and, in particular, British machines would continuously penetrate enemy air space seeking to fulfil its reconnaissance role and also destroy German aircraft and installations. As Trenchard wrote in September 1916:

> The aeroplane is not a defence against the aeroplane … the aeroplane as a weapon of attack cannot be too highly estimated … On the British front, during the operations which began with the Battle of the Somme, we know that, although the enemy had concentrated the greater part of his available forces in the air on this front, the work actually accomplished by their aeroplanes stands, compared to the work done by us, in the proportion of 4 to 100 … British aviation has been guided by a policy of relentless and incessant offensive.[58]

Trenchard pursued this policy of aggression throughout his command. In his January 1918 memorandum 'The Employment of the Royal Flying Corps in Defence', Trenchard concluded that: 'The successful performance of the role of the Royal Flying Corps … must primarily depend on its ability to gain and maintain ascendancy in the air … This can only be done by attacking and defeating the enemy's air forces'.[59] An example of this policy in practice was recorded in Haig's war diary (31 July 1916): 'General Trenchard reported regarding the Flying Corps. More German machines were seen yesterday than at any time previously during this battle [the Somme], but not more than 20 crossed our line, and none got very far. The previous day 8 crossed our line. On the other hand we made 451 separate flights over the Enemy front two days ago, and some 500 yesterday'.[60] And on 18 September 1916, Haig wrote: 'By taking the offensive and carrying the war in the air beyond the Enemy's lines, our artillery airoplanes [*sic*] are free to carry on their important duties of observation and photography unmolested. Our communications too on which so much depends are undisturbed'.[61]

It was also Trenchard who motivated the young aircrew and mechanics to carry out this aggressive policy even during periods of German aircraft superiority and high British casualties. Cecil Lewis wrote that Trenchard: 'infused men's enthusiasm without effort by a certain greatness of heart that made him not so much our superior in rank as in personality … we were all sure that victory was certain'.[62] It was accepted throughout the RFC that, no matter what the circumstances, the work in support of the military must be carried out. When, in November 1917, Trenchard was appointed Chief of Air Staff in London, he wrote a farewell memorandum to his squadrons:

> The splendid courage shown by pilots, observers and aerial gunners has been one of the outstanding features of this time. The fighting has been hard and casualties have been sometimes heavy, but I should like to put on record and impress upon everyone that what has been accomplished has been entirely due to the magnificent spirit shown by all.[63]

That this 'magnificent spirit' existed throughout the RFC was testimony to Trenchard's leadership. Haig fought hard to keep Trenchard in France and wrote to Lord Derby, the then Secretary of State for War: '[Trenchard's] influence and personality carry such weight with various units in the RFC that no new man could hope to fill his place adequately. […] I cannot affirm my conviction too strongly that the removal of Trenchard's personality at the present juncture will be most prejudicial to the fighting efficiency and morale of the RFC in France'.[64] Haig's words were clear evidence of the value he placed on the RFC and of his confidence in Trenchard, but his plea fell on deaf ears.

* * *

That the RFC had a steep and difficult learning experience between 1914 and 1918 is clear. The war began with Britain having virtually no aeronautical industry. Only French co-operation enabled Britain to put squadrons into the air in 1914. However, by 1917, Britain, by rapidly expanding its aircraft industry, had become largely independent of France. Increased rationalization of the industry led to standardization and higher rates of production of both airframes and engines. Aircraft production in Britain rose steadily: in 1915, 2,500; in 1916, 6,600; in 1917, 14,800; and in 1918, 30,800. By August 1916, 114 companies employing a labour force of 20,000 were making aircraft engines. By October 1918 these numbers had increased to 323 companies and almost 100,000 employees.[65] In contrast, German production of aircraft, adversely affected by a shortage of materials, had fallen from around 20,000 in 1917 to 6,000 in 1918.[66]

The training of RFC pilots was an area of weakness particularly at the beginning of the war. Instruction was haphazard and there was no formal syllabus or consistent method of training. Lieutenant Cecil Lewis was posted to his first combat squadron in early 1916 and later wrote: 'My Flight Commander was scandalised at my lack of experience. Twenty hours, the total my logbook showed, was no good to him. I was to take my machine and fly it all day'.[67] It was not until autumn 1917, three-quarters of the way through the war, that the Smith-Barry 'Gosport' principles of pilot training began to have effect.

The pendulum of air supremacy on the Western Front swung from one side to the other and was critically dependent on the effectiveness of fighter aircraft. The periods of the Fokker 'scourge', the 'Jagdstaffel' squadrons, the Richthofen 'Circus' and the Halberstadt and Albatros D saw the Germans in the ascendancy. On the other hand, the early Vickers FB5, the FE2b, the DH2, and the series of Sopwith, Bristol and SE aircraft secured periods of supremacy for the RFC. It can be regarded as fortunate that the periods of

RFC ascendancy coincided with the major British land offensives of Neuve Chapelle, Loos, the Somme, Messines, Passchendaele and the battles of 1918. RFC involvement did not guarantee success in these battles, but its contribution was acknowledged as highly significant.

Liaison between the army and the RFC developed effectively with the allocation of squadrons to armies and corps, providing constant air reconnaissance, artillery support and fighter attacks. Haig and Trenchard, both of whom found difficulty in articulating their thoughts verbally, had a close working relationship starting at the Battle of Neuve Chapelle in March 1915 when Trenchard's First Wing was attached to Haig's First Army. When some artillery officers questioned the use of air observation, Haig informed them that he was going to use the air in the war and they had to use it also.[68] This relationship continued through the war. It was Haig who, in 1916, supported Trenchard's request to the War Office for more fighters and it was Haig who attempted, unsuccessfully, to keep Trenchard on the Western Front in 1918.[69] It was symbolic of the level of co-operation that, in March 1916, RFC HQ was moved from St Omer to Saint-André-aux-Bois to be near Haig's HQ at Montreuil.

RFC flying tactics were developed to suit changing circumstances. While outstanding aces such as Hawker, Ball, Bishop, McCudden and Mannock[70] exercised their own remarkable skills the general trend through the war was to move from individual to group flying. This applied particularly to the bombing of German industrial centres which became increasingly important, culminating in the creation of the Independent Air Force.

Air supremacy moved from one side to the other on several occasions during the war as a result of relative technical improvements in aircraft design and weaponry. However, even when RFC aircraft did not keep technical pace with German developments, the general policy of the RFC remained constant. Support for the army on every possible occasion, even during periods of enemy aircraft superiority, was considered paramount. Trenchard's policy of constant aggression over German-held territory was costly in lives, but it led to ultimate success. As Maurice Baring noted in the dark days of April 1917 when the fortunes of the RFC were low:

> The work of the Army had been done in spite of the weather, in spite of our inferiority in machines, and in spite of the casualties ... our casualties in the air, although heavy, saved thousands of casualties on the ground, for there was no break in artillery work. The enemy's batteries were registered and his trenches were photographed unremittingly. The spirit of the Flying Corps was undefeated.

* * *

From this discussion of the development of the RFC it is possible to identify the key factors that lay behind Britain's eventual domination of the air over the Western Front during the last eighteen months of the war. The first of these factors was the support given by the French. This showed itself, particularly in the early years of the war, through the exchange of information and the British reliance on French aircraft and engines. Indeed, France produced twice as many aero engines than Britain and Germany put together and more aircraft.[71] In 1914 Britain was inadequately prepared for a war in the air and French support was critical to the future success of the RFC. An important aspect of Anglo-French liaison was the constructive relationship that existed between Trenchard and the French air commander, Commandant Paul du Peuty. Learning from the French experience at Verdun in 1916, the two men developed the doctrine of the offensive that was followed by both air forces for the remainder of the war.

The second factor was the outstanding leadership of both Sir David Henderson and Sir Hugh Trenchard. These two men provided the vision, the policies and also the practical 'hands-on' approach that characterized the RFC and encouraged continuous innovation throughout the war. While Trenchard has not been without his critics – an over-emphasis on the offensive leading to heavy losses and his initial objection to an independent RAF[72] – his contribution to the development of the RFC is unquestionable. The third factor, related to the second, was the high morale of RFC personnel and their determination to carry out their work in support of the army regardless of heavy casualties and severe setbacks. Essential to both of these elements of success was the fourth key factor – the encouragement and backing at crucial times from the highest levels. General Smuts was a figure of great influence and considerable foresight in the creation of both the RFC and the RAF. Kitchener and Haig were effective supporters and advocates of the RFC and considered it an integral and essential part of the BEF.

The fifth and arguably the most important factor was the dramatic expansion, after a poor start, of the British aircraft industry. The course of Germany's aeronautical development was quite different from that of Britain. In the early years of the war Germany had placed emphasis on the use of Zeppelins. Zeppelins had indeed caused some panic as a result of their attacks on English targets, but by 1917 they had become the prey of aircraft that were far quicker and more manoeuvrable. The German aircraft industry grew between 1915 and 1917, but inadequate industrial organization and the effects of the Royal Navy blockade meant that from mid-1917 the RFC and its French ally had overwhelming numerical superiority. The performance of British aircraft fell below that of German aircraft during a number of periods of the war, but from mid-1917 the RFC was competing on at least even terms with the enemy.

The above factors eventually led to Britain's air superiority on the Western Front. For most of the war, success in the air, as on the ground, was not assured. When it came, however, it signalled that in any future war, the role of the RAF, acting as an independent force, would be crucial.

## *Chapter 4*

# Tanks on the Western Front

*'The box-like body of the machine suggested that some such name as "reservoir" or "cistern" be employed, in order to conceal its real purpose. "Tank" was adopted on 24 December 1915'.*

*British Official History*[1]

In 1914 neither trenches nor barbed wire were new. They had been used extensively in the American Civil War, the Boer War and the Russo-Japanese War. However, by the end of 1914 the nature of the trench system on the Western Front was of a significantly different order. It stretched from the North Sea to the Swiss Alps – some 480 miles. The trenches were heavily defended by fields of barbed wire together with complex systems of support trenches and strongpoints. After only three months the scene was set for a long and bitter war.

Suggestions for dealing with barbed wire and trenches were not slow in coming. The shipbuilder Sir Charles Parsons proposed that cars should be fitted with front-mounted wire-cutting mowers powered by compressed air. These cars would approach the enemy trenches and the revolving mower would cut a line through the wire for the troops to follow. The difficulty with this idea was that the mowers were unable to deal with the thick iron pickets that supported the wire. A further suggestion came from a Mr Harcourt of Pontarlington, near Dublin, who proposed that a series of heavy wire-cutting rollers could be housed in a wooden frame together with 'an engine or a horse'. This idea was thought to be impractical. These suggestions, along with many others aimed at shortening the war such as the use of water jets and the novel proposal of filling shells with snuff to distract the enemy, caused the Secretary of the Committee of Imperial Defence, Captain Maurice Hankey, to observe: 'For the most part it is found that the "bright ideas" of the outside inventor are not new and the new ideas are not bright'.[2]

More practical ways of dealing with the trench system were being considered by the Military Transport Committee of the War Office, formed in 1900 during the Boer War. The search was for a tracked vehicle that could move over soft and uneven ground, cross trenches, cope with barbed wire and, at the same time, withstand enemy fire. Richard Hornsby & Son of Grantham had produced a number of agricultural tractors between 1906 and 1909 and the Motor Transport Committee considered that they 'approximated to the ideal tractor for military purposes'.[3] However, these tractors were seen as useful mainly for haulage purposes rather than for breaking into trenches and the War Office lost interest. When the Motor Transport Committee sought permission in 1910 to acquire an American Holt 'crawler' for evaluation alongside the Hornsby 'caterpillar' the War Office turned the proposal down. The Hornsby Company, despite the lack of orders from the military, produced in 1911 a practical chain-track machine powered by an internal combustion engine. Again the War Office showed little interest and Hornsby, after five years of profitless effort, sold its foreign patents to Holt Manufacturing of California. It was therefore ironic that, by mid-1915, Britain was placing substantial orders with Holt Manufacturing for tracked vehicles.

In the 1913 British Army manoeuvres there were 45,000 men, 17,000 horses, 2,200 horse-drawn vehicles, but only 192 motorised vehicles and no tracked machines. In retrospect it can be regarded as fortunate that, in 1910, a design that was essentially a tank was submitted to the Austro-Hungarian government who ignored it and that, in 1913, a German inventor gave a demonstration of a 'land-cruiser' which proved unsuccessful.[4]

The man who, in October 1914, saw the urgent need for an armoured tractor on the Western Front and who took it upon himself to champion the cause was Lieutenant Colonel Ernest Swinton. Swinton was a trained engineer and a Regular soldier who had seen service in South Africa and had witnessed trench warfare in the Russo-Japanese conflict. He had been appointed the official correspondent of the British Forces in France and therefore had first-hand knowledge of the fighting conditions on the Western Front. Swinton was aware that the Holt tractor could cross rough terrain and drag heavy loads. On 20 October 1914 Swinton contacted Captain Maurice Hankey and pressed the case for the conversion of the

Holt tractor into an armoured fighting machine. Together with Captain T.G. Tulloch, an explosives expert and a convinced supporter of the armoured vehicle concept, Swinton and Hankey agreed to do whatever was possible to generate some interest at the War Office.

Hankey raised the matter with Lord Kitchener, the Secretary of State for War, on two occasions, but found him 'not receptive of the idea'. Swinton also approached Kitchener, but only received the comment that a caterpillar machine would be 'shot up by guns'.[5] At this point, Hankey was appointed Secretary of the newly-formed War Council. It was in this role that Hankey wrote what became known as the Boxing Day Memorandum and circulated it to Herbert Asquith, the Prime Minister, Winston Churchill at the Admiralty, Kitchener and the other members of the Council. In this Memorandum, Hankey discussed the stalemate situation in France and possible ways of dealing with it including a description of a machine made up of heavy rollers, armed with a Maxim Gun and drawn by caterpillar tracks. 'The object of this device would be to roll down the barbed wire by sheer weight, to give some cover to men creeping up behind and to support the advance with machine gun fire'.[6]

Hankey's Memorandum prompted Churchill, whose RNAS had used a form of armoured car early in the war, to write to Asquith:

> It is extraordinary that the army in the field and the War Office should have allowed nearly three months of trench warfare to progress without addressing their minds to its special problems … It would be quite easy in a short time to fit up a number of steam tractors with small armoured shelters in which men and machine guns could be placed which would be bullet proof … The caterpillar system would enable trenches to be crossed quite easily, and the weight of the machine would destroy all wire entanglements … If the experiment did not answer, what harm would be done?[7]

Hankey's Memorandum had proposed that a small committee should be set up, stressing that it should contain officers of the Royal Engineers who had experience of trench warfare. Churchill took up this proposal and urged Asquith to take action. Asquith immediately sent for Kitchener and showed him Churchill's letter. As a result, Kitchener formed a War Office Committee and agreed to 'set experiments in train without delay'.[8] Such was Churchill's enthusiasm that he established on his own initiative a 'Landship Committee'. It was headed by the Admiralty chief architect, Eustace Tennyson d'Eyncourt, and, quite illegally, Churchill funded it with a grant of £75,000 to cover the cost of trials. The War Office Committee soon lost momentum following an unsuccessful trial of a caterpillar tractor and only regained interest in mid-1915 when the BEF Commander, Sir John French, prompted by Swinton, gave his opinion that the proposed machine would be of 'considerable tactical value'.[9] After some discussion between the Admiralty and the War Office the two committees were merged.

During the following twelve months the Landship Committee reviewed a series of proposals including the Thomas Hetherington 'Land Battleship'; the 'Big Wheel' built by the Lincoln firm of William Foster & Company; the Tritton 'Trench Crawler'; the landship designed by the Pedrail Transport Company; the American Killen-Strait armoured vehicle; the Bullock 'Creeping Grip'; and the first version of the Tritton and Wilson 'Number One Lincoln Machine'. All of these machines were found to be inadequate for one reason or another. It was not until a revised version of the 'Number One Lincoln Machine' was fitted with new tracks that a practical proposal emerged. The new tracks were a significant breakthrough in design. They were made of cast-steel plates which were riveted to hinged links. Guides engaged rails on the track frames and this prevented the track from working loose. The new machine was known as 'Little Willie'. It had a box-like compartment of boiler plate and was powered by a 105hp Daimler engine. It was the first armoured fighting vehicle with a purpose-built body and tracks – in fact, the first tank.

* * *

Even while 'Little Willie' was being built, Tritton and Wilson were working on another design capable of meeting the criteria put forward by the War Office. 'Little Willie' could cross a 5ft gap, but the Landship Committee now required machines to be able to cross gaps of 8ft 6in and climb over obstacles 4ft 6in high. Tritton and Wilson's new machine, named 'Big

Willie', was able to meet these requirements. 'Big Willie' was of a radically different design from previous models. Its shape was rhomboid and the tracks went completely around the body to improve the tracking capability. This restricted the amount of space on top of the machine which meant that there was no room for the turret. Instead the 6-pounder guns were placed on either side in half turrets known as sponsons. 'Big Willie' weighed 28 tons, was operated by an eight-man crew and had a road speed of 4mph. The design incorporated tail-wheels as an aid to steering which was controlled by gears that varied the speed of each track independently.

'Big Willie' was trialled at Hatfield Park on 2 February 1916 in front of His Majesty King George V, Kitchener, Balfour, Lloyd George and a number of military representatives. The trial was sufficiently successful for the Ministry of Munitions to place an order for 100, later increased to 150. To preserve secrecy, the production model was called 'Tank Mark I' and, henceforth, the word 'tank' became part of military vocabulary. As the parent of all future tanks, 'Big Willie' became known as 'Mother'.

About half the Mark I tanks produced in 1916 were 'males' armed with two 6-pounder guns, one in each sponson, and four Hotchkiss machine guns. Tail-wheels were fitted to improve the steering capability. A 'female' version was also produced with modified sponsons that would house two heavy Vickers machine guns and one Hotchkiss gun instead of the 6-pounders. A new unit of the Machine Gun Corps – the Heavy Branch – was formed under the command of Swinton and recruitment and training began. The first manpower plan provided for six Companies each with twenty-five tanks and manned by twenty-five officers and 225 Other Ranks.[10] Recruitment continued throughout the war and in July 1917 the Tank Corps was established.

Work continued on new designs with the Mark II and Mark III tanks which were primarily used for training and only lightly armoured. Both had male and female versions and incorporated several improvements such as a hatch roof to make access easier and wider track shoes. Also, the tail-wheels of the Mark I were abandoned since they tended to get stuck in shell holes and mud. The Mark IV, available from mid-1917, was the most used tank of the war. It had improved armour (12mm thick), a better petrol feed system, armoured fuel tanks and better ventilation. The armaments were also improved. In December 1917 the Medium A tank was commissioned specifically to take advantage of any possible 'breakthrough' situation. Because of its increased speed – it could travel at 8mph – it became known as the 'Whippet'. Finally, in July 1918, the Mark V arrived and was followed by a number of variants. The Mark V had improved steering, a 150hp engine, and the thickness of the armour was increased to 14mm.

* * *

It was Churchill who brought tanks to the attention of Sir Douglas Haig. Churchill's papers 'The Variants of the Offensive' and 'The Attack by Armour' prompted Haig to send Major Hugh Elles, a Royal Engineer at GHQ, to observe the trials of 'Big Willie' at Hatfield Park in February 1916. Elles reported back positively. It was at this point that Haig was planning the Battle of the Somme and was eager to use any means to ensure success. He immediately ordered 150 tanks, but by the first day of the battle none were available. Haig noted: 'This is disappointing as I have been looking forward to obtaining decisive results from the use of these "Tanks" at an early date.'[11] The first Mark I tanks reached France in early September.

There was considerable controversy as to whether tanks should be used on the Somme. Swinton, Churchill, Lloyd George and Hankey were against their use on the grounds that there were not enough available (around fifty) to make a significant impact; their armour was not strong enough to withstand enemy fire; and the advantage of surprise would be squandered and prejudice future attacks. Moreover, the tanks were to be used in 'driblets' of twos and threes in support of the infantry rather than *en masse* leading the infantry as proposed by the tank pioneers. Churchill later commented: 'a secret of war which well used would have procured a world-shaking victory in 1917 had been recklessly revealed to the enemy'.[12] These were certainly important points but, even in 1917, Haig had not received the large number of tanks he had requested. Also, the opportunity of trying out the tanks in battle and discovering their weaknesses would be lost as would the real action experience for the crews who had never before used tanks in battle. Haig was well aware of the potential problems associated with using the few tanks available to him. He stated his position as follows; 'It is not my intention to employ tanks in small numbers unless and until I am convinced that the advantages to be gained by doing so are great enough to outweigh the disadvantages of making known to the enemy the existence of these new engines of war'.[13]

A communiqué from GHQ dated 13 September was circulated to all corps and divisions involved in the attack on the line Morval-Gueudecourt. It read:

> On the front of the attack, besides a superiority of at least four to one in infantry, we have more artillery, practical supremacy in the air, and a large mass of cavalry immediately available to exploit to the full a successful assault by the other arms. In addition, we have a new weapon of war which may well produce great moral[e] and material effects.[14]

General Sir Henry Rawlinson, commanding the operation, was, however, sceptical about the tanks: 'We are puzzling our heads as to how to make use of them and have not yet come to a decision. Some people are rather too optimistic about what these weapons will accomplish.'[15]

On 15 September 1916 tanks were used for the first time in battle. Their performance was mixed. Of the forty-nine tanks employed only thirty-two reached their starting points. Nine pushed ahead of the troops and nine failed to keep pace with the advancing infantry. Of the remaining fourteen, nine broke down and five ditched. The reception of the tank by the British infantry was also mixed. A tank commander, Lieutenant V. Huffan of D Company, later wrote: 'At dawn reported to an Australian Colonel. My reception was rude. I was told to take my bloody stink box away out of it.'[16] On the other hand, Lieutenant B.L.Q. Henriques of C Company wrote: 'We moved off from our camp behind the lines at 5pm … Troops rushed to the side of our route and stood, open-eyed, thousands swarmed around and we seemed to cheer people up as we went.'[17]

Despite the breakdowns, the poor terrain and the inadequate number of tanks, there were some successes. The most publicized achievement was that of D17 'Dinnaken'. Commanded by Lieutenant Stuart Hastie, D17 was to advance with D9 and D14 some one and a half miles to the village of Flers in support of the 41st Division. Shortly after moving off at 6.20 am D14 slid into a disused trench. D9 attempted to pull D14 out of the trench, but the sponsons of the two tanks fouled and they were effectively *hors de combat*. Hastie's D17 went on alone despite damaged tail-wheels and reached Flers with troops of the 122 and 124 Infantry Brigades. 'Dinnaken' flattened various wire entanglements, machine-gunned a trench and then entered Flers. About 300 infantry followed 'Dinnaken' which did further damage to enemy positions in the village. Shortly after moving into Flers, D17 received a direct hit on a track and the engine failed. There was little that Hastie and his crew could do so they evacuated 'Dinnaken' and returned to the British lines.

When reports of D17's exploits reached the Press the event became exaggerated and the myth was born of a tank 'walking up the High Street at Flers with the British Army cheering behind'.[18] Despite this exaggeration, GHQ were well pleased with the day's events. Haig's diary entry for 15 September read: 'Certainly some tanks have done marvels! And have enabled our attack to progress at a surprisingly fast pace'.[19] Lieutenant General Sir Lancelot Kiggell, Haig's chief of staff, wrote to General Sir William Robertson, the CIGS:

> Consider that the ability of the tanks has been proved. It has been established that the magnitude of the success of 15th in certain localities was directly attributable to the employment of tanks. Further, there is no doubt that their employment minimises loss among the attacking troops.[20]

Shortly after the attack at Flers, Haig met Swinton and congratulated him on the success of the operation: 'I then discussed our future Tank policy and decided to ask the Home authorities to send us out quickly as many as possible, at the same time, to improve the armour of the present type, and work out an improved design of a heavier nature (68 tons)'.[21] Haig then sent Major General Richard Butler, his deputy chief of staff, to England to press his views. A thousand tanks were ordered in addition to those already in production.

The feelings of the British infantry towards the tanks were ambivalent. On 15 September tank D1 had been given the task of breaking the German hold on Delville Wood. Lance Corporal Lovell (KOYLI) was one of the bombers following D1. Later he recorded his experience: 'We were awed! We were delighted that [the tank] was ours … The Jerry waited until our tank was only a few yards away and then fled – or hoped to … We would have danced for joy if it had been possible out there'.[22] Shortly afterwards, D1 received a direct hit from a shell. It had been the first tank to go into battle and it was also the first tank casualty.

Lance Corporal Lovell's enthusiasm was not shared by Private Coles (Coldstream Guards). The Guards Division had attacked the Quadrilateral, a heavily defended German strongpoint. They had been allocated three tanks, but all three broke down.

> We manned the parapet at Zero hour waiting to go over and waiting for the tank … The wretched tank never came … We couldn't wait for it, so we had to go over the top. We got cut to pieces. Eventually the tank got going and went over past us. The Germans ran for their lives – couldn't make out what was firing at them. The tank did what it was supposed to have done, but too late![23]

Only a small number of the troops who took part in the Flers-Courcelette attack would have actually witnessed a tank in action. Those who did were quick to realize that although the tank could give valuable support it was also extremely unreliable and a dangerous friend in that it attracted considerable enemy fire.

* * *

While the initial reaction of the German soldiers to this new weapon of war was, understandably, one of alarm – the report in the *Dusseldorfer Generalanzeiger* described the tanks as 'the devil's chariots'[24] – they soon came to regard them as just another weapon and a weapon that they could deal with. The tank of 1916 was clearly vulnerable to field guns and armour-piercing bullets. Even machine-gun bullets were seen to cause enough damage to incapacitate a tank crew who were subject to flying pieces of red-hot metal dislodged from the machine's armour plating.

Indeed, the crew of a tank fought in the most terrible conditions. The badly ventilated machines were filled with noxious fumes, there was no suspension, the noise was deafening and temperatures were generally above 100°F. Crews suffered delirium and vomiting. Speech was impossible and contact was made by banging a spanner on the metal casing to attract attention. Crews were issued with leather helmets and face masks of leather or chainmail, but the heat made them so uncomfortable that they were often unused. After the war Sir Basil Henriques, who as a young subaltern had commanded a tank at Flers, wrote:

> The nervous strain in this first battle of tanks for officers and crew alike was ghastly. Of my Company one officer went mad and shot his engine to make it go faster; another shot himself because he thought he had failed to do as well as he ought; two others had what I suppose could be called a nervous breakdown.[25]

What with mechanical breakdowns, inadequate armour and grim operating conditions there was much to be done to make the tank an effective weapon.

There was also much to be done to produce tanks in the numbers and to the timescale required. Over twenty months had passed from the time of the conversations between Asquith, Churchill and Kitchener in January 1915 and the use of the first tanks at Flers-Courcelette. The design and production of tanks was indeed slow. At a War Cabinet discussion on 22 March 1917 the then Minister of Munitions, Dr Christopher Addison, announced that the final design of the new Mark IV tank had not been approved until 23 November 1916 and the drawings had not been available until 7 January 1917. At the same meeting Lieutenant Colonel Stern of the Department of Munitions stated that: 'When deliveries commenced they would take place in considerable quantities so that during the summer months large numbers would be available.'[26] However, the number of tanks delivered invariably fell short of the plans made by the Department of Munitions. In February 1917 there were only sixty tanks in France and in July 1917 only 136 were available. Robertson, aware that Haig had ordered 1,000 tanks in September 1916, had prudently commented to Haig in November 1916:

> The man Stern who was something to do with the production of tanks has been telling Lloyd George that he can put in hand still another 1,000 tanks for you. Lloyd George is rather in favour of giving out this order, but it seems that the 1,000 you have already asked for is as far as we should think of going at the present experimental stage of these things.[27]

When Churchill took over the Ministry of Munitions in July 1917 he observed: 'Broadly speaking, I consider that a year has been lost in Tank development'.[28] Even with Churchill's promise of 'strenuous efforts … to repair this melancholy state of affairs', only 378 Mark IV tanks, of the original 1,000 ordered by Haig in September 1916, were available in November 1917. The Mark V tank did not appear until March 1918. There were undoubtedly difficulties in design and manufacture and the Tank Corps frequently wanted changes to the tank specification. Ironically, Churchill's previous department, the Admiralty, in commandeering the supply of steel plate for shipbuilding, also contributed to the tardiness of tank production.[29]

* * *

In the weeks following the September 1916 Flers-Courcelette battle tanks were used in small numbers and, most notably, took part in a successful attack on the fortified village of Beaumont-Hamel. The next significant use of tanks was not until April 1917 when twenty-six Mark IIs fought at Arras. The Mark II machines, produced essentially for training purposes, were defective in armour. Moreover, the three weeks' artillery bombardment, which took place before the attack, churned up the ground and turned it into mud. The tanks had some success, but the mud and snow together with the usual breakdowns prevented them from being used effectively.

Arras was not a tank success story. Nor was the use of the new Mark IVs at Messines in June 1917. The poor weather and mud again frustrated the advance and many tanks were bogged down. It was these conditions that gave rise to the use of the 'ditching beam'. This wooden beam was chained to the tracks of the tank. The movement of the tank pulled the beam underneath the tank thus providing some grip to enable the tank to move over the mud.

Rain and Flanders' mud were even more of a problem during the Third Battle of Ypres which began on 29 July 1917. The battlefield soon became a bog and even the tanks' ditching beams proved completely inadequate to move the machines forward. Of the 136 tanks that took place in the first assault, only nineteen were operational at the end of the first day. Tanks continued to be used during the battle which lasted until 10 November. There were occasional successes such as the destruction of critical German strongpoints near St Julien on 19 August. But the terrible conditions ensured that overall the effectiveness of the tanks was minimal. The staff of General Gough's Fifth Army gradually lost faith: 'Tanks are unable to negotiate bad ground. The ground on the battlefield will always be bad. Therefore tanks are no good on the battlefield'.[30] Major J.A. Coughlan, who was a tank commander at Passchendaele, later wrote:

> At that time, though we young officers did not know it, the fate of the young Tank Corps hung in the balance. The High Command was naturally disappointed at the poor results and one school of thought held that persistence in the use of these expensive toys was damaging to the self-reliance of the Infantry.[31]

The Commander of the Tank Corps, Brigadier General Hugh Elles, who had been appointed in September 1916, and his chief of staff, Lieutenant Colonel J.F.C. Fuller, had been dismayed by the inappropriate use of tanks during the Third Ypres offensive and were determined to show how these new weapons should be best employed. The essentials of their plan were that there should be suitable terrain – firm going that had not been churned up by shells – and that the tanks should be used *en masse*, not in penny numbers. A sector that met the Elles-Fuller criteria lay in front of Gouzeaucourt towards Cambrai. The ground was of sand and loam on a chalk base. It was free of mud and had been for some time a relatively quiet sector. Altogether a marked contrast with Flanders. In addition, the nearby Havrincourt Wood was a most convenient place to conceal large numbers of tanks, guns and shells ready for the advance.

The Elles-Fuller plan caught the interest of General Sir Julian Byng, the commander of the Third Army. Independently, Brigadier General Tudor, commanding the artillery of the Third Army's 9th Division, had also developed a plan which preserved secrecy and would use tanks to destroy the enemy wire rather than by the use of guns. The novel feature of Tudor's plan was that the artillery should do away with the usual gun registration that alerted the enemy to a forthcoming attack. Instead 'predicted' fire, using the techniques of flash spotting and sound-ranging, would target specific German gun positions and strongpoints. This bombardment would take place simultaneously with the advance of the tanks and the infantry.

The original Elles-Fuller plan had envisaged a tank raid towards the German lines that would last only a few hours, but Byng's final version was much more ambitious. It aimed at breaking the German defences between the Canal du Nord and the St Quentin Canal, taking Bourlon Wood, Cambrai and the bridges over the River Sensee before advancing in the direction of Valenciennes. This enlarged plan was not without its problems – not least that it entailed crossing the formidable Hindenburg Line. The first line of trenches (Siegfried I) were wide enough to deter tanks and were defended by four rows of barbed wire some 100 yards deep. There was a support system about 2 miles behind the first line and behind that were the main defences, Siegfried II. Undeterred, Byng put the proposed plan to Haig who, after some misgivings but hoping to end a dismal year with a measure of success, authorised the attack which took place on 20 November 1917.

The initial assault would be carried out by the Tank Corps leading six infantry divisions of II and IV Corps and supported by fourteen RFC squadrons. Five cavalry divisions were held ready for the hoped-for breakthrough. In total 378 fighting tanks were to be used along with supply tanks and tanks fitted with grapnels for dragging out the barbed wire and opening up gaps for the cavalry and the infantry. Such was the perceived importance of this operation, both to Byng and to Elles, that the tanks committed to the attack constituted virtually the entire Tank Corps in France. Special Order No. 6 from Brigadier General Elles announced that he personally would lead the attack in his tank 'Hilda'.

Secrecy had been maintained and the German defenders were taken by surprise. At 6.20 am the tanks rolled forwards into no man's land, many of them carrying fascines – 2-ton bundles of wood ready to be dropped into the wide enemy trenches and form bridges. The first day of the attack was a notable success. Despite a setback at Flesquières, the British penetrated the Hindenburg Line on a 6-mile front and captured 7,500 prisoners and 120 guns. When news of the Cambrai advance reached England church bells were rung for the first time in the war. However, the euphoria was premature. Byng had no Reserves – he had committed all his available infantry and tanks in the first attack. The attacks on Bourlon Wood were proving costly and drawn out. The Germans brought forward reinforcements and on 30 November made a successful counter-attack which, while making little progress in the north of the battle area, broke through in the south towards Gouzeaucourt. When the battle was called off on 7 December the British retained part of the Hindenburg system near Flesquières-Ribécourt, but had lost ground to the south. Considering that the Third Army had suffered some 45,000 casualties and that the Tank Corps had lost a third of its personnel and half of its tanks, the outcome, once so promising, was far from satisfactory. The War Cabinet ordered an official enquiry. At least the attack at Cambrai had shown that the Hindenburg Line could be penetrated and that a carefully prepared operation which combined infantry, guns, aircraft and tanks could make considerable progress even against a well-defended enemy. In Hindenburg's words: 'The English attack at Cambrai for the first time revealed the possibilities of a great surprise attack with tanks'.[32] Fuller later wrote: 'there could no longer be any doubt that … armour on the battlefield … could solve the stalemate'.[33]

During the German Spring Offensives of 1918 the faster Medium A tank, the 'Whippet', made its first appearance. However, its intended role as a tank to exploit breakthrough situations was irrelevant during the German advances. In a defensive role the 'Whippet' had some success – for example on the Somme in March 1918 when twelve of these machines broke up a German advance and, on 24 April, when seven 'Whippets' charged two German battalions causing disruption and heavy casualties.[34] One event of note was the first tank-against-tank battle which took place on 24 April just outside Villers-Bretonneux when Lieutenant Mitchell's Mark V engaged and destroyed a German A7V. Later in the same action, Mitchell's tank was attacked by two A7Vs:

> Now thought that we shall not last very long. The two great tanks were creeping forward relentlessly; if they both concentrated their fire on us at once we would be finished. We sprinkled the neighbourhood of one of them with a few sighting shells when, to my joy and amazement, I saw one go slowly backwards. Its companion did likewise and in a few minutes they both have disappeared from sight, leaving our tank the sole possessor of the field.[35]

Generally, however, tanks were of little use in stemming the enemy forward movement in the first half of 1918 and crews were frequently used as Lewis gunners to help the infantry.

From July 1918 onwards the tank played an important part in the British advances. Sir John Monash, the newly appointed Australian commander, used the latest Mark V tanks successfully during the Battle of Hamel on 4 July. On 8 August Rawlinson employed 342 Mark Vs together with 2,000 guns and an air superiority of 5:1 to win a stunning victory at Amiens. General Erich Ludendorff described it as the 'Black Day' for the German army. After Amiens, tanks were never again used in such large numbers. GHQ were becoming alarmed at the high casualty rate among tank crews and also at the significant loss of tanks from breakdowns and enemy fire. More than two-thirds of the tanks that fought between the 8 and 11 August at Amiens were knocked out and 700 tank personnel became casualties.[36] It was the opinion of Lieutenant General Sir Herbert Lawrence, Haig's recently appointed chief of staff, that the Tank Corps had suffered losses 'which were not compensated by the results achieved'.[37]

For the remainder of the war tanks were used in conjunction with other arms. Hence 183 tanks saw action on 21 August at Albert; eighty-one were used on 2 September on the Drocourt-Quéant switch; 181 during the attack on the Hindeburg Line on 29 September; forty-eight at the Battle of Selle on 17 October; and thirty-seven on 4 November on the Sambre. During the final stages of the war the tank had become an integral part of the BEF 'all arms' battle tactics.

* * *

The tank was Britain's unique contribution to the war and the BEF on the Western Front was the first army to use the tank in battle. The main factors that gave the BEF tank supremacy between 1916 and 1918 can be summarised as follows: the tenacity and technical ingenuity of the early tank pioneers; the political and practical support given by Hankey and Churchill; the ready acceptance of tanks by Haig and his senior generals; the leadership given to the Tank Corps by Elles and Fuller; and the almost incomprehensible attitude of the German High Command who ignored the use of tanks until it was too late.

The tank certainly had its limitations. In all the major tank battles the number of machines that survived the initial attack was minimal. At Flers-Courcelette (September 1916) only nine of the original forty-nine tanks committed to the advance were able to keep up with the infantry. The entry in the 39th Division Report of 13 November 1916 was typical: 'One tank succeeded in getting to its starting point, another breaking gear, and a third getting buried en route, in spite of a route having been carefully prepared'.[38] At Messines (July 1917) only nineteen of the sixty-eight tanks that began the attack were able to support the infantry. At Cambrai (November 1917) ninety-two of the 378 tanks committed were operational after three days and at Amiens (August 1918) of the 414 machines used only six were available after four days.[39] It was not an impressive record. In addition to their unreliability, tanks were painfully slow – even the latest Mark Vs could manage only 2mph over rough ground – and they were cumbersome and difficult to manoeuvre. The operating conditions for the crews bordered on the intolerable. The cavalry may have become redundant, but the tank was an inadequate replacement.

Nevertheless, by the end of the war the tank was accepted as a valuable weapon and played a significant part in defeating the German army during the British victories that led to the Armistice. Even from the early days of tank warfare there had been some spectacular achievements. On 26 September 1916, eleven days after the tank attack at Flers-Courcelette, one tank cleared the heavily defended Gird Trench that had been holding up the 21st Division of XV Corps:

> [The tank] started moving south-eastwards along Gird Trench firing its machine guns. As the trench gradually fell into our hands, strongpoints were made in it by two Companies of infantry … No difficulty was experienced. The enemy surrendered freely as the tank moved down the trench … In the capture of Gird Trench eight officers and 362 Other Ranks were made prisoner and a great many Germans were killed. Our casualties only amounted to five. What would have proved a very difficult operation, involving probably heavy losses, was taken with great ease entirely owing to the assistance rendered by the tank.[40]

Individual and small groups of tanks regularly gave dramatic assistance to embattled infantry. On 22 August 1917 in the mud of Third Ypres several tanks of XVIII Corps worked around five German strongpoints near St Julien and opened fire. The defenders either surrendered or fled. The strongpoints were captured in just over two hours with the loss of only twenty-eight British troops.[41] Innumerable such actions took place during the years 1916–1918. In his last despatch of the war Haig praised the role of tanks during the Hundred Days: 'the importance of the part played by them in breaking the resistance of the German infantry can scarcely be exaggerated'.[42]

The tanks of the First World War could never be thought of as 'war winners'. They were just not sufficiently technically advanced. Their role was essentially one of supporting the infantry along with other weapons such as the artillery and aircraft. But it is clear that tanks made a positive contribution to the final defeat of the German army on the Western Front. There is no doubt that the BEF was far better off with tanks than without them and it is worth identifying the main factors that enabled this new weapon to make such a major impact.

The initial development of the tank was due to the commitment of a number of dedicated individuals. The concept was forwarded by enthusiasts such as Swinton, Hankey, Tulloch, Tritton, Hetherington, Wilson and Roberts and, in military operations, by Elles and Fuller. Of these pioneers, and there were others, Swinton deserves special mention. Not only did he bring the concept of the tank to Hankey's attention, he personally lobbied members of the War Office and GHQ. He commanded the first tank unit

– the Heavy Branch of the Machine Gun Corps – and was responsible for the recruitment and training of the first tank crews. His contribution to the early development of the tank and the Tank Corps cannot be over-stressed.

By contrast, the development of the tank took place almost despite the War Office, whose contribution was often slow and negative. In 1910 the War Office turned down the request of the Ministry of Munitions to evaluate the Holt 'Crawler' and the Hornsby 'Caterpillar'. When, in 1912, an Australian engineer, L.E. de Mole, submitted a plan for a caterpillar-tractor to the War Office, it was ignored on the grounds that 'the occasion for its use had not then arisen'.[43] Similarly, the War Office showed little enthusiasm for progressing the tank following an unsuccessful 'caterpillar' trial in June 1915 – a trial that took all of six months to set up. The War Office Committee, formed in 1915 to investigate the possibilities of the tank, was virtually stillborn.

In political terms, Churchill, an advocate of mechanical warfare and spurred by Hankey's Boxing Day Memorandum, was the main supporter of the tank and went out of his way to gain the interest of Prime Minister Asquith. It was Churchill at the Admiralty who championed the early tank, not Kitchener at the War Office. Churchill's 'Memorandum on the Variants of the Offensive', in which he encouraged the use of 'caterpillars', was published in December 1915. This memorandum made a favourable impression on Field Marshal French and paved the way for Swinton's more technical paper to the War Committee which, in turn, gained Haig's approval. It was Churchill who formed his influential 'Landship Committee' at the Admiralty (even though the link between the tank and the sea was somewhat tenuous) and, when serving in the trenches in December 1915, it was Churchill who first brought information about the tank to Haig. The minutes of the Royal Commission on Awards, established in 1919 to assess the claims of inventors who had helped the war effort, summed up the contribution of Churchill to the development of the tank: 'It was primarily due to the receptivity, courage and driving force of Mr Winston Churchill that the general idea of the use of such an instrument of warfare as the "Tank" was converted into practical shape'.[44]

A further key factor in the development of the tank as a fighting machine was the ready acceptance of this new weapon by the leaders of the BEF.

Both of the commanders of the BEF, French (1914–15) and Haig (1916–18), welcomed the tank for the same reason that had led them to use another new weapon, gas – they saw that both innovations could be of great assistance in progressing their military aims. Haig ensured that the new machines were employed in the BEF. When Rawlinson showed a lack of interest for the use of tanks on the Somme, Haig wrote to him: 'I think great boldness should be shown at the outset ... so use tanks boldly'.[45] Later in the war, Rawlinson became a tank enthusiast and in June 1918, for example, he spent time and effort in encouraging Australian troops to understand and use tanks.[46]

Tanks clearly had their limitations and there was inevitably some scepticism. Even in August 1917 Kiggell, who had shown much enthusiasm for tanks after Flers-Courcelette, wrote to Lieutenant General Sir Hubert Gough: 'a check must be kept on the enthusiasts'.[47] But most generals in the BEF followed Haig's lead and doubts gradually gave way to more balanced views. Gough considered that tanks would prove to be of great assistance in trench warfare 'if their mechanical weaknesses could be overcome'.[48] The CIGS, Robertson, wrote to Haig on 7 September 1916 just before the attack at Flers: 'I hope the tank will prove successful. It is rather a desperate innovation.'[49] On 15 September 1917, one year after the Flers attack, Robertson again wrote to Haig: 'I am inclined to think that we may get good things out of the tanks.'[50] And Robertson commented on 12 November 1917, after the initial success of the Cambrai tank battle: 'Your recent operation has been more than splendid'.[51]

In general, British commanders on the Western Front took a positive if guarded view of tanks. General Maxse considered that: 'The tank, if used with discretion, is capable of encouraging manpower and minimising casualties'.[52] In March 1917 Lieutenant General Sir Richard Haking of XI Corps wrote to the First Army commander, General Sir Henry Horne, requesting the use of just one tank: 'If a tank could be attached to my Corps the news of its arrival might be spread to the enemy and we could also test it in this muddy ground with a view to further operations'.[53] Haking was also keen to demonstrate the abilities of a tank to the commander of the Portuguese troops, General Tamagnini, as a means of raising morale. General Byng readily incorporated the proposals of the tank commander, Elles, in his expanded plan of attack at Cambrai. Haig and his generals have frequently been accused of being technophobes, but there is nothing in their acceptance or use of tanks to suggest this – quite the reverse.

Yet another factor in the development and use of the tank on the Western Front was the significantly different approaches taken by the main belligerents. The French acted in this respect quite independently of the British. Having initially investigated the possible conversion of wheeled agricultural tractors and tracked vehicles, the Schneider Company, in May 1915, acquired two Holt tractors and demonstrated them to representatives of the French army. The two leading French champions of the tank were Eugène Brillie, the Schneider Chief engineer, and Colonel Jean Baptiste Estienne, an artillery officer. Between them, Brillie and Estienne produced the first French tank – the Schneider *Char d'Assaut*. After trials, the French Ministry of Armaments placed an order for 400. The Schneider tank weighed about half as much (14 tons) as the British Mark I and was armed with a 75mm gun and two Hotchkiss machine guns. It had a crew of six. A second make of tank soon appeared – the St Chamond – similarly armed but with a much larger body weighing 29 tons and having a crew of nine. The French Ministry of Armaments again ordered 400.

The first French tank operation took place on the Chemin des Dames in April 1917. As with British tanks, the Schneiders proved vulnerable to German artillery fire. Additionally, they found it almost impossible to cross trenches. A major design fault became evident in that the fuel tank was positioned high on the body and a direct hit invariably caused a major explosion. Of the forty-eight Schneiders that took part in this first attack eight broke down and thirty-eight were either destroyed or abandoned.[54] Three weeks later, at Laffracie Mill, thirty-two Schneiders operated with sixteen St Chamonds. This second tank operation was no more successful than the first and the large tanks again failed to deal with the German trenches. Faith in these heavy machines was lost and no further orders were placed for either the Schneiders or the St Chamonds. Thereafter, French production concentrated on a light, two-man tank, designated the FT17, from Renault. The FT17 was novel and quite different from British tank design. It weighed only 6 tons, had a fully rotating turret and was armed by an 8mm machine gun or a 37mm cannon. The FT17 was first used in May

1918 and it became the standard French tank. By the end of the war some 3,000 had been built.

The American contribution to tank development was virtually nil and the American Expiditionary Force (AEF) used either British or French machines. The French government had contracted in November 1917 for 1,200 Renault tanks to be built in America, but only 150 were actually produced and of these twenty reached France before the end of the war. In 1918 the Americans used tanks at St Mihiel and during the Meuse-Argonne offensive, but both experiences, through poor organization and lack of training, were disappointing.[55]

Given Germany's industrial and technical strength, the lack of interest shown by that country in the tank is perplexing. The fact that Germany mainly played a defensive role on the Western Front is almost certainly a factor, though the availability of some tank-like machines at Verdun (1916) and during the spring 1918 offensives might well have provided an important advantage. In the event, the OHL gave priority to aircraft engines rather than to tank development. Also of significance is that Germany had no tank 'champion' – they were without a Swinton or an Estienne. Ludendorff was not impressed by the performance of the British tanks in 1916 and chose to rely on anti-tank weapons such as armour-piercing bullets and field guns. It was only after the British success at Cambrai that Germany became at all serious about tanks. However, Germany produced only twenty of their own heavy and cumbersome A7V tanks, which weighed 33 tons and had a crew of eighteen. Instead they relied mainly on machines captured from the British. The fears of both Lloyd George and Churchill that the Germans would learn and benefit from a premature use of the Mark I tank at Flers-Courcelette were proved to be unfounded. The proceedings of the 'German Official Investigation of the Causes of Collapse in 1918' acknowledged that: 'The importance of the tank was not at first estimated by our Army commanders as highly as was proved necessary by later experience. When the construction of the tank was begun the work was not organised efficiently enough.'[56]

During 1918 all the Western Front participants prepared plans for a continuation of the war into 1919. After the success of the British tanks at Amiens in August 1918 the Germans finally decided to produce tanks on a serious scale and ordered 670 light machines with the aim of having 4,000 by the end of 1919. A heavy tank was also planned, but the Armistice brought all developments to an end.

The French continued to produce Renault tanks right up to the end of the war. They were prepared to continue into 1919 with a programme of 7,000 tanks by March. An Anglo-American project at Châteauroux for the mass production of tanks began operation in October 1918. It had a target of 300 heavy tanks per month. Independently, the British were developing the Mark VIII in Glasgow. GHQ placed an order for 4,000 tanks for spring 1919. Such activity among all those involved on the Western Front showed that the tank had undoubtedly become an essential weapon of war. It also showed that Britain, the originator of the tank, was set to maintain its position as the leader in tank development in the immediate future.

From the early days of tank design there had been discussion as to how the tank could be best used. Churchill had favoured an infantry-carrying vehicle. The Mark V had been designed to carry out that role, but experience showed that troops exposed to the foul interior of a tank became incapable of fighting. The troop-carrier idea was overtaken, following the merger of the War Office and Admiralty Committees in 1915, by Swinton's vision of the tank as a means of breaking through the enemy's wire and trenches and thus ending the stalemate on the Western Front. Fuller had an even more ambitious role for the tank. In his 'Plan 1919' he envisaged large groups of tanks cutting through the enemy's lines and attacking their key control and communications centres. During the period 1916–1918 none of the roles put forward by Churchill, Swinton and Fuller were possible on the Western Front. The then state of tank technology did not allow it. The role that the tank did play, imperfectly but with growing success, was as an adjunct to the infantry. It was not until the advent of the German Panzer divisions in 1940, whose role owed more to Fuller than to either Churchill or Swinton, that the true potential of the tank was realized. Given Germany's negative attitude to tanks in the First World War this was indeed an ironic twist.

*Chapter 5*

# Artillery on the Western Front

*'We would therefore seem to be confronted with the problem that unless we use a great deal of artillery fire we cannot get on'.*

*General Sir William Robertson*[1]

While aeroplanes and tanks were novel and dramatic examples of technological development in the BEF it was artillery that proved to be the decisive weapon of the war. The importance and growth of artillery can be clearly seen from a variety of BEF statistics. In August 1914 there were 2,087 officers and 75,757 Other Ranks. By August 1918 these numbers had increased to 29,990 officers and 488,710 Other Ranks.[2] In August 1914 the BEF possessed 456 guns of all types, while in August 1918 the total number of guns available had risen fifteen-fold to 6,437. The production of guns rose from ninety-one in 1914 to 10,680 in 1918.[3] In terms of human destruction, 59 per cent of all wounds inflicted on British soldiers throughout the war were inflicted by shells or mortar bombs.[4]

From the very earliest days of the war it became clear that guns and shells were to play a crucial part in the conflict. By the afternoon of 4 August German troops had reached Liege. Belgium, anticipating a German invasion, had fortified the whole of the Liege area with a series of forts built by the foremost military engineer of the time, General Henri-Alexis Brialmont. The twelve Brialmont forts around the city were positioned so that they provided mutual cover. They were constructed of reinforced concrete with steel cupolas and the armour-plated gun turrets housed eight 21cm and 15cm guns. They were considered the most formidable forts of their day.

While the advancing Germans were able to infiltrate between the forts and take Liege, the forts themselves were a major obstacle. Their command of the crossing points on the River Meuse seriously delayed the progress of the main German army. In order to deal with this problem the Germans brought up two of their secret 42cm Krupp howitzers. These weapons, known to their gunners as 'Big Berthas', weighed 42.5 tons and could fire a 1,800lb shell some 10,000 yards with considerable accuracy. At 6.40 pm on 12 August the first shell was fired towards Fort Pontisse. It fell short, as did the following six shells, but the massive explosions were so terrifying in intensity that the defenders thought that the fort had been mined. The eighth shell landed directly on the fort. It penetrated the concrete roof and destroyed much of the defensive system. The shelling continued the following morning and by midday Fort Pontisse was little more than rubble with most of its garrison dead.

The next fort to be shelled was Fort Embourg which suffered the same fate as Pontisse and surrendered within a day. This pattern was repeated with crippling effect until all the forts on the east of the city were destroyed. The two Big Berthas were then moved into Liege itself and proceeded to shell the forts on the west of the city. Fort Loncin, which housed the headquarters of the defending force under General Leman, received direct hits from nineteen shells and its resistance ended when the magazine exploded, causing the total destruction of the fort. General Leman survived and was taken prisoner. The remaining forts, seeing the effect of the howitzer shells, surrendered and by 16 August Liege was entirely under German control.

The two German howitzers were now joined by two Austrian Skoda 30.5cm howitzers (known as 'Slim Emmas'[6]) and on 19 August the ring of nine Brialmont forts around Namur were shelled. It was a repeat of the Liege experience and by 23 August Namur had fallen. It was the fall of Namur and the consequent advance of the German First Army through Belgium that precipitated the retreat of the BEF from Mons. The massive destructive effect of the German and Austrian howitzers was the first dramatic demonstration of the importance of artillery power in the war.[5]

It was Germany's geographical position, encircled by potential enemies, that led to the development of the mighty Krupp and Skoda howitzers. Any advancing German army would inevitably meet strongpoints such as the Brialmont forts and the French defences in the areas around Verdun and Belfort. The successful destruction of these fortifications required high-elevation guns that could lob heavy shells onto concrete fortifications and the German and Austrian giant howitzers were designed for just such a purpose. However, these massive guns were not the most manoeuvrable of artillery weapons. The Krupp 42cm howitzer was transported on low-loaders each drawn by an agricultural tractor. The heavy 30.5cm Skoda was carried on two trailers pulled by 100hp Daimler tractors. They were slow and cumbersome and by the start of the Battle of the Marne on 9 September the 'Big Berthas' and 'Slim Emmas' were left well behind and played no part in that action.

It is here worth distinguishing between high elevation guns such as howitzers and mortars whose trajectory gave an advantage in firing over hills and ridges and also into trench systems, and flat trajectory field and long-distance guns which had a somewhat better ability to destroy strongpoints and trench parapets. Confusingly, guns were variously identified by the weight of the shell they fired or by the diameter of the gun barrel. In general, field guns were defined by the weight of the shell while heavy guns were defined by the diameter of the barrel. The heavier the gun the more its potential for destruction, but, compared with the lighter guns, they were far less manoeuvrable and could fire less quickly. As regards the shells that were fired from these guns, there were, in 1914, two kinds – shrapnel and high explosive (HE). Shrapnel balls, made of lead, were packed into a shell. A time fuse at the nose of the shell would ignite a small charge of gunpowder and the balls would be blown out at a high velocity at a height above the ground selected to inflict maximum damage to the soldiers beneath. An 18-pounder shrapnel shell could fire 375 bullets at a velocity of 1,590ft/second. Early HE shells were simply filled with picric acid (trinitrophenol) and, from 1915, by ammonal which was ignited by an impact fuse and exploded with great force sending shards of white-hot metal casing in all directions. Guns, using mainly Cordite as a propellant, could fire either shrapnel or HE shells.

In March 1915 Sir John French wrote to Lloyd George distinguishing between HE and shrapnel shells:

> Large quantities of high-explosive shells for field guns have become essential owing to the form of warfare in which the Army is engaged … Shrapnel, being the man-killing projectile which is used against troops

> in the open, is primarily used in defence. In offensive operations it is used for searching communication trenches, preventing the enemy's reinforcements intervening in the fight, repelling counter-attacks, and as an alternative for high explosive shells, for cutting wire entanglements. It is, however, ineffective against occupants of trenches, breastworks or buildings. It is therefore necessary to have high explosive shells to destroy parapets, obstacles, buildings and many forms of fortified localities that the enemy construct, more particularly his machine gun emplacements. Without an adequate supply the attack is impotent against defenders of field fortifications, as the first steps cannot be taken. Guns require 50% of high explosive shells.[7]

* * *

The British and French had nothing to compare with the giant German and Austrian howitzers. The French had concentrated on producing their 75mm Puteaux field gun, recognized as probably the best of its kind in the war. It was remarkably manoeuvrable, weighing 2,513 pounds; it could fire 12- or 16-pound shells over a distance of 7,500 yards; and its rate of fire was twenty-five rounds per minute. The 75s fitted perfectly into the French philosophy of *elan* and attack, but their weakness was their limited angle of fire which reduced their effectiveness in hilly country. In 1914 the French had 3,800 such guns, but they lacked howitzers and heavy artillery. While the French possessed only around 270 guns in the 120-155mm range, all of which were around thirty years old, the Germans had some 850 guns of a similar size including the outstanding 150mm howitzers. The German artillery weakness was in their field guns which were made up mainly of twenty-year-old 77mm guns and which were much inferior to the French 75s. British artillery, limited in numbers, was made up of the formidable 13- and 18-pounder field guns supported by 4.5 inch howitzers and 60-pound heavy guns together with a variety of old guns left over from the Boer War.

In 1914, while the artillery of the French, German and British armies were of somewhat different compositions, the total number of guns per army corps was similar. A French corps had 126 guns, a German corps had 160

## Men and Machines

Sir Douglas Haig.

Sir Henry Wilson.

Sir Hugh Trenchard.

Sir John French.

Sir William Robertson.

Sir William Birdwood and Anzac soldiers.

Marshal Joffre.

Marshal Ferdinand Foch.

General Erich von Falkenhayn.

Field Marshal Paul von Hindenburg.

General Erich Ludendorff.

Field Marshal Lord Kitchener.

David Lloyd George.

Winston Churchill.

Tsar Nicholas II and King George V.

Kaiser Wilhelm II.

New recruits, 1914.

A British BE2c in 1914.

A squadron of German Albatross DVs.

An Austrian siege gun.

The French 75mm quick firer.

The German U-boat U-9 sank three British destroyers in 1914.

A German defensive position on the Somme, 1916.

A British Mark II tank captured at Arras, 1917.

and a British corps had 154.[8] On the Western Front the British and French had together roughly the same number of guns as the Germans.

The first major use of artillery by the BEF was during the attack at Neuve Chapelle in March 1915. Originally intended to be a joint attack with the French, Field Marshal French and Marshal Joffre disagreed over a proposed extension of the British front line. As a result the joint attack was called off and the British carried on alone. The French had been bearing the brunt of the fighting and Sir John French was determined to establish the BEF as a serious fighting force in the eyes of its ally. The aim was to take the village of Neuve Chapelle and move forward towards the strategically important Aubers Ridge. It was the biggest battle yet fought by the British in terms of troops and guns and it was planned in great detail. During the initial stage of planning it was proposed that there should be a four-day bombardment of the German wire and trenches, but Haig, then commanding the First Army, was anxious to achieve surprise and decided on a three-hour bombardment before the attack, using all the available ammunition. In common with both the French and the Germans, the British had used up the greater part of their artillery ammunition in the early days of the war. Shells were scarce. Major General Henry Wilson noted in his diary on 10 February:

> In no case have we more than 800 rounds per gun in this country and probably not more than 40 of these are H.E. Nor is our output at home of any real use, for in the case of the 18 pounder, which is the most favourable, we are only getting 12 rounds a gun a day, of which 4 are H.E. Now this is a scandalous state of affairs.[9]

In order to preserve secrecy it was arranged that the guns – 340 of them – would move into position well before the attack. The registration of the guns, the firing of trial shots to determine what adjustments were necessary for better accuracy, was carried out at odd times over a period of days so as not to alert the enemy. The final artillery timetable was in three phases. First, the bombardment of the enemy front trenches to destroy men and wire. Second, the bombardment of the support troops in the rear trench lines and, third, a 'box' barrage to seal off Neuve Chapelle and prevent the movement of reinforcements.

On the morning of 10 March at 7 am a few ranging shots were fired to check the accuracy of the guns. Minor adjustments were made and at 7.30 am the artillery bombardment began. It was the heaviest bombardment of the war up to that time. Unfortunately, two batteries of 6-inch howitzers which had arrived from Britain only one day before the attack had no time to register and consequently the artillery support on the extreme left of the attack, where the howitzers were positioned, was far from adequate. All three phases of the artillery plan were completed by 8.35 am. After the first 35-minute bombardment of the German front line, at 8.05 am, three brigades from the Indian and IV Corps left their trenches and went forward towards the enemy lines.

The assault in the centre of the attack area went well. The enemy trenches were captured on a front of 1,800 yards and Neuve Chapelle was taken. The assault on the extreme left failed, mainly because the late-arriving 6-inch howitzer batteries had not destroyed the enemy strongpoints. The German defences on the extreme right also escaped destruction and the attacking troops made little progress. Communication problems after the initial attack meant that the forward troops were uncertain as to their next move. Critical time was lost which allowed German reinforcements to arrive and establish new defence lines. The initiative gained by the British in the first phase was lost and, although the battle continued for two more days, no further gains were made.

In the period 10–13 March the British First Army had 12,892 casualties. Haig's aim, to make a breakthrough towards Aubers Ridge, was only partly achieved. The main lesson learnt from the Neuve Chapelle battle was that a successful advance depended on the destruction of enemy defences by shell fire. Where that had happened, in the centre, the attack had gone well. Where artillery support was lacking the attack had failed. However, the attack had demonstrated that enemy trenches could be taken and it had also shown the French that its ally was quite capable of aggressive action. The discussion after Neuve Chapelle focused on artillery – guns and shells. A break-in had taken place, but it was not exploited and FM Sir John French, on 13 March, claimed that a main reason for this was the shortage of ammunition. During the three days of battle, the 18-pounder guns had fired one-sixth of all the 18-pounder shells available in France – equivalent to seventeen days' production from the munitions factories in the UK.[10] Field Marshal French made his view clear to Kitchener: 'Cessation of the forward movement is necessitated … by the fatigue of the troops and, above all, by the want of ammunition.' French added that unless more shells arrived 'the offensive efforts of the army must be spasmodic and separated by a considerable interval of time. They cannot, therefore, lead to decisive results'.[11]

Two months after Neuve Chapelle, on 8 May, Field Marshal French made a second attempt, again in support of a major French offensive in Artois, to take the Aubers Ridge. Again Haig's First Army was to carry out the attack and some of the lessons from Neuve Chapelle were taken into account. Haig was convinced that the surprise of a short, intense bombardment, as at Neuve Chapelle, was worth repeating. At Aubers, Haig was to have 121 heavy guns and 516 field guns and howitzers. The bombardment, mainly of shrapnel shells, was to last forty minutes. Communication had been a serious problem at Neuve Chapelle and while little could be done about the destruction of telegraph wires during battle, Haig planned to make greater use of the RFC. The role of the RFC was to prevent enemy aircraft from observing the British preparations; to seek out German batteries; and, in a new role, to follow and report back on the progress of infantry identified by white panels that would be laid on the ground. For the first time three aircraft were fitted with radio and during the battle forty-two messages were sent. A third lesson from Neuve Chapelle concerned the use of reserves, including the Cavalry Corps, which would be held at two hours' notice to provide rapid support in the event of a breakthrough. Finally, Haig planned for the forward movement of the artillery, a feature lacking at Neuve Chapelle. Some heavy mortars and field artillery would be attached to the assault battalions for use against enemy strongpoints.

All these plans, however, failed to take account of work done by the Germans on their defensive systems. They too had learnt some lessons from Neuve Chapelle. The barbed wire had been doubled and, in some places, trebled in thickness. The front line trenches had been strengthened and a second line included dug-outs for its garrison with communication trenches linking the first and second lines. Behind the second line was a third line of concrete machine-gun posts. The British artillery, because of ammunition restrictions, were able to bombard these much strengthened defences with only a fifth of the shells used at Neuve Chapelle.

The attack at Aubers was a disaster. The British shelling had not destroyed the German defences and the British First Army lost 11,500 men without any territorial gain. The artillery reported that their stocks of ammunition were severely depleted and that many guns were becoming useless with their barrels and recoil mechanisms worn out. The artillery lesson from Aubers contradicted that of Neuve Chapelle. It was now decided that the considerably stronger enemy defence systems could only be destroyed by long and more powerful artillery bombardments using, predominantly, HE shells. Sir John French wrote: 'It's simple murder to send infantry against powerfully fortified entrenchments until they have been heavily hammered'.[12]

The blame for the failure of Aubers Ridge was placed squarely on the shortage of HE ammunition and the lack of heavy guns – a view that was later supported by the British Official History which attributed the lack of success to: 'the strength of the German defences … the lack of sufficient shells of large calibre and … the inferior quality of much of the ammunition supplied and the difficulties of ranging'.[13] That the British generals had failed to recognize that the Germans had revised their defences was a factor lost in the growing argument about the lack of guns and shells. In April and May 1915 the BEF field guns had available, respectively, ten and eleven rounds per gun per day. The estimated requirement was for fifty rounds per gun per day. When the 27th and 28th British Divisions took over a part of the front line from the French XVI Corps they found that the French had possessed 120 75mm field guns, twenty-four 90mm guns and six 120mm guns. The two British Divisions had only seventy-two 18-pounders between them.[14]

* * *

Sir John French had pleaded for additional guns and ammunition on numerous occasions. During a meeting with journalists on 22 March 1915 he said: 'It is a rough war, but the problem itself is a comparatively simple one – munitions, more munitions, always more munitions'.[15] And in an interview with *The Times* on 27 March he stressed that: 'the protraction of the war depends entirely upon the supply of men and munitions … I dwell emphatically on the need for munitions'.[16] The situation was not helped when, on 20 April, Asquith told munition workers in Newcastle that there was plenty of ammunition, a statement based on information provided by Kitchener.[17]

The Battle of Aubers Ridge was followed on 16 May by an attack at Festubert, this time with a bombardment lasting three days. However, as noted in the British Official History: 'On the material side, heavy guns and high explosive shell were necessary to prepare the way and deal with machine-gun nests … these guns and shells were not forthcoming'.[18] Less than 8 per cent of shells were high explosive. Again the strengthened German defences were only partially destroyed. The limited gains at Festubert were at the cost of 16,500 men.

When Sir John French returned to his headquarters after the Battle of Festubert he found a message waiting for him. He was ordered to send shells to the campaign in Gallipoli. He was outraged. As he later wrote: 'If any additional proof were required of the hopelessness of any relief coming from the War Office I found waiting for me a telegram from the Secretary of State for War, directing that 20 per cent of our scanty reserve supply of ammunition was to be shipped to the Dardanelles'.[19]

The issue of the inadequate supply of guns and ammunition came to a head following an article in *The Times* by Charles Repington, a friend of Sir John French. The headline of Repington's article of 14 May, which claimed that the failure at Aubers Ridge was caused by the lack of shells, read: 'Need for Shells: British Attack Checked: Limited Supply the Cause: A Lesson from France'.[20] The 'Shell Scandal' was underway and it became a major political issue. Field Marshal French sent two of his staff to London to report on the shell situation to Lloyd George and to the leading members of the Opposition, Andrew Bonar Law and Arthur Balfour. The figures were damning: the requirement for 18lb shells was 50 per gun per day while actual supplies from November 1914 to May 1915 had averaged 8 per gun per day. The requirement for the 4.5-inch howitzer shells was 40 per gun per day and the supply averaged 6.[21] Sir John French's actions were a blatant attempt to embarrass Kitchener who, as Secretary of State for War, was responsible for munitions of all kinds. On 21 May Lord Northcliffe, the proprietor of both *The Times* and the *Daily Mail* and no admirer of Kitchener, published a story in the *Daily Mail* headed: 'The Shell Scandal: Lord Kitchener's Tragic Blunder: Our Terrible Casualty Lists'.[22]

The Asquith government was facing not only the shell crisis but also the resignation of the First Sea Lord, Fisher, who was opposed to the Gallipoli campaign. Asquith, fearing that these two events would threaten his leadership and destabilise the government, decided in May 1915 to form a coalition administration. Asquith remained Prime Minister and Lloyd George was appointed to the new Ministry of Munitions. Kitchener continued in the War Office, but his reputation among his colleagues in government, if not with the general population, was seriously damaged.

It was now abundantly clear to everyone that the BEF needed more guns and more shells, particularly high explosives. What was less obvious was how these weapons would be provided. The War Office had taken the view, as it had with the production of aircraft, that private industry and supplies from overseas would solve the problem. The assumption was that increased production, backed by lucrative government contracts, would meet the growing demand. But this approach was far from successful. Skilled labour was scarce – many had enlisted in the early days of the war. Machine tools were in short supply and had to be imported from North America. Even the basic premise, that entrepreneurs would grasp the opportunity to make money, proved unsound. Private industry was unlikely to make significant investment in the armaments business if a short war removed the need for its products. Nevertheless, the War Office pursued this policy with some energy and the Master General of the Ordnance, Major General von Donop, vastly increased the number of armaments contracts with private firms. But the required increases in production were unprecedented and unforeseen. In the whole of the South African war 273,000 rounds had been fired whereas over one million rounds had been fired by the BEF in the six months between August 1914 and January 1915.[23] Large orders were placed, but promises for completion were not met and the quality of the shells produced was uneven.

Matters were not helped by the reluctance of workers in the munitions factories to alter their traditional practices. Many refused to increase production by working nightshifts. Trade unions resented the 'dilution' of labour whereby unskilled workers were able to carry out the work of more skilled craftsmen. The War Office may have been grappling with these problems in 1914 and early 1915, but by the time of the battles of Neuve Chapelle, Aubers Ridge and Festubert there was little to encourage Field Marshal French and his army commanders that an end to their munitions problems was in sight. On 15 March 1915 Kitchener acknowledged this problem:

> The work of supplying and equipping new Armies depends largely on our ability to obtain the war material required … Notwithstanding these efforts to meet our requirements, we have unfortunately found that the output is not only not equal to our necessities but does not fulfil our expectations, for a very large measure of our orders have not been completed by the dates on which they were promised'.[24]

* * *

Even from the beginning of the war, Lloyd George, as Chancellor of the Exchequer, had taken a real interest in the production of armaments. In September 1914 he guaranteed firms against financial loss in the event of peace. In March 1915 he was influential in reaching the Treasury Agreement with a large number of unions who agreed to remove certain constraints on production and accept dilution at least until the end of hostilities. At the same time, a cap was placed on the profits made by the companies in the engineering and shipbuilding industries. He supported the idea of state-owned National Munitions Factories which would give the government more direct control. However, as time passed and results were slow, his general feeling was that the Ordnance Department, run by von Donop under Kitchener, was 'halting and hesitating in front of the munitions problem'.[25]

The need was for greatly increased production supported by an adequately skilled labour force and when Lloyd George moved from the Exchequer to the Ministry of Munitions in May 1915 he immediately set about the task of gaining the cooperation of both employers and employees. In the first week of June he met employer representatives of the main engineering firms in Manchester, Liverpool, Birmingham, Cardiff and Bristol together with the trade unions. His message was: 'We have been employing too much the haphazard, leisurely, go-as-you-please methods. The nation now needs all the machinery it is capable of using for turning out munitions or equipment, all the skill that is available for that purpose'.[26] He stressed that it was no longer 'business as usual' – a phrase he himself had used in the opening days of the war.

His Majesty King George V played an important part in winning the cooperation of the munitions workers. He visited Woolwich Arsenal in March, Enfield and Walton Abbey in April and toured factories on the Clyde and the Tyne in May. He expressed his appreciation of the workers' efforts and encouraged them to 'press forward as efficiently and rapidly as possible'. On the Tyne he urged that 'all restrictive rules and regulations' should be removed and that all should 'work to one common end and purpose'. It was just the sort of support that Lloyd George needed.[27]

It was Lloyd George who persuaded the King and members of the Royal Household to abstain from alcohol for the duration of the war.[28] Lost time among munitions workers because of over-indulgence was seen to be a significant factor in restricting production and the 'King's Pledge' was intended to encourage the population in general and the munitions workers in particular to abstain from excessive drinking. The gesture, however, went largely unheeded. The House of Commons refused to support abstention and Lloyd George himself never gave up alcohol. In November 1915 Lloyd George, characteristically, resorted to legislation using the Defence of the Realm Act. Opening hours were curtailed and beer was watered down. As a result, convictions for drunkenness fell 75 per cent between 1914 and 1918 and the consumption of alcohol fell 50 per cent in the same period. The problem of over-indulgence was not unique to Britain. The drinking of vodka was forbidden in Russia and in France absinthe was prohibited.[29]

Lloyd George believed that state control was the key to higher munitions production. Using the Defence of the Realm Act he converted engineering factories across the country to the manufacture of armaments and the government assumed control of their production. Despite the Treasury Agreement, the support of engineering workers was still a problem. Local union officials considered that their leaders had been taken in by Lloyd George's oratory and resented the loss of their time-honoured practices.

The Treasury Agreement was not working – there was just too much local opposition. The government response, in July 1915, was the Munitions of War Act which designated any industry or production unit considered as essential to the war effort a 'controlled establishment'. This meant that all strikes were outlawed and had to be solved by arbitration; that unofficial strikes and undue absenteeism would be liable to a fine; and that dilution was to take place as required.

Serious labour unrest did take place in the South Wales mining industry over wage rates and this led to strike action. A wage settlement, largely in favour of the union, was agreed, but only after Lloyd George had declared that mining was a 'controlled industry'. On Clydeside, engineers also took strike action with grievances against profiteering landlords and the issue was only settled by the passing of the Rent Restrictions Act which curbed excessive rent rises. The Clydeside workers also refused to cooperate with the principle of dilution and at a meeting on Christmas Day 1915 Lloyd George was shouted down by the Clyde Workers Committee (CWC) of shop stewards and the meeting ended in disorder. In response, Lloyd George imprisoned the CWC leaders, who carried little local support, and dilution was finally accepted. Both in South Wales and on the Clyde Lloyd George had contrived by judicious concession and by a firm application of the law to forward the essential interests of the country.

During the time that Lloyd George was at the Ministry of Munitions (May 1915–June 1916) its powers expanded until it controlled every aspect of munitions development and production. It supervised both the state and the private factories that produced guns and shells. It became responsible for buying supplies of non-ferrous metals, linen, flax, iron and steel and also for the import of mica from India and steel from Sweden. Ball bearings, which had been imported from Germany before the war, were now either made in Britain or imported from Sweden. By 1918 the Ministry of Munitions, then under Winston Churchill, employed 25,000 workers in fifty different departments. It directly managed 250 government factories and supervised 20,000 'controlled' manufacturing units.

* * *

Thanks to the efforts of the Ministry of Munitions and British industry, Sir Douglas Haig had far more guns and shells at his disposal than ever before as he prepared, in spring 1916, for the 'Big Push' on the Somme. The Somme offensive had been planned in December 1915 as a joint French-British attack, but by May 1916 the French were fighting for survival at Verdun. The Somme became a predominantly British battle and while Haig planned for a breakthough, the relief of pressure on the French at Verdun was an equal objective.

By mid-1916 the BEF had a formidable array of guns. New models included 8-inch and 12-inch howitzers. In addition, for the first time there was a range of trench mortars; the 2-inch 'toffee apple' mortar so-called because it fired a 40lb bomb on a 12-inch shaft; the 3-inch and 4-inch Stokes mortars and a 9.45-inch heavy trench mortar (the 'Flying Pig') which had the power to destroy dug-outs. Some 3,000 field and heavy guns together with 1,400 trench mortars were used in the opening Somme bombardment.[30]

Rawlinson's Fourth Army was to carry out the attack and there was immediate disagreement as to the length of the bombardment. Haig was in favour of a two-day hurricane bombardment, giving as much surprise as possible. Rawlinson wanted the bombardment to last five days – and only gained Haig's agreement to this plan by successfully arguing that two days was insufficient to destroy the strengthened German lines of defence and the barbed wire that protected them.

In the week before the attack, British guns fired 1.5 million shells. The 18-pounders concentrated on the wire and trenches while the heavier guns shelled the German strongpoints. In addition, nineteen mines were exploded shortly before zero hour. The British had a 3:1 superiority in the air and observation of enemy positions by aircraft and balloon could take place without interruption. The overall effect on the front-line German troops was traumatic: 'One's head is like a madman's. The tongue sticks to the mouth in terror. Continued bombardment and nothing to eat or drink and little sleep for five days and nights. How much longer can this go on?'[31]

However, the results of the British shelling were mixed. Yard for yard, the intensity of the shelling was less than at Neuve Chapelle where the German defences were less well constructed. 'Dud' shells, many of them imported from America, were also a problem and an estimated 30 per cent failed to explode. The Germans had dug deep into the Somme chalk and many of their dug-outs were undamaged. When the British infantry began their attack the Germans emerged and fired their machine guns into the lines of the advancing troops. The first day of the Somme, 1 July 1916, was a disaster with some 58,000 casualties.

The British did make some ground, but it was slow and costly. Some first-day objectives were not achieved, for example Thiepval, which was not taken until September. Other first-day objectives, such as Serre, were never taken. There were some artillery successes, notably that of 14 July when a night attack followed a heavy two-day bombardment with five minutes of hurricane fire just before the attack. The combination of darkness and concentrated fire on a narrow front destroyed the German trenches from Bazentin-le-Petit to Longueville and the enemy was overrun.

The hoped-for breakthrough never occurred. The Somme became a battle of attrition. When the offensive was called off in October the British and French casualties amounted to 680,000. The Germans had lost around 600,000. At best, the Somme offensive served to weaken the German army both numerically and in morale. About 60 per cent of the German divisions on the Western Front fought on the Somme. Von Kuhl, the chief of staff to Crown Prince Rupprecht of the Bavarian Army Group, stated in January 1917 that: 'We can no longer reckon on the old troops; there is no doubt that in the past summer and autumn our troops have been fearfully harried and wasted'.[32] Ludendorff described his army as 'completely exhausted'.

* * *

By the time of the Somme, the BEF was receiving at least an adequate supply of guns and shells even if the quality was uneven. Through the remainder of 1916 and during 1917 the supplies of armaments increased and quality improved. The proper provision of armaments was crucial, but so too was the development of artillery technology and tactics. The necessities of war provided the impetus for a variety of developments. The introduction of the 'creeping barrage' provided some much needed cover for attacking troops advancing towards enemy trenches. It took the form of a rolling curtain of shell-fire, usually shrapnel, which moved forward 50–100 yards in front of the infantry at a predetermined rate of approximately 100 yards every four minutes. Its purpose was to force the defenders to stay undercover and thereby shield the attackers from rifle and machine-gun fire. The barrage lifted once the advancing troops had reached the first enemy line. The creeping barrage was not without its problems. If the curtain of fire advanced faster than the line of attacking troops it left them vulnerable once the curtain had lifted. It was also possible for advancing troops to be caught up in the barrage and suffer from 'friendly fire'. It was, however, a marked improvement on the previous standard bombardment whereby the infantry left their trenches only after the bombardment had lifted from the enemy front line. The creeping barrage may have been first used by a British heavy battery in October 1914.[33] The French General, Nivelle, used it during his 1915 Champagne offensive and also at Verdun in 1916. It has also been accredited to Major General C.E.D. Budworth, Rawlinson's MGRA, who promoted its use during the later stages of the Somme. As with many such initiatives in the First World War, the idea probably occurred to a number of people all trying to deal with a common problem. One of the most powerful creeping barrages of the war took place on 31 July 1917 during the opening barrage of the Passchendaele offensive when 24 tons of shells were fired per minute. The poet Edmund Blunden wrote: 'A flooded Amazon of steel flowed immensely fast, over our heads'.[34]

The 'Chinese barrage' was used by the French in mid-1915 when irregular pauses were incorporated into an artillery bombardment. The purpose was to confuse the enemy as to the real time of an attack. When the defenders prematurely emerged from their dug-outs during a pause they became exposed to the next stage of the bombardment and so on. The British soon adopted this tactic. At Fromelles in July 1916, for example, the fire plan of the 184th Infantry Brigade included a series of 'lifts':

> During these lifts the infantry in the trenches will show their bayonets over the parapet: dummy heads and shoulders will be shown over the parapet. Officers will whistle and shout in order to induce the enemy to man his parapet. At the end of each of these lifts the Artillery will shorten the range to the enemy's front parapet and continue the intense bombardment of the front and support lines.[35]

An observing British officer described the 'lifts' as 'picturesque' and as giving a 'biblical flavour to the proceedings, and the shouting and waving of bayonets took one back to the walls of Jericho'.[36] The Germans on the receiving end of these 'lifts' appeared, on this occasion, to be unimpressed and dismissed them as 'only a ruse which the English are very fond of playing'.[37]

At Verdun, the Germans experimented with artillery 'corridors' of concentrated fire power along which the infantry could attack. Several simultaneous 'corridors', some of them false, made it difficult for the French to predict which sections of the line were to be attacked and, as General Petain noted, 'ignorant of the points threatened by the attack, defenders are obliged to be strong everywhere and to place in the front line increased numbers of personnel who must be replaced often'.[38] Corridors were also used by the British in September 1916 on the Somme when tanks were used for the first time. Because tanks were extremely vulnerable to shell fire from field guns, corridors 100 yards wide were left open during the barrage to protect them from 'friendly fire'. The idea was not altogether successful since a number of tanks broke down, leaving the supporting infantry isolated in the corridors without covering fire.

From Neuve Chapelle onwards fire plans became a standard feature of an artillery action detailing the type of shells, targets and timings for each battery. 'Interdiction' barrages designed to disrupt the movement of enemy reserves and communications were used by the British on the Somme. 'Curtain barrages' aimed at preventing enemy support troops from reaching the front line. These 'curtain barrages' were further developed to cover both the sides and rear of an objective such as the 'box' fire, which sealed off the village of Neuve Chapelle in March 1915. A hurricane bombardment, also used at Neuve Chapelle, was of short duration to give an element of surprise. However, to be effective a hurricane bombardment needed to be especially heavy and concentrated against relatively thin defences. At Festubert (May 1915) and Loos (September 1915) hurricane bombardments were not used because of the strong German trench system and the opening attacks were preceded by the lengthier shelling of the enemy front line.

The 'registration' of guns was carried out by firing ranging rounds with direction and length adjustments fed back by forward observers before the actual bombardment took place. The downside of this approach was the loss of any element of surprise. 'Bracketing' (which the French termed *rafale*) was used as an alternative to registration. Each gun in a battery would fire on a given range but with different settings to blanket a large area. Observers would then identify and feed back the most accurate shots.

A significant step forward in identifying and destroying enemy targets, particularly gun emplacements, was the development of 'counter-battery' work used by both the Germans and the British from 1917. This technique is associated with the German gunner Colonel Georg Bruchmüller who first used a counter-battery plan in 1917 at Riga against the Russians. On the British side this approach was advocated by Brigadier General H.H. Tudor and Major B.F.E. Keeling who argued that reliance should be placed on topographical survey information. Major Keeling of the Third Army Field Survey Company worked with the RFC to build up a survey of the Western Front on a scale 1:20,000. This was the basis of 'artillery boards' – mounted maps – on which targets were marked so that the range and bearing could be accurately plotted.

Counter-battery targets were identified and plotted by the RFC and also by 'flash spotting' – taking bearings on enemy guns – and by 'sound-ranging' – an electronic device which was able to identify the type of enemy gun by its firing sound and calculate its ground position. Both of these important techniques were available for the British attack at Cambrai in November 1917. At around the same time there was a further major advance in achieving artillery accuracy – calibration. This entailed a careful study of each gun's individual characteristics – the wear and tear on the barrel and other moving parts and its recent performance. Keeping a detailed record for every gun became standard procedure. Just before firing, some final adjustments were made to the setting of the gun according to thermometer and barometer readings and to the force and direction of the wind. The use of artillery was rapidly moving from trial and error towards mathematical precision.[39]

There were other technical developments that enhanced the effectiveness of shell fire. Fuse 106 was first used at Vimy in April 1917. This was an instantaneous fuse that splintered on contact. Such was the sensitivity of fuse 106 that it could cut barbed wire, thus removing the problem of high explosive shells churning up the ground in front of the advancing infantry.

Smoke shells became available in 1917. Again for the first time, attacking troops had the benefit of a cover entirely under the control of the supporting artillery.

Gas shells were used by the Germans in January 1915 on the Eastern Front at Bolimov between Lodz and Warsaw. These were 15cm shells filled with xylyl bromide, a tear-inducing compound. However, these shells were largely ineffective since the extreme cold prevented the substance vaporising into gas. The French used gas grenades early in the war, but again the effects were more of an irritant than life-threatening. Nevertheless, gas had become a weapon of war. It became clear, after the experiences of the Germans during the Second Battle of Ypres and of the British at Loos in 1915, that gas shells were a far more reliable and more accurate method of delivery than gas released from cylinders, which were subject to the vagaries of the wind. The first use of gas shells on the Western Front was by the Germans at Hill 60 near Ypres in April 1915, though in small quantities. From then onwards all the belligerents experimented with various forms of lethal gas shells – in total more than sixty different varieties.[40] Both the Allies and the Germans used shells filled with phosgene gas (codenamed Green Cross), a more virulent form of gas than chlorine which attacked the respiratory system. Phosgene was particularly lethal since it had a delayed action causing death as long as forty-eight hours after exposure. Germany pioneered arsenic gas (Blue Cross) which was able to penetrate protective masks and also mustard gas shells (Yellow Cross), which caused blisters, burned the skin and could cause blindness. The Germans first used mustard gas in 1917. It took the French and the British a further twelve months before they were able to produce their own mustard gas shells.

Fortunately for those who suffered from gas shells, protective equipment developed to the extent that, apart from mustard gas, the effects were much reduced. In July 1915 the BEF was supplied with an impregnated flannel head cover which had a celluloid window and then, in 1916, the effective box respirator came into general use. While horrific for those who were personally affected, gas was far from the weapon of mass destruction that it was expected to be. Some 5,900 British and Commonwealth soldiers died as a result of gas during the war, representing 1.2 per cent of the total BEF fatalities on the Western Front.[41] Mainly through the efforts of Fritz Haber, the head of the Kaiser Wilhelm Research Institute in Berlin, Germany was always ahead in gas weaponry and used an estimated 68,000 tons during the war – equal to the sum of French and British gas usage.[42]

* * *

In his account of the events of 1915 Brigadier General J.E. Edmonds, the compiler of the British Official History, wrote: 'The Allies were in reality confronted by siege warfare…it was an engineer and artillery war'.[43] Once the opposing trench lines had solidified they defined, give or take a few hundred yards, the Western Front until March 1918. In such a conflict, the provision and effective use of guns and ammunition were of crucial importance. As in other aspects of the war, Britain started the war at a serious disadvantage. It was not until 1917 that the BEF's requirements for guns and shells were being met. This immense fire-power, together with the considerable technical and tactical development that had taken place during the years of the war, made artillery the key weapon in the BEF victories of 1918.

The main factors that had made possible the far-reaching developments in the role of the artillery in the BEF are readily identifiable. Kitchener and von Donop at the War Office in 1914 and 1915 had made a start on the massive task of improving the supply of armaments. Civilian experts such as Lord Moulton who chaired the High Explosives Committee, George Macauley Booth who was concerned with the problem of labour supply and Sir Percy Girouard who headed Kitchener's Armaments Output Committee, were drafted into service. Contracts were awarded to private manufacturers to increase the supply of guns and shells. Shell production under Kitchener increased from 1.4 million in the first five months of the war to 5.3 million in the first six months of 1915. Things were moving, but moving too slowly.

It was Lloyd George, as Minister of Munitions, who galvanized the country's efforts to control and improve the production of armaments and the supply of other vital materials. The recruitment of experienced businessmen and scientists, considered essential by Lloyd George, was accelerated. Eric Geddes became the Deputy Director of Munitions Supply. Chaim Weizmann, a biochemist, provided expertise in the area of weapons propellants such as cordite. Wilfred Stokes, the managing director of an engineering company, designed the most widely used trench mortar despite a marked lack of support from the War Office. James Stevenson moved from being a managing director of Johnnie Walker Whisky to become the coordinator of munitions production. Lloyd George wrote in his *War Memoirs*: 'A copious correspondence poured in from businessmen offering their services and asking for instructions in regard to requirements'.[44]

One such businessman was Lord Chetwynd. Lloyd George wrote:

> We told him he was wanted to build and run a factory that would fill a thousand tons a week of high explosives into shells. He stipulated and got a very free hand ... He found a site at Chilwell, near Nottingham ... Lord Chetwynd designed his own plant and processes, aiming always at speed, simplicity, and the fullest use of machinery on mass production lines.

Chilwell started shell-filling, mainly high explosives for heavy guns, in January 1916 and by the end of the war had produced over 19 million shells. In 1914, the only factory available for shell-filling was at Woolwich. By 1918 there were eighteen national filling factories.

The great majority of employees in these factories were women. In July 1914 some 212,000 women were employed in metal and engineering work. One year later this number had risen to 256,000 and by July 1916 there were 520,000 women working in war-related industries.[45] Shell-filling, in particular, was inherently dangerous. In the years 1916 to 1918 there were 404 cases of toxic jaundice, resulting from TNT poisoning, of which 109 were fatal. An explosion at the filling factory at Barnbow killed thirty-five women in December 1916 and thirty-five more women died in an explosion at Chilwell in July 1918. The largest single explosion took place at the Chemical Works in Silvertown in January 1917 when sixty-nine workers were killed, including seventeen women, and a further 1,000 were injured.[46]

The production of guns and ammunition for artillery purposes was the prime example in the war not only of state intervention but also of the joint efforts and shared dangers of those working in the factories at home and those fighting at the Front. A Public Recruitment Committee poster showed a soldier and a munitions worker with the words: 'We're both needed to serve the guns'. As Edwin Montagu, the Minister of Munitions, said in August 1916: 'This war is not a soldiers' war or a civilians' war, but a whole nation's war.'

As far as Lloyd George was concerned, not only had Kitchener and the War Office failed to get to grips with the shell problem, they were also a 'perpetual source of obstruction'[47] to the work of the Ministry of Munitions. An example of this 'obstruction' was an issue concerning the responsibility for the design and specification of armaments. In January 1916 a letter from the War Office stated that approval for 'designs or amendments to existing designs' should come from the War Office. Lloyd George, who insisted that approval for this work had already been allocated to his Ministry, brought the matter to the Cabinet War Committee and, after several meetings, established that 'The responsibility for designs, patterns, and specifications and for testing of arms and ammunition rests with the Ministry of Munitions.'[48] By such means, Lloyd George gradually engineered the reduction of Kitchener's authority and the expansion of the Ministry of Munitions. When Lloyd George first became responsible for munitions he received a note from Kitchener: 'Delighted to hear that you are coming to help me'. The implication was that the Ministry of Munitions would be subordinate to the War Office. Such an implication was a serious misunderstanding on Kitchener's part and was quite contrary to the intentions of Lloyd George.[49]

Lloyd George's work with the Ministry officials, the entrepreneurs and scientists was matched by his work with the trade unions. Overall, Britain had a poor labour relations record. An estimated 17.8 million days were lost between 1915 and 1918 compared to 2.7 million days lost in France in the same period.[50] On the more positive side, the number of working days lost in Britain dropped from 10 million in 1913 and 1914 respectively to an average of 4.4 million per year in the years 1915–1918.[51] In this context, Lloyd George's tactics of persuasion mixed with the force of the law were essential in bringing about significant changes in working practices and an acceptance of dilution.

The results of Lloyd George's actions were startling. A summary by Eric Geddes dated 15 July 1916 showed the increase in shell production per week during the first year of the Ministry of Munitions. High explosive shells had increased from 33,111 to 593,396 per week while shrapnel shells had increased from 86,790 to 432,263 per week. Given the pleas from the BEF during the first half of 1915 for more and more high explosives, this eighteen-fold increase was both appropriate and remarkable. Similar progress was made in the production of guns: 1,105 were manufactured in the first ten months of the war, while 5,006 were produced in the twelve months between July 1915 and June 1916. Within these numbers the production of heavy guns had increased by a factor of nine.[52] By the time of the Somme offensive in July 1916 the BEF had more artillery resources than ever before. During the preliminary bombardment some 3,000 field and heavy guns fired over one million shells and more were available in the supply dumps.[53] The artillery problem on the Somme was not the supply of guns and ammunition, it was the fact that the German defences were too strong to be totally destroyed.

While much of Lloyd George's account of his time at the Ministry of Munitions as written in his *War Memoirs* is considered as an exercise in self-promotion, there can be little doubt that his determination, energy and organizing skills were essential to the development of British artillery power from 1916 onwards. Nor was the production of other weapons ignored. Lloyd George promoted the manufacture of the Stokes mortar, the Mills bomb and the Lewis gun. The production of trench mortars increased from twelve in 1914 to 5,554 in 1916 while grenade production rose from 2,164 to 34,867,966 and machine guns from 287 to 33,507 in the same period.[54]

The contribution of Sir John French to the development of artillery power should not be overlooked. By provoking the 'Shell Scandal' of 1915 he contributed to his own eventual downfall, but he also placed a spotlight on the lack of guns and shells in the BEF and indirectly paved the way for Lloyd George and the Ministry of Munitions. Credit should also go to other heads of the Ministry of Munitions who built on the work of Lloyd George – Edwin Montagu, Christopher Addison and particularly Winston Churchill who increased the size of the Ministry and carried through a major reorganization. And Churchill was fulsome in his praise of those who worked for him: 'I worked with incomparably the largest and most powerful staff in my experience. Here were gathered the finest business brains of the country working with might and main and with disinterested loyalty for the common cause.'[55]

The significant developments relating to artillery in the BEF between 1914 and 1918 were evident not only in the quantity and types of guns and shells available, but also in the technical and tactical advances that improved their effectiveness. Some of these developments can be illustrated by comparing the artillery arrangements at Neuve Chapelle in March 1915 with those at Amiens in August 1918. Both battles were prepared in great detail under the command of Sir Henry Rawlinson and both battles made use of the technical and tactical experience available at the time. At Neuve Chapelle the BEF used all the guns it could muster, some 340 of all types, but shells were in short supply. At Amiens Rawlinson had over 2,000 guns, of which 684 were heavy, and all the shells he needed. Ranging shots that would alert the enemy to an impending attack were avoided at both Neuve Chapelle and Amiens, but at Amiens the gunners had the advantage of more accurate maps to plot targets and the technical ability to make allowances for atmospheric variations. The thirty-five-minute bombardment at Neuve Chapelle concentrated on the enemy trenches and on the village of Neuve Chapelle itself. There was no creeping barrage. At Amiens the attack followed a creeping barrage to the German lines using smoke shells, not available at Neuve Chapelle, to obscure the advancing infantry. The bombardment plan at Amiens allowed for lanes to be made through the enemy wire to help the subsequent forward movement of field artillery. Most crucially, two-thirds of the heavy guns at Amiens concentrated on accurate counter-battery work – a technique not available at Neuve Chapelle. At Amiens, 95 per cent of German guns in the attack sector had been identified by sophisticated aerial photography and sound-spotting and the great majority had been put out of action by gas and high explosive shells early in the attack.[56] Of course, Rawlinson had other advantages at Amiens, not least the presence of tanks and a massive superiority in aircraft and troops, and was able to move forward eight miles. At Neuve Chapelle, with limited artillery power and none of these advantages, he advanced no more than 1,000 yards.

Germany was also intent on increasing the supply of guns and shells. The Hindenburg programme of August 1916 planned to increase the production of guns by a third and double the output of ammunition. The Amerikaprogram of June 1917 set a target of 2,000 aircraft per month. These targets were never met largely because the plans were not integrated into the general running of the economy. Steel production in February 1917, for example, was less than that of August 1916 and 252,000 tons short of the production target. Aircraft production was 1,000 in June 1917, but never reached the Amerikaprogram target. The hard winter of 1916/17 was a major blow to the German plans. The waterways were frozen over and the country's transport system collapsed. The Germans had the capable Max Bauer to lead the Hindenburg programme, but, unlike Lloyd George in Britain, he was unable to harness the full strength of his country's economy.[57] The Germans were never short of munitions, but their ambitious expansion plans failed.

A further factor in the development of artillery in the BEF was simply the demands and circumstances of the war and the efforts and talents of the many individuals who reacted to them. Among those who made significant personal contributions to improve British artillery technology were Captain B.T. James, Lieutenant D.S. Lewis and Major W.G.H. Salmond (pioneers of aerial observation); Major E.M. Jack and Captain H. St-J. Winterbotham (survey work and the location of enemy batteries); Sir Lawrence Bragg, H.H. Hemming, Corporal Tucker, Lieutenant Lloyd Owen and J.A. Gray (sound and flash spotting); and Brigadier General H.H. Tudor and Major B.F.E. Keeting (topography and accurate mapping). By the summer of 1917 the data available from the BEF sound rangers and flash spotters was so accurate that enemy guns could be located to within 15 yards. Counter-battery work became an essential feature of any plan of attack and was used to great effect at Arras (April 1917), Messines (June 1917) and Cambrai (November 1917). During the last year of the war British artillery, using these various techniques, was out-performing that of the Germans. It is also worth noting that many of the developments associated with artillery, for example counter-battery work and the use of gas shells, were introduced independently and at much the same time by the British, the French and the Germans. If it was seen to be a useful idea, it was worth copying. There was no monopoly on inventiveness when it came to survival or gaining the upper hand.

An interesting feature in the development of British artillery practice on the Western Front was the lack of an artillery commander with strong executive powers. The Royal Artillery did not have a Henderson or a

Trenchard, as did the RFC, nor a Swinton, Elles or Fuller as did the Tank Corps. When Edmonds wrote that the Western Front was 'siege warfare' there was an implication that an artilleryman should play a major command role. Certainly, Haig did have a series of artillery advisers such as H. Horne, F.D.V. Wing, H.F. Mercer, J. Headlam and N. Birch all with the rank of Major General. But these advisers, unlike the German Bruchmüller who held the rank of Colonel, were not allowed to do more than advise.[58] The plans for an attack were made by army, corps or division commanders and the role of the artillery adviser was to make the necessary artillery arrangements to meet the plan. An Army level artillery adviser was not able to give orders to corps or divisions. At Neuve Chapelle Brigadier General A.C.A. Holland, the CRA of 8th Division, proposed a bombardment of two and a half hours, but Rawlinson insisted on 35 minutes. During the preparations for the Somme offensive, Haig and Rawlinson had different opinions as to the length of the opening bombardment. Noel Birch, who was Haig's artillery adviser, was unable to resolve the differences between the two commanders. There were many competent and experienced artillerymen at all levels, not least, for example, Major General H.C.C. Uniacke who was Gough's MGRA in the Fifth Army at Ypres in 1917. Uniacke was an expert in his trade yet he was not consulted before Gough made his plan for the Passchendaele offensive. Even at less senior levels, infantry officers had a habit of thinking they knew best. On 29 September 1918 the experienced Lieutenant F.J. Rice of the 82nd Brigade RFA, 18 Division, advised the use of shrapnel shell against the German-held Eagle trench near Vendhuile, but was ordered to fire HE instead. Rice noted that Lieutenant Colonel Smeltzer of the 6th Buffs 'like most infantrymen, thought HE was better than shrapnel. Of course, timed shrapnel at an enfilade target at 1700 yards was ideal. Still, I turned on some HE 106, but it was no good unless it burst in the trenches. I very soon went back to shrapnel'.[59] Artillery was subordinate to the infantry line and there was no overall artillery commander to press the artillery view and to insist on and coordinate the new techniques. The effectiveness of the artillery no doubt suffered as a consequence.

Nevertheless, the role of the Royal Artillery was paramount on the Western Front. On 26 May 1916 Sir Douglas Haig issued a Special Order of the Day to mark the 200th anniversary of the formation of the Royal Regiment of

Artillery. The Order emphasized 'the efficiency with which [the regiment] has supported the other Arms in every action in which it has been enjoined. The discipline by the Officers, NCOs and Men of the Royal Artillery … has been in accordance with the highest traditions of their Regiment'.[60] These high standards continued throughout the war and a stirring example took place at Messines in April 1918. 'A' Battery of 88 Brigade RFA found that the British infantry was falling back on the guns with the Germans close behind. Lieutenant Dougall, the Battery Commander, rushed two guns to the top of a ridge and began firing over open sights. He rallied the infantry with the shout: 'So long as you stick to your trenches I will keep my guns here'. This action delayed the enemy's entry into Messines for twelve hours. Lieutenant Dougall was killed and was awarded a posthumous VC.

*Chapter 6*

# Tactics: Attack and Defence on the Western Front

*'Strategy decides where to act ... tactics decide the manner of execution and the employment of the troops'.*

*Antoine-Henri de Jomini*[1]

The period 1915–18 was one of continuous experimentation in methods of attack and defence. The attackers soon learnt that an 'offensive spirit', personal courage and a robust morale, supported by the rifle and bayonet, were only some of the ingredients required to carry out a successful assault. Technical proficiency in the use of artillery, new trench weapons, aircraft and tanks together with improved munitions and tactical expertise, were also essential. It took four years to develop these elements and bring them together as a cohesive fighting system. Similarly, the defenders also refined their methods. The hastily dug trenches of 1914 became complex, multi-layered defensive networks incorporating deep dug-outs, concrete bunkers, machine-gun nests and barbed wire entanglements many yards wide. The tactics of both defence and attack were subject to frequent review and revision throughout the war as the opposing commanders searched for the elusive formula that would lead to military success.

During the opening months of the war there was a confusion of offensive tactics as the armies of Germany, France and Britain clashed along the Western Front. The recognized pre-war method of infantry attack, accepted by all the belligerents, was based on the principle of 'fire and movement'. Once the enemy's fire had been adequately suppressed by artillery or machine guns then the infantry would advance in groups, one group giving covering fire as another group made a short rush forward. When within 200 yards of the enemy position, the infantry would charge forward together and take the enemy line using rifle and bayonet. A British military manual summarized the manoeuvre as follows: 'as the enemy's fire is gradually subdued, further progress will be made by bounds from place to place, the movement gathering renewed force at each pause until the enemy can be assaulted with the bayonet'.[2] In fact, the BEF had few opportunities in 1914 to use fire and movement though on 22 October the British 2nd Brigade was able to put this tactic into practice. The 2nd Brigade had been ordered to retake a position near Kortekeer held by the German 46 Reserve Division. The attack was described by 2nd Lieutenant J.G.W. Hyndson of the 1st Loyal North Lancs:

> The time had now come to put the finishing touches to the battle, and we work forward in small groups until only two hundred yards separated us from the enemy. From this point of vantage the whole regiment rises up and with rousing cheers, which must have put fear into the heart of the Germans, we surge forward with fixed bayonets and charge.

The position was taken and the Commander of the 2nd Brigade, Brigadier General E.S. Bulfin, recorded that the Germans lost 1,200 dead and 600 were taken prisoner.[3]

For most of 1914 the British soldier was on the defensive – at Mons, Le Cateau and Ypres. On the Marne there were some clashes with retreating German troops, but on the heights above the Aisne the BEF advance came to a halt in front of the enemy's line of entrenchments. The advice given by a pre-war military adviser was of little help: 'The so-called frontal attack, or attempt to pierce the centre of the enemy's line, leads only to self-destruction, therefore a choice of either flank remains.'[4] With the gradual extension of the trench lines, the option of an attack from the flank disappeared. In any event, many of the original Regulars of the BEF, who would have been familiar with the tactic of 'fire and movement', no longer existed. By the end of the year a third of them had been killed and many more wounded. As the British official historian noted: 'The vast majority of trained men had fallen before the enemy in 1914'.[5] Their replacements, a few Regular divisions from abroad, the Territorials, the Dominion troops and the New Army battalions, began the long and difficult learning process associated with trench warfare on the Western Front.

The massed German armies, attacking through Belgium, swept forward with patriotic enthusiasm and tactical subtleties were often forgotten. The German Army *Regulations* dealing with the attack made it clear that 'defence could only be overcome by the attacker gaining localized fire suppression through the coordination of rifle and artillery fire'.[6] But such an approach was singularly absent at Mons when six German divisions supported by cavalry attacked two British divisions. An eyewitness later wrote:

> [The Germans] advanced in companies of quite 150 men in files five deep. We could steady our rifles on the trench and take deliberate aim. The first company was simply blasted away to Heaven by a volley at 700 yards and, in their insane formation, every bullet was bound to find two billets. The other companies kept advancing very slowly, using their dead comrades as cover, but they had no chance.[7]

Similarly, Corporal Bernard Denmore of the 1st Royal Berkshire Regiment noted in his diary for 23 August: 'We saw the Germans attack on our left in great masses, but they were beaten back by the Coldstream Guards'.[8] Among the German troops fighting at Ypres in October 1914 was the 51st Reserve Division which had been raised from volunteers with no previous military training. Many were students or school-leavers who had received only two months' training. On 25 October the 51st Reserve Division launched an attack towards Ypres in the area of Langemarck. Captain H.C. Rees of the 2nd Welch Regiment noted:

> We actually saw the Germans form up for the attack and opened fire on their front line at 1,250 yards. From that time forward we had every form of target from a Company in mass to a battalion in fours … Sgt Longden, who was firing the [machine] gun, told me that evening that he reckoned he'd killed a thousand Germans … I never saw the Germans make a worse attack or suffer heavier losses.[9]

In the German cemetery at Langemarck the bodies of 25,000 young, inexperienced soldiers lie together in a mass grave. The Langemarck attack became known as the *Kindermord* – the Massacre of the Innocents.

The French, attacking into Alsace-Lorraine, also adopted the tactic of advancing in close formation over open ground against concealed German infantry and machine guns. Captain André Laffargue of the French 155 Regiment put forward the case for advancing in line, especially when inexperienced troops were involved: 'The alignment holds each in his place, carries along those who hesitate, holds back the enthusiasts, and gives everyone a warm irresistible feeling of mutual confidence'.[10] It also fitted the French philosophy of all-out attack – *attaque à l'outrance* – and their penchant for *elan*.

Edward Spears, who was a British liaison officer with the French V Army, had observed the French pre-war manoeuvres. He later wrote:

> I had the misfortune to see these troops animated by the highest courage, led to their doom in the same close formations I had watched at manoeuvres a few years before ... The sense of the tragic futility of it will never quite fade from the minds of those who saw these brave men, dashing across the open to the sound of drums and bugles, clad in the old red caps and trousers which turned every man into a target. The gallant officers who led them were entirely ignorant of the stopping power of modern firearms, and many of them thought it *chic* to die in white gloves.[11]

The French lost heavily. By the end of the first month of the war 75,000 French soldiers had been killed and a further 200,000 were wounded or prisoners. By the end of 1914 the French had lost 855,000 men.

* * *

The initial war of movement on the Western Front was over by the end of November 1914. The German Schlieffen Plan had failed and so had the French Plan XVII. Trench warfare had taken over and the resulting deadlock caused General Falkenhayn, the Chief of the German Supreme

Command (OHL), to make his decision to transfer all available troops to the Eastern Front. The transfer of eight infantry and six cavalry divisions began in January 1915 and Falkenhayn declared the Western Front a defensive area.[12] Thereafter, until the offensive at Verdun in February 1916, the Germans made only one major attack on the Western Front – that at Ypres in April 1915. Even the Ypres attack, though partly inspired by the German wish to try out their new weapon, gas, was aimed at reducing the Ypres salient and the length of their defensive line rather that at piercing the British front.

Falkenhayn emphasized his defensive strategy in two memoranda which he circulated on 7 and 25 January 1915. He ordered that the existing German line should be fortified in such a way that it could resist attacks from a large force. The front line was to be the main line of resistance. If it was lost, it was to be retaken immediately. Behind the main line other defences were to be built. A second line, not far behind the front line and incorporating machine-gun nests, would house the main body of troops. Further back, outside the range of enemy guns, there would be more defences. In such a way, reasoned Falkenhayn, a 'bend' in the line might take place but there could be no breakthrough.[13]

Not all the German commanders agreed with this form of defence. Crown Prince Rupprecht of Bavaria (German VI Army), for example, believed that a strong second line would reduce the efforts of the soldiers in the first line who might be tempted to fall back when attacked. But this view was balanced by those who thought that since the first line troops had themselves constructed the trench, they would have built them as strong as possible for their own protection. In any event, Falkenhayn persisted with his policy. It took until Autumn 1915 to complete this major task.

Apart from a strongly held trench system, the Germans had two other significant advantages on the Western Front. Their policy of falling back to the nearest high ground was of great tactical importance. Further, the area in Northern France behind the German lines contained a well-developed rail network based on Lille. The Reserves of the German VI Army could arrive at any point of the front within twenty-four hours. By the second day of the Battle of Neuve Chapelle, for example, the Germans were able to increase the total number of defenders from 4,000 to 20,000.[14] The corollary of Falkenhayn's defensive policy was that France and Britain were obliged to take on the role of the attacker.

* * *

It is understandable that the BEF generals were perplexed at the situation that faced them. The German trench system was becoming stronger and more permanent by the day, as the German artilleryman Herbert Sulzbach wrote:

> At the battery they have made themselves much more cosy. The dugouts have tables and stoves and one even has a piano in it … Now we have been two months in this position … everything is becoming a habit … We are preparing more and more for a static campaign. The infantry positions have been surrounded by strong barbed-wire entanglements.[15]

Furthermore, the fresh troops arriving from Britain were inexperienced, only partly trained and, while full of enthusiasm and courage, were inadequate replacements for the professional soldiers of the original BEF. Under these circumstances there is little wonder that the years 1915–17 saw continuous tactical experimentation accompanied by heavy casualties.

The BEF generals realized that there were numerous tactical possibilities. The problem was selecting the most effective of the available courses of action. The differing artillery tactics in 1915 were a case in point. Although beset by supply and quality problems in both guns and shells the British commanders experimented with different forms of bombardment. At Neuve Chapelle there were 340 guns on a front of 1,200 yards – a gun every 4 yards. The opening bombardment, to gain surprise, lasted only 35 minutes. At Aubers Ridge the bombardment covered two attacking fronts which amounted to some 5,000 yards. There were 630 guns (one every 8 yards) and the bombardment lasted 40 minutes. The lack of success of these two attacks brought a different approach that emphasized the destruction of the German trenches through longer bombardments. At Festubert the bombardment lasted three days on a front of 5,000 yards. At Loos the length of the front was 11,000 yards. There were 533 guns (one every 23 yards) and the bombardment lasted four days. At Neuve Chapelle the bombardment did gain the advantage of surprise, but the Germans were not prevented from bringing up their reserves. Overall, none of these bombardments was particularly effective – even when, at Loos, the guns were supplemented by the use of gas. The German barbed wire and strongpoints were not totally destroyed and the infantry had to advance into no man's land facing enemy artillery and machine guns with disastrous results.

The attacks of 1915 had revealed a further major problem for the British generals. In previous wars – at Waterloo, the Crimea and during the South African war – the commander had been able to exert a personal influence on the course of the battle. During the First World War this was no longer the case. The role of the general was to devise strategy and agree plans of attack, but once battle had begun he found himself completely out of touch with the developing events. At both Neuve Chapelle and Loos the advantage gained by the initial British attack was lost because the generals, well behind the front line, lacked the information to commit their reserves at the right time. The problem was that communication between the attacking troops at the front and headquarters in the rear was virtually nil. Radio sets were available but were so heavy and large as to be useless on the battlefield. Visual signals such as semaphore were unseen because of smoke and general confusion. Telephone wires connecting the forward troops and the commanders were buried in the ground but were invariably destroyed by shell-fire. Pigeons were used but often went missing. Human message-carriers, in the form of Runners, were the most reliable form of communication but all too often they became casualties and failed to reach their destination. Even when a Runner did manage to survive and deliver his message events had generally moved on and his information had become worthless.

Throughout the war the generals found themselves, once an attack had begun, to be impotent onlookers. Such was their frustration that many generals insisted on moving forward into the battle area. Haig noted in his diary that during the attack at Neuve Chapelle there was 'so much uncertainty regarding the position of units of 8th Division that Rawlinson himself went up … to see what was going on'.[16] Inevitably this courageous but foolhardy behaviour led to casualties. No fewer than fifteen BEF generals were killed between 1914 and 1915 while taking part in front-line activities.

Among these casualties were three Major Generals – Sir Thompson Capper, GOC 7th Division, who died leading his men into battle at Loos in September 1915; General G.H. Thesinger who also died at Loos while personally investigating a hold-up at Fosse 8; and General F.D.V. Wing who died of shell wounds after visiting the front line trenches at Mazingarbe on 2 October 1915. These losses were so serious that on 3 October Lieutenant General Sir William Robertson, then chief of staff of the BEF, wrote to the Army Commanders:

> Three divisional commanders have been killed in action during the past week. These are losses which the Army can ill-afford, and the Field Marshal/C in C desires to call attention to the necessity of guarding against a tendency by senior officers such as Corps and Division Commanders to take up positions too far forward when fighting is in progress.[17]

During the four and a quarter years of war more than 200 generals were either killed or wounded. The evidence is that many generals went into the battle area to keep in touch with events. Captain Cyril Falls, who fought on the Somme and was later a Staff Officer with both the 36th and 62nd Divisions, noted that: 'In general, British commanders and staffs went forward much more often than the French and indeed too often during a battle. It was absurd that the divisional commander and GSO 1 should be absent at the same time on such occasions, but that was too often the case'.[18] The problem was not how to get generals out of their HQs, but how to prevent these highly experienced men from going forward and taking unnecessary risks.[19]

* * *

Various tactics were employed by the BEF in 1915 to pierce the enemy lines but none had resulted in the desired 'breakthrough'. A BEF memo from GHQ dated 2 December 1915 stated:

> In the battles of last September we achieved important tactical successes but failed in our object, which was to break through the enemy's lines. The lessons of these attacks, as of all previous attacks, are that given

> adequate artillery preparation, or some form of surprise such as a gas attack, there is no insuperable difficulty in overwhelming the enemy's troops in the front line and in support, but that there is the greatest difficulty in defeating the enemy's reserves which have not been subjected to the strain of a long bombardment and come up in good order fresh from their billets to meet our troops at a time when they are somewhat exhausted in the confusion unavoidable in a modern battle.

The same memo proposed a solution to the problem which read more like a hopeful speculation than a firm expectation: 'sufficient force should be employed to exhaust the enemy and force him to use up his reserves, and that then, and then only, the decisive attack which is to win victory should be driven home'.[20]

The year 1915 had been, to say the least, an unsatisfactory one for the BEF. A GHQ memorandum summed up the situation on the Western Front:

> During the past 6 months the Germans have taken the offensive on the Western Front on a considerable scale on four occasions; twice at Ypres, once at Soissons, and once at Givenchy. The French in the same period have taken the offensive in Champagne, near Verdun, and at Arras. We have taken the offensive at Neuve Chapelle and about Festubert. Thus nine serious attempts to break the opposing lines have been made. All of these have had some degree of success, but none have had any material effect upon the general situation.[21]

This memorandum was written in June 1915. It would have described the situation at the beginning of 1918 just as well.

However, while definite signs of a formula for victory were difficult to see in 1915, there was evidence of new and imaginative thinking. General Robertson wrote in a memorandum dated 8 February 1915: 'If the Germans are to be defeated they must be beaten by a process of slow attrition, by slow and gradual advance on our part, each step being prepared by a predominant artillery fire and great expenditure of ammunition'.[22] Robertson was probably the first to advocate this 'step by step' or 'bite and hold' approach as opposed to 'breakthrough' tactics. At Neuve Chapelle, Rawlinson, the IV

Corps Commander, had advocated a 'bite and hold' attack – an approach rejected by Haig who insisted that a breakthrough was possible. Both of these methods of attack were designed to deal with the stalemate of the Western Front. The 'bite and hold' approach called for a preliminary bombardment followed by an attack to 'bite off' a section of the enemy line. Once that had been achieved, fresh troops would move forward to consolidate the new position. The artillery would then be brought forward and the process would be repeated using the captured territory as a base for the next stage. The 'bite and hold' tactic had its supporters. Robertson and Rawlinson in particular considered that it was the most practical method of gaining ground and also the most effective use of troops because it resulted in the fewest possible casualties. Objectives were clear and attainable and, if necessary, the operation could be called off without having undertaken a major commitment. Probably the best executed example of 'bite and hold' took place in June 1917 by General Plumer's Second Army. By thorough and detailed preparation, including the detonation of twenty mines under the German lines, the limited objective of the Messines Ridge was taken with minimal losses. But the 'bite and hold' system did have its shortcomings. Such attacks were normally suited to a narrow frontage thus creating a salient into enemy territory that could be counter-attacked from three sides. Moreover, there were inevitable logistical difficulties in moving artillery and munitions forward over ground that had only recently been destroyed by shell fire. It was also clear that since 'bite and hold' attacks were aimed at gaining only a limited amount of territory, the end of the war would be a very long-term prospect. John Buchan, the author, writing in *The Times* of 29 September 1915 was clearly of the opinion that an attack on a narrow front was pointless:

> the summer's war has brought certain military facts into high relief, and one is the futility of attacks on a narrow front. You may pierce the enemy's line on a front of several miles, as the Allies did in May in Festubert and Artois. But the front closes up before you and hardens like asphalt, and what began as a breach ends as an ordinary salient. You have driven in a wedge, but you are no further forward.[23]

A narrow frontage automatically meant that a serious breakthrough was impossible. Breakthroughs were much larger operations planned on a larger scale. The initial bombardment would be on an extensive front thus minimising enemy counter-attacks from the sides. If the enemy line could be broken then the cavalry could push through the gap and fan out behind the front trenches, rolling up the enemy defences from the flanks. Such an advance, if successful, could indeed result in a major victory. But the breakthrough approach also had its downside. A large front needed a virtually unlimited supply of artillery and such a luxury was not available until well into 1916. Even if a large breach could be made in the enemy's line, there would be insuperable communication problems which would frustrate efforts to press forward using cavalry and support troops. The problems associated with supplying large bodies of men and horses with food, ammunition and other equipment were immense. In the meantime, the enemy, warned by the lengthy artillery bombardment, would have had time to reorganize their defences and bring in reserves from other areas of the front. A GHQ memorandum of June 1915 described the problem in this way: 'A long line of trenches thus resembles an elastic band which can be pushed back if sufficient force is applied but which is very difficult to break through'.[24] During the four years of the war both 'bite and hold' and 'breakthrough' tactics were employed by the Allies, but it was not until the second half of 1918 that real success was achieved.

Haig consistently held ambitions for an infantry breakthrough followed by a cavalry advance. Just before the British attack at Neuve Chapelle, Haig wrote in his diary:

> We are embarking on a serious offensive operation with the object of breaking the German line. There is no idea of merely taking a trench here, or a trench there. My objective is to surprise the Germans and push forward to Aubers Ridge with as little delay as possible, and exploit the success thus gained by pushing forward mounted troops as quickly as possible so as to threaten La Bassée from the north-east in which direction there are no fortifications.[25]

In April 1915 he had told his cavalry officers, Brigadier General MacAndrew and Major Baird, that: 'We cannot hope to reap the fruits of victory without a large force of mounted troops'.[26] Also, when discussing with his senior officers his plans for the Loos offensive, Haig announced that the objective was to 'break the Enemy's front and reach Pont-à-Vendin'. To this end, he would have 'a brigade or two of cavalry ready to go forward to seize the rising ground north-east of Pont-à-Vendin'.[27] Even on the Somme, Haig held out hopes that 'after the next attack the crisis of the battle is likely to be reached, and the moment might be favourable for cavalry action'.[28]

Haig had considerable difficulty in convincing some of his senior subordinates that a breakthrough was the correct tactic. In March 1915, both Rawlinson and the Commander of the 8th Division, Major General Francis Davies, planned to pause and consolidate after the village of Neuve Chapelle had been taken. Similarly, Rawlinson and Major General Anderson of the Meerut Division planned a two-phase attack on Bois du Biez. Both of these suggestions were turned down by Haig leaving Rawlinson and his Division commanders with the problem of planning the supply arrangements associated with a possible breakthrough. Meanwhile Haig arranged for two cavalry divisions 'to support … if circumstances are favourable'.[29]

Evidence of tactical confusion was clearly evident when the BEF undertook its major offensive on the Somme in July 1916. Haig and Rawlinson again differed as to the best form of attack. Haig had in mind a significant breakthrough that would end the war. Rawlinson, on the other hand, again preferred the 'bite and hold' approach. The opening assault would capture the German front line and once that had been accomplished his artillery and troops would move forward and take the second German line, and so on. Eventually the entire German defence system would fall and the cavalry would burst through into open territory. As regards the role of the artillery, Rawlinson preferred an opening bombardment lasting five days to destroy the German front line in accordance with his 'bite and hold' approach. Haig wanted a short 'hurricane' bombardment and a massive infantry assault. What actually took place was a seven-day bombardment but with Rawlinson accepting Haig's plan for a breakthrough.

The breakthrough concept meant that 120,000 troops were committed on the first day of the battle, 1 July. Rawlinson doubted that his troops of the Fourth Army, sixty per cent of whom were undertrained, inexperienced ex-civilians, would be able to maintain a 'fire and movement' advance: discipline and cohesion would be lost. In his tactical notes, Rawlinson prescribed four waves 'each line adding fresh impetus to the proceeding line ... and carrying on the forward movement'.[30] Consequently, in the centre of the attack, General Pultenay's III Corps advanced in a series of straight lines towards Ovillers and La Boisselle and suffered terrible losses as a result. It has been estimated that around two-thirds of the attacking troops advanced shoulder-to-shoulder in 'close order'. Private Sidney Williamson of the 1/8th Royal Warwickshire Regiment, in VIII Corps, noted in his diary for 1 July: 'At 7.30 am whistles were blown and the attack started. What did I see! To left as far as Gommecourt and to the right as far as Beaumont-Hamel, lines of soldiers were going forward as though on parade in line formation'.[31]

However, other tactics were employed along the 18-mile front reflecting the preference of the local commander.[32] On the right of the Fourth Army, Lieutenant General Sir Walter Congreve's XIII Corps used trench mortars for wire cutting and 'lifts' of 50–90 yards from one enemy trench to another. The 30th Division of XIII Corps moved into no man's land before the opening bombardment had finished and the 21st and 89th Brigades took their first objective, Dublin Trench, which they found deserted. Their passage across no man's land was not in close lines moving at a sedate pace, but at a run. XV Corps, on the left of XIII Corps, had, contrary to orders, used twice its allocation of shells and succeeded in cutting the enemy wire and destroying the first line trenches. When the 7th Division of XV Corps attacked they were able to take Cemetery Trench and Bulgar Alley in front of their objective, the village of Mametz. Altogether, the first day of the Somme has gone down in history as a disaster. It was a terrible confusion of tactics with little overall control and a shocking number of casualties. Only three of the thirteen German-held villages that constituted first-day objectives were taken. By 12.15 pm Rawlinson announced: 'there is, of course, no hope of getting the cavalry through today'.[33]

After 1 July, the Battle of the Somme developed into a series of 'bite and hold' operations which, although costly, brought some success. On 14 July, for example, 22,000 men assaulted the Longueville Ridge. Again Haig and Rawlinson had disagreed about tactics but Rawlinson, on this occasion, prevailed. The attack took place, unusually, at night. There was a whirlwind bombardment of just five minutes with the troops well out into no man's land. By 10 am men of the 3rd and 9th Divisions (XIII Corps) and of the 21st and 7th Divisions (XV Corps) had taken the German second lines of resistance. Not all such attacks during the early weeks of the Somme were as successful. Those on High Wood and Guillemont failed, but at Pozieres, Australian and British Territorial troops were able to take and hold a key position on high ground. The Somme battle continued in this way with the British commanders experimenting with whatever might bring success – hence the first use of the tank on 15 September at Flers. Nevertheless, even in September 1916 some battalions 'took pride in preserving their dressing whilst advancing to the assault, regardless of the fact that lines of men proved ideal targets for machine guns firing in enfilade'.[34] By mid-November, after Beaumont-Hamel had been taken, the weather had broken and the Somme campaign was called off. Much tactical learning had taken place but at a massive cost. Significantly, Haig, in his despatch following the Somme offensive, referred to the fighting as 'the opening of the wearing-out battle'. The emphasis had moved from a quick victorious breakthrough into enemy territory to a war of attrition – the continuous killing of enemy soldiers until their reserves had been used up and they could wage war no longer. It was a policy that placed greater importance on the number of dead than on the amount of ground gained. The Germans had pursued this policy at Verdun and the British followed the same policy on the Somme in 1916 and at Passchendaele in 1917. It was a policy that was condemned by the politicians, particularly Lloyd George and Churchill, but which Haig later rationalized as: 'the period of real struggle in which the main forces of the two belligerent armies are pitted against each other in close and costly combat … losses will necessarily be high on both sides, for in it the price of victory is paid'.[35]

* * *

The major BEF set-pieces of 1915–17 – Neuve Chapelle, Aubers Ridge, Festubert, Loos, Arras, the Somme, Passchendaele and Cambrai – caught the attention of the public mainly because of the massive casualty lists associated with them. Each one, however, was like the tip of an iceberg. After the Second Battle of Ypres in April 1915, for example, the German General

Balck noted that 'while no more major operations should be undertaken … raids and mining did not cease on either side'.[36] The greater part of the BEF was rarely involved in major attacks; rather it was concerned with the day-to-day grind of trench warfare which gradually developed its own tactical sophistication. Trench raids, aimed at entering enemy trenches, causing mayhem and perhaps taking prisoners, together with patrols into no man's land to spy out landmarks and defensive positions, were frequent occurrences. Once the trench system became established it was inevitable that the opposing forces would make small-scale attacks. They were useful to gain information about the enemy trenches and troops and they provided the opportunity for soldiers new to the front to gain some battle experience. It is unclear when the first BEF trench raid took place. The I Corps War Diary recorded 'a small bomb raid' by the 1st Irish Guards on 2 January 1915,[37] but the British Official History suggests that the first 'raid' was carried out on the night of 3/4 February 1915 by men of the 1st Worcesters.[38] Field Marshal French soon gave official authority to such raids: 'Such enterprises are highly valuable and should receive every encouragement since they relieve the monotony of our troops, while they have a corresponding detrimental effect on the moral[e] of the enemy troops and tend in a variety of ways to their exhaustion and general disquiet'.[39] In October 1915 FM French wrote that 'minor operations' were essential as part of the policy to 'wear out and exhaust the enemy's troops, to foster and enhance the offensive spirit of our own troops and to encourage them to feel superior to the enemy in every respect … Pressure on the enemy should be relentless'.[40] 'Minor operations' were to include local attacks, the use of smoke, gas, mining and bombing. When Haig became commander-in-chief in December 1915 he not only endorsed French's policy on raids but he made raiding and general aggression in no man's land a key part of his strategy of attrition. On 19 December 1915 Haig set out his views as to the future conduct of the war: 'At the present time I think that actions should take the form of (1) "Winter Sports" or raids continued into spring, i.e. capturing lengths of enemy trenches at favourable points (2) wearing out fights similar to (1) but on a larger scale, along the whole Front'.[41] Confirming his support of 'minor enterprises', Haig wrote to the First Army on 27 January 1916 referring to some recent local raids: 'the success achieved reflects credit on all concerned. The effect of such enterprises lowers the enemy's moral[e] and raises the moral[e] not only of the troops engaged in the particular operation, but also of the Division and the Corps'.[42]

Raids, which started as 'hit and run' stunts carried out by a handful of volunteers, eventually became large operations often involving companies and even battalions. The 2/5th Battalion of the Gloucester Regiment, for example, was selected to carry out a raid on the First Army front in June 1916 and in the same month the 12th and 13th Battalions of the Royal Sussex Regiment attacked a German strongpoint, the Boar's Head. Pressure from both GHQ and Army levels for continued local aggression was persistent. At his Corps Commanders' Conference on 29 February 1916 the First Army Commander, General Sir Charles Monro, raised the subject of 'minor enterprises':

> stress was laid on the value of minor enterprises ... Ruses and schemes by infantry should always be combined with artillery bombardment in order to induce the enemy to man his parapets and thus inflict loss on him by shell fire. All minor enterprises of the kind referred to were useful not only in bringing infantry and artillery into closer touch, but also in encouraging the offensive spirit and initiative in all ranks. The GOC hoped that Corp Commanders would continue and even increase their efforts to arrange for the carrying out of such enterprises.[43]

The British Official History noted that in the period July–November 1916 the First Army had carried out 166 raids and the Second Army 104.[44] It also noted that the three BEF Armies positioned outside the area of the Somme offensive carried out no fewer than 310 raids during the same period.

As was to be expected, the Germans carried out their own 'minor enterprises'. The First Army War Diary for May 1916 reported a series of German raids along the length of its front. I Corps suffered attacks on 11, 14, 20 and 27 May. On the XI Corps front the 39th Division trenches were raided on 26 and 29 May. On occasions the German raids were large scale. On 11 May I Corps trenches near the Hohenzollern Redoubt were assaulted by an estimated German force of two battalions resulting in 552 British casualties. On 21 May a German raid in the Vimy area prompted a counter-attack by the British 99th and 142nd Brigades which led to them losing 695 men.

What were once ad hoc incursions into the enemy trenches became well-planned and sophisticated set-pieces which were seen by senior commanders as necessary training for future battles. In March 1916 the XI Corps Commander told his divisions:

> We must get at least small parties of one or more platoons into the German trenches opposite the front of each Division in the line. This is absolutely essential if we are to maintain the offensive spirit which we have created and nourished ... We must make our men realise that they have the power of getting into the enemy's trenches and driving him out; nothing short of that will render us fit for greater operations later on when we shall end the war with one or two great battles.[45]

Raids were preceded by detailed preparation. Provision was made for artillery support before and during the raid and by 1916 the 'box barrage' was frequently used to seal off the attack area and prevent the advance of enemy reinforcements. Ground behind the front was laid out to replicate the actual area to be attacked. Those involved in the raid practised on these areas until they were familiar with the terrain and the obstacles they would meet. Sir Charles Monro at a conference on 8 June 1916 'called attention to the fact that in XI Corps a model of the German trenches on a portion of the Corps' front had been laid out on a reduced scale in the vicinity of each Divisional HQ. The model was of considerable use in arranging raids or any other operation as it was possible to get the officers concerned to come to the Division HQ and show them exactly what had to be done'.[46] XI Corps went to the extent of organizing a Raids Competition, encouraging battalions to submit suitable schemes. In one week thirty such schemes were received.[47]

An example of the preparations for one such raid, carried out by eighty men of the 32nd Battalion of the Royal Fusiliers on German trenches near Ypres in December 1916, was described by 2nd Lieutenant Wilfrid Pym Trotter. The aim was to take prisoners and cause as much damage as possible:

> A definite scheme of training was drawn up, consisting of bombing and trench fighting, while practice attacks were carried out daily over ground on which were laid out tapes representing the trenches we were going to raid … Each day, too, we had a practice attack … So perfect did we become at carrying out these manoeuvres that we could do it without the slightest trouble or confusion on the darkest nights.

The raid was successful though four fusiliers were killed, one was missing and six were wounded. Wilfrid Trotter was awarded the MC for his part in the raid.[48]

* * *

The weapons used in trench fighting also became more sophisticated. The Germans, at the beginning of the war, were better provided with both mortars and grenades, essential trench weapons, than the British. For much of the first year of the war, British soldiers with blackened faces and stripped of all items that might identify their unit, improvized using clubs, maces, knives, knuckle-dusters and sharpened spades. Hand grenades were made out of old jam tins. When, on 13 July 1916, a party from A Company of 2/4th Royal Berkshire Regiment raided an enemy trench in the La Ferme du Bois sector, they were equipped with bombs, wire clippers, butchers' cleavers and electric torches.[49] Gradually new weapons were introduced. The portable 2-inch medium trench mortar and the Stokes mortar were designed in 1915 and were widely used during 1916. The Mills grenade, having a cast-iron shell with a detonator that ignited at a set time after releasing the safety pin, together with the rifle-grenade became the main weapons for close quarter fighting. The flamethrower was first used by the Germans at Hooge in July 1915. Its 20ft jet of flame was terrifying, but it could only be used at close quarters and the flames and smoke made the operator a prime target. The Allies experimented with the flamethrower, but it remained principally a German weapon.[50]

Sniping became an important trench activity not only because of the resulting casualties but because it restricted movement and seriously undermined morale. Again the Germans were well equipped. By the end of 1914, some 20,000 Mauser Gewehr 98 service rifles fitted with telescopic sights had been sent to the front. Individual British officers responded by using their own sporting guns. Lieutenant Leysters Greener of the Royal Warwickshire Regiment, for example, brought his 1905 .280 Ross Model fitted with a Carl Zeiss prismatic sight and shot fifty-four Germans with it. Other sporting guns were sent from Britain. Lieutenant Stuart Cloete of the 9th King's Own Yorkshire Light Infantry recorded that 'we used a heavy sporting rifle – a .600 Express. These heavy rifles had been donated by British big-game hunters and when we hit a [loophole] plate we stove it right in, into the German snipers face'.[51]

It was not until May 1915 that the first British Lee Enfield rifles were adapted for sniping using telescopic sights. Losses on both sides were not insignificant. In early 1915 a British officer recorded that: 'Sergeant Doherty was killed by a sniper ... this is the eighteenth casualty and the fourth NCO we have lost in this way since we came into the line on Tuesday – it is a frustrating business'. In the Vermelles section in September 1916 an officer of the West Yorkshires was hit twice by two different snipers. An NCO sniper in the 2nd Royal Welch Regiment had over a hundred notches on his rifle.[52]

The Germans were the first to use snipers in a methodical way. They wore camouflaged capes, carried their own steel loop-holes and often had rifles with telescopic sights. British units were left to organize their own sniping – generally one sniper per company supervised by a battalion sniping officer. In July 1917, however, each company was ordered to supply two of its best shots to join a sniper section attached to a brigade or a division. These men were to work in pairs – one observing and the other firing. Under the guidance of an ex-big game hunter, Major Hesketh-Pritchard, a series of specialist schools were established – the first in October 1915 for the sniping officers of the 48th Division – and by 1917 each of the five BEF armies had a Sniping School.[53]

Mining was endemic along the Western Front with both sides attempting to destroy the opposing trench system. Counter-mining became an art form as the tunnellers attempted to anticipate the enemy's explosions. When the tunnels under Arras were being constructed in 1917, over forty New Zealanders were killed and 150 injured as a result of German counter-mining. General Plumer's mining of the Messines Ridge in 1917 involved

3 miles of deep tunnelling. As an indicator of the frequency of mining activity the Germans exploded 653 mines between 1 January and 31 May 1916 – an average of thirty per week.[54] Seventeen mines were exploded by the British under the German lines in preparation for the Somme offensive. The massive craters near Beaumont-Hamel and La Boisselle are testimony to the destructive power of this form of trench warfare.

The machine gun was a key weapon. At the beginning of the war the Vickers gun was widely used and the first Machine Gun School was opened in December 1914. Courses were initially held monthly but in June 1915 were increased to two per month, each attended by 500 men. In October 1915 the Machine Gun Corps was founded and organized at brigade level with the aim of providing specific attacks with a greater density of fire. At battalion level the allocation of four Vickers guns was replaced by eight Lewis guns which had a similar rate of fire but were half the weight (28lbs) and therefore much more mobile. Lewis Gun Schools operated from June 1915. Such was the importance of the Lewis gun that by July 1916 each battalion possessed sixteen guns and by July 1918 there were thirty Lewis guns per battalion.

* * *

The necessity and value of 'minor enterprises', emphasized continuously by senior BEF officers, were not readily apparent to the rank and file. There is plenty of evidence to indicate that trench raids were far from appreciated by those who might be called on to carry them out. The author of the history of the Guards Division wrote that 'troops came to resent continually being called upon to carry out raids and reconnaissances for apparently no other purpose than to satisfy the insatiable curiosity of the Intelligence Branch of the General Staff'.[55] Similarly, the historian of the 2/5th Gloucesters noted: 'It was never ascertained that [raids] produced the effect that was intended, but they were very unpopular with the men, as they never failed to draw retaliation from the enemy, the full brunt of which fell on the front line troops. Many casualties were suffered in this way'.[56]

Such feelings among front line soldiers, apart perhaps from those in elite regiments such as the Royal Welch Fusiliers, the 1st Royal West Kents and the 11th Royal Scots who prided themselves on their raiding ability, gave rise to 'live and let live' practices. In some sectors an 'understanding' developed between the opposing troops for their mutual protection. This involved, for example, firing high or firing only at set times of the day, or finding reasons why a raid should not take place. In the 19th Division, five of the Division's twelve battalions did not plan or initiate a single trench raid in the period November 1915–April 1916 even though exhorted by their Corps Commander to do so.[57] An American soldier, Einar Eklof of the 23rd Infantry Regiment, noted in March 1918:

> In Flanders we learned trench warfare. On our left flank was a British unit and on our right, a French. We were at first surprised by the stillness and we asked the French why it was so. They told us that if the Germans were not disturbed by us, they didn't disturb us. We often saw the Germans hanging out their washing on their barbed wire.[58]

The average frequency of trench raids on the First Army front in the period 1916–17 was only 1.5 raids per division per month – not a particularly high level of aggression.[59] Live and let live practices thwarted many a general's efforts to demonstrate an offensive spirit. There have been mixed opinions among post-war commentators as to the real value of raids and other minor enterprises. Some have contended that: 'Overall, the balance sheet might just read in favour of raids … In static positional warfare raiding was the only way to test and sharpen infantry skills short of major offensive operations'.[60] Others have written that while raids may have been 'wearying to the enemy, they were probably more costly to ourselves in life and energy'.[61]

Nevertheless, some of the more positive practices that developed as a result of 'minor operations' became important aspects of activity during major battles. The 90th Brigade, fighting on the Somme, for example, were given the difficult task of taking the fortified village at Montauban. As part of their pre-attack training they laid out a large area behind their lines with trenches to represent no man's land and a mock-up of the village itself. Everything was to scale and based on aerial photographs: 'Trenches, streets, etc., are marked with names that we shall christen them when we get across there, and here the Brigade goes *en bloc* everyday to practise step by step'.[62] Montauban was one of the few first-day objectives taken on 1 July 1916.

* * *

The German defensive tactics on the Somme followed the Falkenhayn emphasis on a strong front line and immediate counter-attacks to retake any lost ground. On the whole the method was successful, but it was also very costly in terms of casualties. It was because of this, together with his failure at Verdun, that Falkenhayn was dismissed. In August 1916 he was replaced by the formidable duo Paul von Hindenburg as Chief of the General Staff and Erich Ludendorff as First Quarter-Master General. Both had operated successfully on the fluid Eastern Front and they brought their experience to the stalemate of the West. They were particularly concerned with the arrangements for defence which they considered to be vulnerable to the ever increasing artillery power of the Allies. Hindenburg later outlined his thinking:

> [The current arrangements] were based upon our experiences of earlier battles. In future our defensive positions were no longer to consist of single-lines and strongpoints, but of a network of lines and groups of strongpoints. In the deep zones thus formed we did not intend to disperse our troops on a rigid and continuous front, but in a complex system of nuclei and distributed in breadth and depth. The defender had to keep his forces mobile to avoid the destructive effects of the enemy fire during periods of artillery preparation as well as to voluntarily abandon any parts of the line which could no longer be held, and then to recover by counter-attack all points that were essential to the maintenance of the whole position … At the same time we developed the principle of saving men in the forward lines by increasing the number of our machine guns and so economising troops.

Hindenburg was well aware that the new defensive system involved considerable risk and would meet opposition:

> So far-reaching a change … involved a certain amount of exaggeration of the new features … and a very stubborn adhesion to the old. Even the most carefully worded instructions left room for misunderstanding … additionally, our new defensive system made heavy demands on the moral resolution and capacity of the troops because it abandoned the firm external rigidity of the serried lines of defence, and thereby made the independent actions, even of the smallest body of troops, the supreme consideration. Tactical co-operation was no longer obtained by defences that were continuous to the eye, but consisted of the invincible moral bond between the men engaged in such tactical co-operation.[63]

Discussions about a new German defensive system had begun in May 1915 when a French map was captured and sent to Colonel von Lossberg of the OHL Operations Section on the Western Front. The map showed a proposed French front line made up of listening posts behind which, by some 200 yards, was a first line of resistance. Behind this line was a main line of resistance and some 600 yards behind that were a series of shelters for local reserves. The main line of resistance was made up of a number of strongpoints about 200 yards apart, the garrisons of which were ordered to hold out at all costs until relieved by the counter-attack of the third line reserves.

Von Lossberg, together with his OHL colleagues Colonel Max Bauer and Captain Hermann Geyer, elaborated these French defence proposals and their work gave rise to Ludendorff's 'Principles of Field Construction' (November 1916) and 'The Principles of Command in the Defence Battle in Trench Warfare' (December 1916). The new German defences were to be both elastic and in-depth. There were to be three zones – a lightly held front zone with machine-gun posts some 600 yards deep, a battle zone heavily defended by concrete machine-gun emplacements and up to 300 yards deep, and a rear zone with trenches outside the range of enemy artillery, for reserves. Unlike the Falkenhayn system, the defenders would be positioned on reverse slopes to gain maximum protection. The effect of such a system was to allow enemy troops to enter the defence area after which it met increasingly powerful resistance. As the enemy attack weakened then fresh reserves would drive them from the defended area. The British Official History described the new German defences: 'In short, the German concept of a defence in depth was a chequered system of strongpoints to break up and delay an assault, backed by a succession of counter-attack formations ready to recapture any lost ground immediately'.[64]

The major example of the new German system of defence in depth was the Hindenburg Line made up of the *Siegfriedstellung* running from Arras to St Quentin, the *Wotanstellung* from Quant to Drocourt/Lille and the *Flandernstellung* towards the northern coast. Later, and continuing the use of Wagnerian names, the *Brunhild Stellung* was constructed in Champagne and the *Kriemhilde Stellung* defended the Meuse-Argonne sector. Of all these *Stellung*, the *Siegfried* was the most heavily defended with a total depth varying from 5,000 to 9,000 yards. It was described as 'an iron wall that no human power can overcome'.[65] Over four days in March 1917 the Germans withdrew some 18,000 yards to their new position. Apart from providing an immensely formidable defence, the Hindenburg Line gave the additional advantage of reducing the length of the German front line and releasing divisions. The effectiveness of the Hindenburg Line was tested at Cambrai in 1917 and even more so in the second half of 1918.

By the end of 1917 it was clear to the British that with the transfer of German divisions from the Eastern Front a major defensive battle in the West was imminent. GHQ had accumulated a mass of information, including captured copies of certain Ludendorff and Lossberg papers, which gave details of the German defence system. A small committee, comprising of Generals Edmonds, Jeudwine and McMullen, was set up to examine the suitability of the German methods for the BEF. The committee recommended modifications of the German system and proposed a deep outpost zone, which would be given up in the face of a major attack, and a main line of defence outside the range of enemy guns. This proposal was turned down since it seemed to imply a form of delaying action rather than a defensive battle. In its place GHQ adopted what they thought was the German system in full.

Unfortunately, the captured German papers in the hands of GHQ were incomplete. In particular, GHQ misunderstood the role of the reserves. In the German defence system the bulk of the defence force was to be kept back behind the battle zone ready to counter-attack, but GHQ placed its reserves further forward in the actual battle zone. The result of this and other misunderstandings was disastrous in terms of the distribution of infantry in the three defence zones. At Passchendaele, for example, the German divisions were distributed (front zone: battle zone: reserves) in a ratio of 1:1:4 whereas in spring 1918 the battalions of the BEF Third Army were distributed in a ratio of 7:12:1. The British Fifth Army was split 37:44:29, but since the twenty-nine reserve divisions were spread over 35 miles they could not be considered as an effective counter-attack force. Taking both the Third Army and the Fifth Army together, a total of 190 divisions, 157 were placed in the forward battle zones. There was therefore hardly any 'elasticity' and inevitably the majority of the British troops placed in the forward zones became casualties during the opening German bombardment. It is significant that the GHQ pamphlet SS 210 'The Division in Defence' of May 1918 made no mention of a strong counter-attacking force.[66]

The result of the confused GHQ version of defence in depth was lack of cohesion among the BEF corps commanders. Lieutenant General Sir Richard Haking of XI Corps expressed his view that such a system 'does not agree with the system of defence which is in accordance with our native characteristics, i.e. the defence of the front line at all costs ... our experience has been that counter-strikes to regain lost trenches are more costly in casualties than the stubborn defence of the front line system'.[67] Haking was not alone in opting to hold the front line in strength rather than developing a defence in depth. The III Corps Commander, Sir Richard Butler, also adopted the same view even though he was positioned in spring 1918 next to Sir Ivor Maxse's XVIIII Corps who had organized an in depth defence. When the difference in views of Butler and Maxse was brought to the attention of the Fifth Army HQ the response was that they would have to settle the matter between themselves.[68] Further evidence of confusion within the BEF came from Major General Jeudwine of the 55th Division, who wrote in 1931: 'To this day I don't clearly comprehend what the term [Battle zone] implies – nor have I met anybody who did'.[69] At Givenchy in April 1918, Haking and Jeudwine ignored any form of 'in depth' defence and insisted that the front line should be held in strength. Haking later wrote to Brigadier Sir James Edmonds, the official historian: 'We would have no truck with the "defence in depth" idea at Givenchy and we should have lost the battle if we had'.[70] It is noteworthy that despite the great effort that

Ludendorff had put into the three-zone method of defence, he eventually lost confidence in the concept and by the end of 1917 was favouring a 'one line and a strong one' defence tactic.[71]

* * *

Considerations about defence tactics were accompanied by new thinking about methods of attack. In May 1915 a company of the French 153 Infantry Regiment commanded by Captain André Laffargue was held up near Neuville-Saint-Vaast by two German machine guns. As a result of that experience, Laffargue argued that progress could have been made if there had been available small units of men, well-trained and heavily armed, who could infiltrate between enemy strongpoints which would then be encircled by follow-up troops. Laffargue recorded his thoughts in a pamphlet *Etude sur L'Attaque dans la période actuelle de la Guerre*. Whether Laffargue was the first to advocate such infiltration tactics is unclear. On 16 April 1915 Note 5779 from the French HQ stated that in an attack the first waves of infantry should penetrate as far as possible and leave strongpoints to succeeding waves. However, the French failed to follow up these new ideas and the British even declined to translate Laffargue's pamphlet. It was left to the Germans to adopt infiltration tactics.

In the summer of 1916 a copy of Laffargue's pamphlet fell into German hands. It was translated and circulated and, with some elaboration, became an official training manual. This approach certainly seemed to answer some of the problems faced during an attack against a solid front as experienced in the 1915 battles. The troops who were to carry out this infiltration tactic would have to be specially selected and trained – an elite group. They would be armed with light machine guns, grenades and bombs and their success would depend on surprise and speed. Their aim would be to disrupt enemy defences and communications and advance, as independent groups, towards the enemy artillery positions.

It is likely that these new tactics were not originated by one man, but rather emerged gradually as front-line soldiers attempted to deal with the problems of strong and complex defence systems. In the summer of 1915 Captains Rohr and Reidemann, working with Colonel Bauer of the

German OHL Operations section, had put forward the idea of special attack battalions armed with light mortars and flamethrowers and equipped with new steel helmets and protective metal shields. What Laffargue had called *groups de tirailleurs*, Rohr and Reidemann termed *sturm- or strosstrupps*. Infiltration tactics were employed by the Russian General Aleksei Brusilov in his June 1916 offensive and also by the Germans at Riga in September 1917 and at Caporetto in October 1917. The German counter-attack at Cambrai in November 1917 used similar methods. They were a return, in an elaborate form, to the pre-war 'fire and movement' tactics and the German *sturmtrupps* were to play a key role in the battles of spring 1918.

BEF attack tactics developed along somewhat different lines. Arising from its experience on the Somme, the BEF produced a series of manuals that, between them, constituted a major change in tactical thought. The two principal manuals were SS 135 'Instructions for the Training of Divisions for Offensive Actions' issued in December 1916 and SS 143 'Instructions for the Training of Platoons for Offensive Actions' issued in February 1917. SS 135 stressed the crucial importance of the artillery creeping barrage with infantry following closely behind, while SS 143 abandoned the concept of solid lines of infantry and in its place emphasized the role of the platoon. The platoon was to be an independent tactical unit with its four sections each having its own speciality: bomb throwers in one; a Lewis gun in the second; nine riflemen and a sniper in the third; and men with rifle-grenades in the fourth. SS 143 stated: 'The organisation of the Platoon has been decided [by GHQ]. The guiding principles of this organisation are that the Platoon shall consist of a combination of all weapons with which the Infantry are now armed'.[72] When in action the rifle and bombing sections would attack the enemy position from the sides, while the Lewis gunners and those with rifle-grenades would attack from the centre. These important developments were reinforced by numerous training schools organized by Brigadier General Solly-Flood and, towards the end of the war, by Lieutenant General Sir Ivor Maxse.[73] During the battles of Arras and Passchendaele (despite the mud and spells of bad weather) these tactics met with some success. But it was not until the second half of 1918 that the potential of these tactics was realized.

* * *

This chapter has shown that there was considerable tactical development on the Western Front between 1914 and 1917. During the entire period the opposing armies, evenly matched, sought on the one hand to discover a successful method of attack with the aim of destroying enemy forces, gaining ground and, ultimately, to effect a war-winning breakthrough. On the other hand they endeavoured to establish impregnable lines of defence that would prevent a successful attack from taking place. These were the elements of stalemate with the Germans, after 1914, adopting a predominantly defensive policy thus obliging the French and the British to take on the role of the attacker.

The year 1914 saw a variety of tactics as the advancing armies met in Belgium and Alsace-Lorraine. The BEF was on the defensive at Mons, Le Cateau and at Ypres and it was only briefly on the Marne and the Aisne that it was able to demonstrate its professional skills of attack. Both the French and the Germans, eager to prove their offensive qualities, too often committed their troops to attacks *en masse* with catastrophic results. The onset of trench warfare was a novel experience for the generals of both sides. They were faced with problems they had never before encountered. Far from being rendered inactive and impotent by the circumstances,[74] they attempted, for four years, to develop tactics in both attack and defence that would lead to victory, or at least avert defeat. The war on the Western Front was, therefore, one of continuous experimentation. If one method failed or was shown to be inappropriate, then another was devised and put into practice.

The various artillery tactics used by the British were examples of this process which, in essence, amounted to trial and error. The tactics at Neuve Chapelle and Aubers Ridge (1915) were, in principle, different from those at Loos (1915) or on the Somme (1916) or at Passchendaele (1917), but they were similar to those adopted at Cambrai (1917). For at least half the war the BEF generals had to contend with a lack of guns and munitions and this problem provided the backdrop to various tactical issues. How could the available fire-power be best used? The options were numerous. Would a short bombardment lasting minutes be more effective than one lasting days? What was the most effective combination of shells – high explosive, shrapnel or gas? And as artillery tactics and technology developed, what was the most effective combination of artillery and infantry?

Taking all these factors into account, should infantry attacks be on a narrow front of a few hundred yards or on an extended front of several miles? Should an attack be aimed at gaining ground using 'bite and hold' tactics or should there be an attempt to achieve a major breakthrough? Or was 'attrition' the answer – killing more and more of the enemy until they could no longer wage war? What was the most effective role of the aeroplane and the tank, both entirely new weapons? There were also problems associated with the inherent nature of trench warfare. Should troops sit in their trenches until a set-piece attack took place or should 'minor enterprises' be encouraged and carried out on a continuous basis? How was an 'offensive spirit' and a high morale developed and maintained and green troops given battle experience?

As regards defence, was the practice of keeping a strong front line superior to the alternative of having a lightly held front line and a defence 'in depth'? What was the best way to counter the ever-increasing fire power of the artillery? And how could the headquartes of the belligerent armies ensure that changes in both attack and defence tactics were communicated, understood and followed at the various levels of command?

The senior generals of the British, French and German armies made tremendous efforts to deal with all these issues during the course of the war. The changes in tactics were the result of ideas initiated and implemented at various levels in the military hierarchy from Haig, Rawlinson, Falkenhayn and Ludendorff to Lossberg, Bauer and Laffargue. And since they were aimed at dealing with problems common to all the belligerents it is not surprising that the opposing armies adopted similar solutions at around the same time. Nor were the generals averse to copying tactics that seemed effective. Infiltration tactics in attack were used at different times by the French, the Russians, the Germans and the British. Defence in depth may have started as a German procedure, but the BEF soon made an attempt, even if largely unsuccessful, to replicate the system.

The tactics developed within the BEF by the beginning of 1918 had evolved, unevenly, during the preceding years. Emphasis had moved from attacks by large groups – companies, battalions and divisions – to infiltration tactics at platoon level. The infantry and the artillery had begun to work together taking advantage of the now abundant supply of guns and shells to provide more accurate fire, counter-battery work and the creeping barrage. Trench warfare had become more sophisticated and trench weapons, particularly the Lewis gun, had become more numerous. Tanks and aircraft had proved their worth and were considered essential in any plan of attack. The highly successful initial phase of the British attack at Cambrai (November 1917) had used such tactics, only to founder against a strong German counter-attack. Much tactical progress had been achieved, but, in the opening weeks of 1918, there was still no sign of an early end to the war.

*Chapter 7*

# The Western Front in 1918

*'Our losses are huge and we are still being steadily pushed back. It is all so sad'.*

*John Charteris – a British soldier*[1]

*'Things were no longer what they had been: our power of resistance had lost its kick. A soldier still did his duty – yet … things weren't as they had been'.*

*Georg Bucher – a German soldier*[2]

The course of the war on the Western Front in 1918 was determined by three major inter-related events: Germany's adoption of unrestricted submarine warfare; the decision of the United States to enter the war; and the revolution in Russia. These pivotal events took place in 1917 and far from the Western Front but their repercussions had a critical effect on the campaigns in France and Flanders during the last year of the war.

In 1914 there was no accepted international law governing the conduct of war at sea. The Declaration of London, which had aimed at codifying the rules of naval conflict, had been drawn up in 1909 but its provisions were largely ignored. They were followed in neither the war between Italy and Turkey of 1911–12 nor in the Balkans war of 1912–13. It was particularly unacceptable to Britain that many items important to Germany's war effort – oil, copper, rubber and cotton – were omitted from the Declaration's list of goods that might legitimately be confiscated from neutral ships heading for German ports. However, this lack of an agreed *modus operandi* at sea suited the British government who had no hesitation on 20 August 1914 in imposing a blockade on German ports. The British Fleet was in control of the North Sea and in 1915 intercepted over 3,000 foreign ships. German merchant shipping came to a halt almost immediately. Where a neutral ship was involved, any goods being carried for the benefit of the Central Powers, mainly by the Dutch and Scandinavian countries, were purchased and the vessel was allowed to continue on its way. In carrying through this policy, which was certainly illegal under the proposed terms of the Declaration of London, Britain took great care not to antagonize the most powerful of the neutrals, the United States. For example, cotton, which was an important US export, was excluded from the British embargo for a period of a year and, responding to American demands, Britain allowed foodstuffs to be sent to Germany through neutral ports.

Despite this last concession, Germany condemned Britain's actions as a 'hunger blockade' and, in retaliation, Admiral von Tirpitz announced unrestricted submarine warfare from 18 February 1915. This meant that every Allied merchant ship found within the waters surrounding the British Isles, the war zone, would be destroyed. Neutral ships were warned to avoid British waters. If they did not, they would be subject to possible attack. Germany's instrument of destruction was to be the U-boat. Traditional naval practice would normally follow what were known as 'cruiser rules' when dealing with passenger and merchant ships. These 'rules' required threatened ships to be warned of imminent sinking and their crews given the opportunity to take to their boats. However, the application of such 'rules' was hardly relevant in submarine warfare. It would mean that a submarine would have to surface, thus unnecessarily giving its position away and putting itself at risk from any weapons concealed on its prey. Consequently, in unrestricted warfare, such rules were ignored. As Sir John Fisher, the First Sea Lord 1904–10, wrote to Churchill in 1913:

> The submarine cannot capture the merchant ship; she has no spare hands to put a prize crew on board … she cannot convoy her into harbour … There is nothing else the submarine can do except sink her capture, and it must therefore be admitted that this submarine menace is a truly terrible one for British commerce and Great Britain alike, for no means can be suggested at present for meeting it except for reprisals.[3]

Fortunately for Britain, Germany had, at the early stages of the war, only twenty-five mainly aged U-boats.[4] Of these, because of repairs and general refitting, only seven or eight were at sea at any one time. Nevertheless, the U-boat threat was far from a token gesture. On 22 September 1914 the German U-boat U-9 sank the British cruisers *Aboukir*, *Cressy* and *Hogue*. Losses of Allied and neutral shipping through enemy action, which had averaged 61,000 tons per month in the first six months of the war, rose to a monthly average of 116,000 tons during March–August 1915.[5] In a memorandum to the British Cabinet dated 17 July 1915 the Foreign Secretary, Sir Edward Grey, expressed his concern:

> Our blockade … has barely commenced as yet to be seriously inconvenient to Germany, whilst, on the other hand, the German submarine depredations have, from the start, been steadily destructive of British shipping, together with the lives of non-combatants, including women and children, and valuable cargoes, nearly 300,000 tons of British shipping … have been destroyed since February 18.[6]

A variety of measures was taken by the Admiralty to counter the U-boat threat. Nets with mines attached were spread across the Straits of Dover forcing the submarines to take a longer route to the Atlantic around the north of Scotland and thereby reducing the time they could spend on active patrol. Surface patrols were increased. Merchant ships were armed. Q-boats – old steamers with concealed guns – were introduced as decoys and British ships were not averse to flying neutral flags. But U-boats were difficult to track. In Churchill's words it was 'a game of blind man's bluff in an unlimited space of three dimensions'.[7] There appeared to be no counter to submarine action.

During May 1915 a series of U-boat attacks brought strong protests from America. On 1 May the US oil tanker *Gulflight* was torpedoed off the Scilly Isles. On 7 May the British Cunard liner the *Lusitania* (which was allegedly carrying munitions as well as passengers) was attacked by the submarine U-20 off the Irish coast at Kinsale Head. It sank in eighteen minutes with the loss of 1,198 passengers and crew. Of these 128 were Americans. Two days earlier the U-20 had sunk without warning two British merchant ships, the *Candidate* and the *Centurion*. There were further US losses in July when the steamer *Leelanaw* was torpedoed, while in August the White Star passenger steamer *Arabic* was sunk in the Irish Sea with three US citizens among the forty-four dead. The protests of the American President, Woodrow Wilson, did have some effect. On 27 August Germany, anxious that America should remain neutral, called off the *Handelskrieg* – trade warfare. U-boat activity in the Channel and off the west coast of Britain was forbidden by the Kaiser and 'cruiser rules' were imposed.

But submarine warfare, even though 'restricted', continued and 'cruiser rules' did not prevent the ubiquitous U-20 from sinking the liner *Hesperian* off the Irish coast with the loss of thirty-two lives. The German naval commanders, Admiral Reinhardt Scheer and Admiral von Turpitz, both argued for a return to all-out warfare. In February 1916 von Turpitz pressed his case:

> Immediate and relentless recourse to the submarine weapon is absolutely necessary. Any further delay in the introduction of unrestricted warfare will give England time for further naval and economic defensive measures and cause us greater losses in the end and endanger quick success. The sooner the campaign be opened, the sooner will success be realised, and the more rapidly and energetically will England's hopes of defeating us by a war of exhaustion be destroyed.[8]

However, the Kaiser and the Chancellor, Theobald von Bethmann-Hollweg, were unwilling to endanger relations with America and von Turpitz's plea for an immediate return to unrestricted warfare went unheaded. Von Turpitz resigned in protest on 16 March 1916.

The debate within Germany concerning U-boat warfare polarized between the politicians, led by the Chancellor, and the military which, apart from the Admirals, included Falkenhayn, Ludendorff and Hindenburg. The politicians urged caution fearing that the United States might enter the war. The military saw the submarine as an essential tool in the defeat of England and believed, in the words of von Turpitz: 'If we break England we break the backbone of the hostile coalition'.[9] The Kaiser swayed between the two factions and on 28 March 1916 was persuaded by the military to re-open a second phase of unrestricted submarine warfare. By this stage of the war at sea any pretence of following 'rules' had disappeared. Less than a week before Germany's second phase of unrestricted warfare was declared a U-boat torpedoed and sank the Folkestone-Dieppe ferry *Sussex*. Fifty passengers were drowned including three Americans. Five weeks later the liner *Cymric* heading for the United States was torpedoed and became the thirty-seventh unarmed liner since the *Lusitania* to be sunk by U-boats.[10]

The sinking of the *Sussex* brought further US protests and President Wilson demanded an end to unrestricted warfare. The mood in Germany changed once again and the outcome was the 'Sussex Pledge' whereby Germany undertook to use submarines only to attack warships. Other vessels would not be sunk without warning. This Pledge had been negotiated by the American Ambassador to Germany, James W. Gerard, who one week later expressed his opinion that the Germans would keep to the Pledge only for as long as it suited them and that unrestricted warfare would start again within a year. The Pledge had little effect. In April 1916 Britain had lost 140,000 tons of shipping. In October the losses amounted to 175,000 tons.[11] Further measures to defeat the U-boat – the depth charge and hydrophonic equipment to detect submarines underwater – were introduced, but Germany lost only fifteen U-boats in 1916. Britain was far from having control of the seas.

By the end of 1916, following the exhausting battles of the Somme and Verdun, Germany was again ready to resort to unrestricted warfare. Technical development meant that U-boats, which could carry only four torpedoes in 1914, could now carry ten or twelve. They could remain submerged for longer periods. Moreover, Germany now had some 120 submarines at its disposal and they were being built at a faster rate than they were being lost. Forty could be at sea at any one time. The generals were adamant that unrestricted warfare should begin immediately. Hindenburg later wrote:

> It was perfectly obvious on purely military grounds we should desire the commencement of the U-boat campaign. The advantages that it would bring to our operations on land was plain to every eye. It would have been an immense relief to us if the enemy's manufacture of war materials, or its transport overseas, could be materially hampered … Further there would be a chance of restricting the imports of raw materials and food into the Entente countries and placing England,

> if not her Allies, before the fateful alternative of either holding out the hand of reconciliation to us or losing her place in world trade. The U-boat campaign seemed likely to have a decisive effect on the course of the war; indeed, at the beginning of 1917 it appeared to be the only means we could employ to secure a victorious conclusion to the war ...[12]

On 9 January 1917 the Kaiser presided over a Crown Council on the subject of unrestricted warfare. Both the head of the Navy Staff, Admiral von Holtzendorff and the head of the Army, Hindenburg, spoke in favour. Bethmann-Hollweg was well aware of the possible consequences: 'We must reckon, however, on the entry of America into the war, her help will consist of the delivery of food to England, financial assistance, the supply of aeroplanes and a force of volunteers'. Hindenburg replied: 'We are already prepared to deal with that. The chances of the submarine operations are more favourable than they are ever likely to be again. We can and must begin them'.[13] The Naval Staff believed that it was possible to sink Allied shipping at a rate of 600,000 tons per month and Admiral Holtzendorff was convinced that at that rate 'we can bring Britain to her knees within five months'.[14] Bethmann-Hollweg had no alternative but to go along, albeit reluctantly, with the military. In July Bethmann-Hollweg was replaced as Chancellor.

The third phase of unrestricted submarine warfare began on 1 February 1917. The results were dramatic. The monthly losses of British, Allied and neutral ships were, in February 234 (500,000 tons), in March 281 (600,000 tons) and in April a staggering 373 (870,000 tons). In April one in four merchant ships that left British ports never returned and 1,150 seamen were lost. In the first six months of the campaign 3.75 million tons of world shipping was destroyed. Britain was not yet 'on her knees', but it was a grim situation. In April Britain had only a six weeks' supply of food available.[15] Sir William Robertson wrote on 19 April:

> Ever since I can remember and years before then it has always been assumed that we would have command of the sea and everything was based on that hypothesis, and if anybody had thought that it should be based on any other hypothesis they would have been classed as fools. As

> a matter of fact we have not got command of the sea. In every theatre we are suffering from shipping shortage.[16]

Clearly a new approach was urgently needed and it appeared in the form of the convoy. Convoys were not new – they had been used to shield troop ships – but they had never been used to protect merchant shipping. The Admiralty was convinced that they would not work. It was argued that convoys would be a better target for U-boats; that they would be able to move only at the speed of the slowest thus lengthening the period of exposure; that receiving ports would be unable to deal with the arrival of a large number of merchant ships all at the same time; and that there were just not enough destroyers available to provide an escort. But the immense losses of April 1917, together with the insistence of the Prime Minister Lloyd George and the Secretary to the Committee of Imperial Defence, Sir Maurice Hankey, galvanized action within the Admiralty. On 10 May a convoy of seventeen merchant ships sailed from Gibraltar and on 20 May every ship arrived safely in Britain. It was a resounding justification of the convoy system. By the end of 1917 more than half of Britain's overseas shipping sailed in convoy. The number of ships lost in May 1917 was 230 and losses gradually fell to 107 in December.[17] Thereafter the U-boat still presented a danger, but the German aim of crippling Britain through unrestricted warfare had failed.

* * *

America's reaction to the losses of ships and citizens from U-boat action – the *Gulflight*, the *Leelanaw*, the *Lusitania*, the *Arabic* and the *Sussex*, to name but a few – was vigorously verbal but largely ineffective. President Wilson faced a number of dilemmas – political, economic and moral. Politically, Wilson was by inclination a liberal intellectual who believed that a negotiated peace was desirable and that neutrality was in the best interests of his country. Churchill described him as 'a good American, an academic liberal, and a sincere hater of war and violence'.[18] Between August and November 1914 Wilson issued no fewer than ten declarations of neutrality.[19] Indeed, it was estimated in 1915 that 90 per cent of Americans did not wish to enter the war.[20] The ethnic mix complicated matters. The 1910 Census showed that

13.3 million Americans (about 14 per cent) had been born abroad. Some 2.5 million of them had been born in Germany and they made up the largest ethnic groups in Chicago, San Francisco and Pittsburg. In Milwaukee half the population were of German extraction. The Irish dominated the east coast cities such as Boston and Philadelphia and could hardly be considered as supporters of Britain. On the other hand, there was sympathy for the Allied cause based on America's English-speaking origin and a common liberal, non-militaristic tradition. Wilson gauged that a stance of neutrality was the best way forward. He had been elected by a narrow majority in 1912 and in the 1916 Election he presented himself as the peace candidate against the Republican Charles Hughes who was known to sympathize with Britain and its Allies. Wilson's slogan was: 'He kept us out of the War'. He won the election with three million more votes than in 1912.[21] As a result of the war, the economy of the United States was thriving. The banking industry was buoyant with the Allies taking the majority of the loans granted from America. By Easter 1917 Allied governments had borrowed $2,000,000,000 against $27,000,000 borrowed by the Central Powers.[22] Before the war America's munitions industry hardly existed, but from 1914 it grew considerably because of Allied demand. Large organizations such as the Bethlehem Steel Corporation, Du Pont, Hercules Powder and New England Westinghouse built production facilities on a large scale and sold armaments at a considerable profit to the extent that the US government introduced a special war profits tax. During the war the United States sold to Britain 926 million rounds of small arms ammunition, 31 million shells, 1.2 million rifles, 569 tons of explosives, 42,000 trucks, 3,400 aero-engines, 1,400 gun carriages and 866 aeroplanes.[23] Some 75 per cent of the light field artillery shells used by the British army on the Somme in 1916 came from America.[24] In addition, Britain imported vast amounts of meat and cereals. The world shortage of shipping resulted in North America becoming the preferred grain supplier instead of the more distant producers in the southern hemisphere – Argentina, South Africa, Australia and New Zealand. The proportion of grain exported from America and Canada doubled between 1913 and 1919.[25]

There were good reasons, therefore, for the United States to remain neutral and this policy enabled President Wilson, a peace-maker by inclination, to adopt the role of mediator. In February 1915 he despatched his special envoy, Colonel Edward House, to broker peace in Europe. In December 1916 he again attempted to clarify and reconcile the differences between Germany and the Allies calling for 'peace without annexation'. The chances of brokering a peace, however, were extremely small. The restoration of complete Belgian independence was a key issue that separated the two sides, both of whom still believed that they were capable of winning the war.

America's policy had a moral dimension: it had adopted neutrality and acted as a mediator, but at the same time it had grown daily more powerful, economically and financially, as a result of the war. This was viewed with no small measure of contempt by both the Entente and the Central Powers. It was seen as a policy based entirely on self-interest. The Central Powers pointed to the loans, foodstuffs and munitions that America provided to the Allies, while the Entente considered the United States as weak and hypocritical in standing by when Belgium's neutrality was violated and when American lives were being lost through illegal U-boat action. When President Wilson announced in a speech in Philadelphia three days after the sinking of the *Lusitania* that 'there is such a thing as a man being too proud to fight' the comment was greeted in Britain with a mixture of scorn and derision. General John Pershing, America's foremost soldier, considered that America had 'made a grievous error' in not making an early entry into the war in defence of Belgium: 'Thus we presented the spectacle of the most powerful nation in the world sitting on the sidelines, almost idly watching the enactment of the greatest tragedy of all time … The inaction played into the hands of Germany'.[26] Following the loss of the *Lusitania* Wilson's special adviser, Colonel House, commented: 'America has come to a parting of the ways, when she must determine whether she stands for civilized or uncivilized warfare'.[27]

By February 1917 President Wilson had become frustrated with his lack of success in persuading the belligerents to respond to his peace initiatives. He had also completely lost faith in Germany's worthless undertakings to abandon unrestricted U-boat action. American public opinion had hardened against Germany as American ships and lives were lost. On 25 February 1917 a German submarine sank the Cunard liner *Laconia*. Twelve passengers were drowned and four of them were American. On 5 March the American steamship *Algonquin* was torpedoed without warning and a week later three more American ships were sunk. Even then President Wilson maintained his stance on neutrality. As he told the United States Congress on 5 March: 'We stand fast on armed neutrality'. But the patience of President Wilson and of America was fast running out.

What settled the matter was the 'Zimmermann Telegram'. On 17 January 1917 British naval intelligence intercepted a message from the German Foreign Secretary, Arthur Zimmermann, to Heinrich von Eckhardt, the German Minister in Mexico. The message proposed that, in the event of a war between Germany and the United States, Mexico and Germany should form an alliance. Mexico would attack the United States, possibly with German assistance, and, given a successful outcome of the war, Mexico would be rewarded by regaining the territories that it had lost to America in 1848 – Texas, Arizona, and New Mexico. The telegram ended: 'Please call to the attention of the President of Mexico the fact that the employment of ruthless submarine warfare promises to compel England to make peace in a few months'. The Zimmermann telegram was passed to President Wilson on 24 February and, amazingly, Zimmermann confirmed its authenticity. The telegram was published in America on 1 March and caused outrage.[28]

The combination of Germany's declaration of unrestricted submarine warfare on 1 February, which had caused America to break off diplomatic relations, together with the interception of the Zimmermann Telegram, provoked America to enter the war. Wilson now asked for a declaration of war to make the world 'safe for democracy'. The Senate and the House of Representatives passed the resolution on 4 April and 6 April respectively by vast majorities. One month later, conscription was introduced and Major-General John J. Pershing was appointed commander of the American Expeditionary Force (AEF) which was to be sent to the Western Front.

* * *

Events in Russia during the first quarter of 1917 were no less momentous than those that had taken place on the high seas and in America. Russia was poised for revolution. The Duma, an elected assembly composed of mainly middle-class representatives, was rarely allowed to meet and the Zemstvo, local committees of self-government, were banned. The Press was heavily censored. The Tsar, Nicholas II, believed that he had been divinely appointed and his extreme autocratic rule was supported by his wife Alexandra who discouraged any suggestion of reform. Moreover, it was widely known that both the Tsar and the Tsarina were under the malignant influence of a mystic and corrupt group led by the monk Rasputin. Rasputin was assassinated in the most gruesome circumstances by members of the Imperial court, but Nicholas continued to act as though oblivious to the threat to his rule. His despotic behaviour forfeited him the support of his subjects – aristocrats, middle-class and workers. Even the army had become disaffected and the lack of adequate clothing, food and medical supplies during the harsh winter of 1916/17 had resulted in spasmodic riots and mutinies.

Ironically, the 1917 revolution first showed itself among the relatively better-off group, the industrial workers. The production of war materials had brought about economic expansion in the larger cities, particularly Moscow and in the capital, St Petersburg. Those peasants who had avoided military service flocked to the cities drawn by work and high wages. The labour force in heavy industry quadrupled between 1914 and 1916 and the urban population increased from 22 million in 1914 to 28 million in 1916.[29] The bitterly cold weather of February and March 1917 was accompanied by lack of housing, fuel, food and rampant inflation. In St Petersburg prices had doubled between 1914 and 1916 while in Moscow they had trebled. Food queues gathered daily and stood for hours in the snow often to be told that supplies had run out. The rail system had failed and St Petersburg received only half the food it required. Moscow was even worse off.

Such was the background to the February Revolution.[30] On 25 February 200,000 workers rioted in St Petersburg. Shops were looted and destroyed and the police, attempting to keep order, were attacked. There was revolt in the navy and on 28 February a mutiny broke out on the ship *Aurora*. Also on 28 February the strikers were joined by the Tsar's own Guard and what had begun as a revolt against the food and housing shortages developed into a political uprising. An eyewitness recorded a significant event:

> the Pavlovsky Regiment marched from its headquarters ... To my surprise they marched towards the Winter Palace, went in, saluted by the sentries, and invaded and occupied it. I waited a few moments and

> saw the Imperial flag come down slowly ... Soon after, alone on this snow-clad square, my heart heavy, I saw a red flag floating over the palace.[31]

On 27 February the Tsar was obliged to appoint a Provisional government to maintain order as best it could. On the same day the St Petersburg workers formed a Soviet – a committee made up of representatives of industrial workers and soldiers. Three days later the Tsar, having lost all credibility and support, abdicated. Both Britain and France welcomed the fall of its erstwhile friend, the despotic Tsar, and sent fraternal greetings to the provisional government.[32] Russia was hailed as a new democracy and a side-effect of the February Revolution concerned America. In Lloyd George's words America had previously 'shuddered at the idea of any close association with the [Tsarist] Government of Russia – brutal, tyrannical and corrupt, in fact, rotten to the core'. The revolution served to remove a barrier to America's entry into the war.[33]

Meanwhile the Russian army was disintegrating. Thousands were deserting. The peasant soldiers, demoralized by poor food and equipment, lacking faith in the ability of the army to gain victory and desperate to return to their starving families, returned to their villages. A further blow to discipline was the 'Order Number One' issued by the St Petersburg Soviet in early March. This Order authorized each army unit to elect a council which gradually assumed authority previously held by the officers. Germany saw this disruption in the Russian army as a step towards Russia leaving the war. Rather than start an offensive on the Eastern Front, Germany took a subtler approach. They encouraged the Bolshevik Party leader Vladimir Lenin, exiled in Switzerland since an abortive attempt at revolution in 1905, to return in a sealed train, via Germany, to Russia. He was joined by other Bolshevik exiles –Trotsky and Bukharin from New York and Stalin from Siberia. While the Provisional government was inclined to continue the Russian war effort in line with its treaties with the Entente powers, Lenin, who arrived in St Petersburg in April 1917, immediately called, as Germany hoped he would, for peace on whatever terms could be negotiated.

But the Provisional government pursued its war aims. Thanks to the superhuman efforts of the new Russian Minister of War, Kerensky, who personally visited the front and addressed the Russian troops, an army of some 200,000 was gathered in Galicia. It attacked on 1 July 1917 against an Austro-German force and it proved the last Russian offensive of the war. A German counter-attack smashed the disorganized and demoralized Russian army which retreated ignominiously and in complete disarray. The final humiliation of the Russian military took place on 1 September when the important port of Riga was lost in a matter of hours. The German commanders at Riga, General von Hutier and the artillery specialist Lieutenant Colonel Georg Bruchmüller, employed a variety of sophisticated techniques including a creeping barrage, gas shells and specially trained stormtroopers. Riga was a rehearsal for future events on the Western Front.

The position of Kerensky, who had proclaimed himself Prime Minister and, later, commander-in-chief, was severely weakened by the military failures. It was the opportunity for the Bolsheviks to assert their growing power. In November 1917 Lenin and Trotsky, supported by their Red Guard, seized control of St Petersburg and the Provisional government fell. An All-Russian Congress of Soviets put forward a programme of land redistribution, workers' control of the factories, complete democratization of the army and, crucially, an immediate armistice. After three months of negotiation, including some further humiliating military clashes which only served to show that Russia was now unable to defend itself, the Congress of Soviets signed a peace treaty with the Central Powers. The terms of the Brest-Litovsk Treaty were punitive and made under duress, but with an army that had virtually stopped functioning, Russia had no option but to make a settlement. Germany gained Poland, Lithuania, and the Baltic states of Estonia, Livonia and Courland. Finland and the Ukraine took the opportunity to break away from Russia and the Turks gained land in the Caucusus. Russia gave up a million square miles of territory, which included a third of its agricultural land and most of its coal, oil and iron-ore producing areas. It lost a third of its population – about 55 million people.[34] The Russian army had suffered terribly. The casualty figures, generally regarded as understated, were between 1.7 and 3 million dead and around 5 million wounded.[35] Russia had been thoroughly defeated. Even before Russia's capitulation at Brest-Litovsk, Sir William Robertson, the Chief of the Imperial General Staff, had written to FM Haig, no doubt echoing a general feeling among the Allies: 'One thing seems for certain, that is that we shall get no more effective assistance from Russia during the war.'[36]

For the Central Powers the defeat of Russia was of immense strategic importance. The Austrians could move its divisions to the Italian Front. Germany, while retaining around a million men in the East to safeguard its interests[37], was still able, between November 1917 and 21 March 1918, to move forty-four of its best divisions to the Western Front. As Hindenburg wrote in 1919:

> I am entitled to claim that on our side nothing was neglected to concentrate all the fighting forces of Germany for the decision in the West. We had at last the object of three years' strivings and longings. No longer threatened in the rear, we could turn to [...] the West and now address ourselves to this passage of arms ... We had a new enemy, economically the most powerful in the world ... It was the United States of America and her advent was perilously near. Would she appear in time to snatch the victor's laurels from our brow?[38]

Germany's insistence on waging unrestricted submarine warfare had brought the United States into the war. The autocratic rule of Tsar Nicholas II together with the policies of Lenin's Bolshevik Party had taken Russia out of the war. The problem, from the point of view of the British and French on the Western Front, was that the repercussions of the first of these two seismic events was somewhat long term, while the impact of the second was immediate. As Hindenburg pointed out: 'For the first time in the whole of the war the Germans would have the advantage in numbers on one of their fronts! ... we were now in a position to concentrate an immense force to overwhelm the enemy's lines at some point of the Western Front'.[39] Germany was well aware that almost limitless forces would eventually arrive from America, but that was in the future. Germany's gamble was that it would win the war in the West before those forces could appear in strength.

* * *

Certainly 1917 had been a bad year for the Allies. Apart from Russia leaving the war, Italy had lost around 700,000 men in 1917 alone and, in October, had suffered a humiliating defeat at Caporetto. The French army was fragile following the failure of Nivelle's offensive in April. No fewer than 110 units in fifty-four divisions on the Western Front had mutinied. The French commander, General Petain, had gradually restored discipline and stability, but at the end of the year the army was still in a state of recuperation. Internally there was political disruption with anti-war marches in Paris.[40] Britain had lost heavily during the Passchendaele offensive and the fleeting promise of Cambrai had ended in disappointment. At home the British, despite food shortages, were stubbornly stoical and determined, but the army was nearing exhaustion. The few territorial gains made by the Allies in 1917 around Ypres and Rheims hardly dented the vast areas of Belgium and Northern France that remained firmly in the hands of the Germans.

Germany was not without its own problems. It too had experienced severe losses at Passchendaele and by the end of 1917 the total number of killed or missing in the war had reached 1.3 million. The U-boat warfare had failed to bring Britain to her knees. Austria-Hungary was considered more of a liability than an asset and, unknown to Germany, had made peace overtures to the Allies. The British blockade, together with the 'Turnip Winter' of 1916/17 when the potato crop failed, had caused a severe shortage of food. Strikes, both political and economic, were on the increase. And the arrival of the Americans was imminent. It was difficult under these circumstances to judge how long the war could go on, but there was no doubt as to where the outcome would be decided. It could only be the Western Front. The main British, French and German armies were already concentrated there. The German troops released from the East were directed there and Pershing's American army was on its way there. The scene was set for the great Western Front battles of 1918.

Germany's strategy in the West for 1918 was decided at a conference in Mons on 11 November 1917. To Ludendorff and Hindenburg there was no choice. A long, drawn-out struggle on the Western Front was no longer a tenable option. What was required was a major breakthrough carried out with surprise and with maximum strength. The troops transferred from the East would give Ludendorff a significant superiority in numbers – 192 divisions against 178 Allied divisions, but since this advantage was only likely to be temporary then a 1918 Spring Offensive was essential. It was almost a repeat of the situation in 1914. Then, Germany had aimed at defeating the French before the Russians entered the war. Now, it was a question of defeating the Allies before the Americans appeared.

It took two months of discussion to decide where exactly the offensive should take place. One possibility was to attack on either side of Verdun and defeat the French army. Ludendorff himself, however, favoured an attack against the British and decided on Operation Michael which would take place in the Arras-St Quentin area over the old Somme battlefields. The aim was to separate the French and British armies and advance along the river Somme. Once the front was broken, the German troops would move north and threaten the British flank and rear. At that stage a second operation, codenamed George, would attack between the La Bassée canal and the Ypres-Commines canal, cross the river Lys and head towards Hazebrouck and the Channel ports. In this way the British would be encircled and defeated. Such a breakthrough, reckoned Ludendorff, would inevitably lead to the collapse of France and to Germany winning the war.

Ludendorff's plan, now given the overall title of *Kaiserschlacht* – the Emperor's Battle – almost succeeded.[41] Before March 1918 the BEF had agreed to extend its line by 28 miles south of the Somme to the River Oise. This sector had recently been taken over from the French by Gough's Fifth Army. The area had been devastated by the 1916 battles and the defence system was far from complete. Moreover, being the stretch of line furthest from the Channel it had received least attention. Gough was allocated thirteen divisions to hold 42 miles of front whereas General Byng's Third Army on Gough's left held 28 miles with fourteen divisions.

It was the Fifth Army, unprepared and vastly outnumbered and outgunned, that faced the brunt of the Michael attack. The Germans used tactics that had already proved effective at Riga, Caporetto and Cambrai. Artillery, over 6,000 guns compared with Gough's 3,000, was brought up to the front, having been registered well behind the German lines. At 9.30 am on 21 March, after a five-hour bombardment of high explosive and gas shells, the highly trained stormtroopers, helped by a creeping barrage and a thick mist, moved forward. Within one and a half hours the Fifth Army front zone had been captured. By the end of the day, the German troops had penetrated to a depth of 4.5 miles. British casualties amounted to 38,500, of whom 21,000 were prisoners. The Germans had lost 40,000.

During 22 and 23 March a gap opened between the British Fifth and Third armies and the Third Army fell back, giving up the key Flesquières salient – a position gained at great cost during the 1917 Cambrai attack. By 24 March the British Fifth Army had collapsed and was retreating, pulling the right wing of the Third Army with it. In the centre and on the left the Third Army stood firm. On the Fifth Army front only a thin and barely organized resistance separated the German troops from the strategically important rail centre of Amiens.

A crisis occurred on the evening of 24 March. Petain, who had sent a division to help Gough, now announced to Haig that in the event of any further German advance, he would order the French armies on the British right to fall back in order to cover Paris. Petain was no doubt influenced by the shelling of Paris from Loan 75 miles away. On 21 March a shell fell close to Notre Dame and another near the Gare de l'Est. Petain had forty divisions in reserve – the result of the extension of the British front line – but, believing that the next German attack would be against his own troops in Champagne, was not prepared to use them. Haig immediately realized that if Petain's forces fell back then a gap would open in the Allied line through which the Germans could advance without opposition. Haig lost no time in contacting the newly appointed CIGS, Wilson, and Lord Milner, a member of the War Cabinet, insisting that the French General Foch should take control of the situation. This duly happened on 26 March at Doullens and Foch became commander-in-chief. One of his first orders was to annul Petain's plan to withdraw the French troops and instead moved French reinforcements to the Amiens area.

Meanwhile the German advance was losing momentum. Instead of concentrating his forces on Amiens, Ludendorff gave each of his three armies different directions of advance thus weakening the overall impetus. In any event, German supplies were now short and the troops were exhausted. They were having to advance over the difficult terrain of the old Somme battlefield – a maze of abandoned trenches and shell craters – which took a heavy toll on artillery and lorries The last major attack of the Michael offensive, codenamed Mars, took place on 28 March. It aimed at driving a wedge between the British Fifth and Third armies and advancing towards Arras. But here the Third Army defences were well prepared. Mars was a complete failure. On 4 April, a mixed Australian and British force successfully counter-attacked at Villers-Bretonneux, only 10 miles from Amiens, and the German High Command finally recognized that Michael had been brought to a halt. Ludendorff was forced to concede that 'the enemy's resistance was beyond our powers'.[42] Michael may have failed, but the British and the French were fortunate to have avoided a catastrophic defeat. The Germans had pushed forward 40 miles and had taken 1,200 square miles of territory. They had inflicted 240,000 casualties, mainly British, and had themselves lost 250,000 men. Gough was made the scapegoat for the British retreat and was sent home.

Ludendorff now launched Operation Georgette, a scaled down version of the original George. The direction of the attack, which later became known as the Battle of the Lys, was over the 1915 battlefields of Neuve Chapelle, Festubert and Aubers towards the important rail centre of Hazebrouck and the Channel ports. Operation Georgette began on 9 April and the Germans made immediate gains. The attack was helped by a number of factors. Eight German divisions faced only three British divisions, one of which had already taken part in the March retreat. A heavy mist again favoured the infiltration tactics of the German stormtroopers. The ground, normally marshy around the River Lys, had dried out. In particular, the centre of the attack area was defended by Portuguese troops of doubtful morale and fighting capability.

The Portuguese troops broke and the Germans, reinforced by a further seven divisions, thrust forwards and by the evening of 9 April had reached and crossed the rivers Lawe and Lys – an advance of 4 miles on a front of some 10 miles. On 10 April the German attack continued in a north-westerly direction and succeeded in taking Armentières, Messines, Ploegsteert and Hollebeke. Three days later German troops were less than 5 miles from their first major objective, Hazebrouck, itself only 22 miles from the Channel.

This was yet another crisis situation for the British army and it caused Haig to issue his famous Order of the Day: 'There is no other course open to us but to fight it out … Every position must be held to the last man … With our backs to the wall and believing in the justice of our cause, each of us must fight to the end'.[43] As though in response, the approach to Hazebrouck was successfully blocked by the 4th Guards Brigade supported by the 1st Australian Division. The Germans were now obliged to head north towards Ypres. On 15 April they gained Bailleul and the Ravelsberg Ridge but were stopped at Meteren. Foch, somewhat belatedly, introduced French troops to defend the Kemmel area. Although Mt Kemmel was taken by the Germans on 25 April, the power of Georgette was now lost. On 29 April Ludendorff abandoned the offensive. Since the opening of Operation Michael on 21 March both the Germans and the Allies had each lost 350,000 men. But the British army, the destruction of which was the aim of Michael and Georgette, was still intact and time was running out for the German High Command. At the beginning of May there were 430,000 American soldiers in France. By the end of that month there were over 650,000. Germany's superiority in numbers was fast diminishing.

Ludendorff still held to the view that defeating the British in Flanders would end the war. Foch had placed thirteen French infantry divisions and three cavalry divisions to support the British forces and Ludendorff was well aware that before any further attack could be made against the British it was necessary to draw the French reserves to the south. It was this thinking that caused Ludendorff to launch his offensive Blucher in Champagne on the Chemin des Dames. It was more than unfortunate that four British divisions, relocated to the Champagne area to recuperate after suffering heavily in the March attacks, now found themselves at the centre of the German offensive.

On 27 May seventeen German divisions, supported by a 4,000-gun bombardment, attacked poorly prepared French defences. The front broke and by the end of the day the river Aisne had been crossed. The breakthrough was on a 25-mile front and on 3 June the Germans were on the banks of the Marne only 37 miles from Paris. On 8 June Ludendorff carried out a second attack in the Champagne area, named Gneisenau, but this time he achieved only limited success. A third attack on 15 July, Friedensturm, managed to cross the Marne near Rheims, but it petered out against strong French resistance.

Had Ludendorff's three offensives in the south done enough to weaken the British position in Flanders? On 18 July Ludendorff was discussing this question with his commanders and preparing for the final attack in Flanders against the British – it was codenamed Hagen – when news reached him that the French, under Mangin, had launched a major counter-stroke at Villers-Cotterets. The Germans were faced by twenty-four experienced divisions, 2,000 guns, 900 aircraft and 400 tanks. Preparations for Hagen were put to one side and were never taken up again. Mangin's attack was the first Allied initiative of any significance in 1918 and it showed the way for future action. Also, it would not have escaped Ludendorff's attention that American troops had fought with the British on the Somme on 28 May capturing the village of Cantigny; that the 2nd United States Division had fought at Belleau Wood on 6 July and that the 2nd and 3rd US Divisions had joined the French on the Marne in June and July. It was now clear to the German High Command that the *Kaiserschlacht* had failed and the Americans had finally arrived. The German troops fell back from the Marne to the river Vesle.

* * *

On Bank Holiday Monday, 1918, exactly four years after the declaration of war, Lloyd George told the people of Britain: 'Hold fast, our prospects of victory have never been so bright'.[44] On 8 August Haig attacked the German positions east of Amiens to clear the enemy from the important Paris-Amiens-Calais railway. Rawlinson was put in command of the attack using British, Dominion and American soldiers, around 450,000 men. He also had 342 heavy tanks and seventy-two of the faster Whippets. In the air, Allied aircraft outnumbered the Germans by five to one. The outcome was a rout of the German forces who were forced back 7 miles on an 11-mile front. The Germans lost 27,000 compared to British casualties of 9,000. Progress on the Amiens front slowed over the next three days, but it was a clear victory. Haig, in a letter to his wife, wrote: 'Who would have believed this possible even 2 months ago? How much easier it is to attack, than to stand and await an enemy's attack!'[45] Ludendorff, still reeling from the attack by Mangin, was in a state of nervous collapse. He called 8 August 'the black day of the German army in the history of this war. This was the worst experience I had to go through … 8 August made things clear for both army commands, both for the German and for the enemy'.[46] On 10 August he reported the situation to the Kaiser whose response was: 'We are at the limit of our powers. The war must be brought to an end'.[47] Ludendorff offered his resignation to the Kaiser on 11 August, but it was refused.

Among the soldiers and politicians in Britain and France the possibility of the war ending in 1918 was never a foregone conclusion. In January Lord Derby bet Lloyd George 100 cigars that the war would end in 1918, but Lloyd George disagreed.[48] Even in October 1918 Lloyd George was of the opinion that: 'The military advice we obtained did not encourage us to expect an immediate termination of the war. All our plans and preparations were therefore made on the assumption that the war would certainly not conclude before 1919'.[49] In July the BEF General Staff issued a document entitled 'British Military Policy 1918–1919'. It concluded that there was little chance of breaking the stalemate in France before mid-1919.[50] Churchill believed that 'all should be staked upon a battle in the spring and summer 1919'[51] and, on another occasion, even suggested that manpower should be conserved 'for the decisive struggle of 1920'.[52] Foch wrote in July: 'To reach the final decision of the war as early as possible in 1919 each of the Allied nations should prepare for the commencement of that year its maximum effort'.[53] Even Haig had his doubts. Discussing the general situation with Sir Henry Wilson in October 1918, Haig said: 'the enemy was not ready for unconditional surrender. In that case, there would be no armistice, and the war would continue for another year'.[54]

However, as Churchill later commented: 'Fortune had earlier and happier solutions in store'.[55] In the period now known as the Hundred Days, from 8 August until the Armistice of 11 November, the Allied forces finally defeated the German army on the Western Front. During the last week of July Foch wrote: 'The Allied Armies have reached the turning of the road'.[56] But at that point the German army, although weakened and generally having to make the best of poor defensive positions gained during the Spring Offensives, was not yet beaten.

The eventual victory did not take the form of one or two major battles. The pattern of warfare on the Western Front had changed. The offensive on the grand scale of the Somme, the Chemin des Dames and Passchendaele gave way to a series of rapid blows which forced the Germans to retreat from one hastily constructed defence system to another. Foch described the Allied attack policy in a memorandum to all the commanders in chief: 'These operations, in order to have their full success, should follow one another without leaving the enemy time to recover himself.'[57] Between 20 and 26 August six British and French armies, co-ordinated by Foch, made successive attacks on a 75-mile front from Soissons to Arras. From 26 to 29 September a similar series of attacks by British, French and American armies pushed forwards towards Mézières, the Canal d'Escaut and the main Hindenburg Line system. All along the front steady advances took place when and where possible. German Reserves were now in desperately short supply. In July eighty-one divisions were in reserve. By November this number had fallen to seventeen.[58] Moreover, the persistent and widespread nature of the Allies' attacks prevented them from being concentrated in any particular area. On 30 September Hindenburg was obliged to tell his army commanders that they could no longer expect to receive Reserves – they must rely on their own resources.[59]

* * *

The BEF played a leading role in these high tempo advances. On 22 August Haig wrote to General Birdwood:

> The methods which we have followed hitherto in our battles with limited objectives when the enemy were strong are no longer suited to his present condition … To turn the present situation to account the most resolute offensive is everywhere desirable. Risks which a month ago would have been criminal to incur ought now to be incurred as a duty. It is now no longer necessary to advance in regular lines and step by step. On the contrary, each Division should be given distant objectives which must be reached independently of its neighbour.[60]

Haig repeated this new approach during a discussion with General Byng: 'Now is the time to act with boldness and in full confidence'.[61] On 21 August the British Third Army took Albert and then advanced across the old Somme battlefield in just three days. On 26 August the First Army reached the River Scarpe. Bapaume fell to the New Zealand Division on 29 August and two days later the Australian Corps took the formidable German position of Mont St Quentin near Peronne.

On 12 September the United States First Army carried out the first all-American attack of the war taking the St Mihiel salient near Verdun. They captured 15,000 prisoners and themselves lost 7,000. On 14 September President Wilson sent his congratulations: 'The boys have done what we have expected of them and done it in a way that we most admire.'[62] The French were now making in-roads into the Noyon salient. It was, as Foch had ordered, '*Tout le monde a la bataille!*'.

The Allied advances continued. On 26 September the French Fourth Army and the US First Army, redeployed from St Mihiel to the Argonne, captured the high ground around Montfaucon taking 18,000 prisoners. The BEF was now approaching the strongly defended Hindenburg Line and on 27 September the Canadian Corps of the First Army attacked the Canal du Nord and managed to gain a foothold along a front of 12 miles. The following day Belgian and British troops advanced over the ground that had taken four months to win during the Passchendaele offensive. September ended with what was one of the most dramatic achievements of the war on the Western Front. The British Fourth Army and the French First Army attacked the Hindenburg Line along the St Quentin Canal. The general advance faultered, but a brilliantly improvized assault by the British 46th (South Midland) Territorial Division crossed the canal at Riqueval using lifebelts from Channel steamers and collapsible boats.

They advanced more than three miles into enemy territory.

By 5 October the BEF had taken most of the Hindenburg Line. Panic had seized the German leaders. Ludendorff wanted an immediate armistice and the Reichstag was told that a reasonable peace settlement could only be gained if overtures of peace were made without delay. Prince Max of Baden was appointed Imperial Chancellor. His prime responsibility was to negotiate an armistice. On 25 October Ludendorff was dismissed. During the first week of November the Germans abandoned the Belgian coast; the BEF advanced to Valenciennes and the French and Americans took Mézières and Sedan. Within Germany there were riots and strikes fuelled by despair and shortage of food. The German communist group, the Spartacists, took control of the Berlin Imperial Palace and the Social Democrats announced a Socialist Republic. The High Seas Fleet mutinied. It had all the elements of the 1917 Russian revolution. The Kaiser abdicated on 9 November and two days later the German delegation signed an unconditional armistice at Compiègne. Haig noted in his diary: 'Fine day but cold and dull … The Armistice came into force at 11 am'.[63] The fighting was over.

* * *

During 1918 the BEF had fought with great determination and considerable skill. The German Spring offensives – Michael and Georgette – had tested the endurance of the British troops to the extreme and while much ground had been lost, the battle line was never completely broken. Both in March and April, at Amiens and in Flanders, desperate last ditch efforts had avoided catastrophe. From July onwards the pendulum had swung in the Allies' favour and it was the British army that led the way to victory during the final hundred days of the war.

Haig himself had no doubts about the contribution of the BEF to the defeat of the German army. On 15 November following a discussion between Haig and Foch about the recent advances, Haig noted, somewhat inaccurately, in his diary:

> of the 3 Allied Armies, only the British were fighting and pressing back the Enemy! The French had stopped fighting being exhausted, and divisions very weak in numbers. The Americans had lost the greater part of their trained personnel, and their administrative arrangements had broken down. I therefore come to the conclusion that there remained only the British Army sufficiently strong and determined to get a decision.[64]

Even allowing for Haig's justifiable pride in the achievements of the BEF, their record during the Hundred Days can only be described as outstanding. The British troops had gone from one success to another. The victories at Amiens (8–13 August); Bapaume (21 August–4 September); Havrincourt and Épehy (12–18 September); Cambrai and the Hindenburg Line (7 September–5 October); in Flanders (8 September–14 October); Le Cateau (6–12 October); the Selle (17–25 October); and the Sambre (1–11

November) saw the BEF defeat the German army in the field and caused Foch to deliver the accolade: 'Never at any time in history has the British Army achieved greater results in attack than this unbroken offensive'.[65]

What were the factors behind the survival of the British army during the dark days of March and April and behind its eventual victories during the period August–November? The German Spring Offensives of Michael and Georgette were planned with great care. The techniques of Bruchmüller and von Hutier, honed at Cambrai and Riga, were applied with great destructive effect. The stormtroopers were well trained and armed and both attacks fortuitously benefitted from a thick morning mist which masked their infiltration tactics. The points of attack were favourable to the Germans – in March against the weak Fifth Army whose defences were disorganized and incomplete and, in April, against the demotivated and poorly-led Portuguese troops. The Germans also had the advantages of numbers and of surprise. On both occasions, a breakthrough was a distinct possibility. What stopped the German advance was the same problem that had stopped the advances of both French and British troops during the earlier years of the war: fatigue, loss of men, and the lack of reinforcements and essential materials as the lines of supply and communication became extended to breaking point. Hindenburg later wrote: 'Ammunition could only be brought up in quite inadequate quantities'.[66] Indicative of the supply problem was the shortage of food. A German soldier, Edwin Kuhns, noted in his diary in the last week of March: 'At this time the food got worse … on Easter Sunday, we had nothing except a half a loaf of bread per man'.[67] Ernst Jünger, a Lieutenant in the 73rd Hanoverian Fusilier Regiment, recorded his amazement when he came across provisions in a captured English dugout:

> The dugout was furnished with extreme comfort … There was a whole box of fresh eggs. We sucked a large number on the spot, as we had long since forgotten their very name. Against the walls were stacks of tinned meat, cases of priceless thick jam, bottles of coffee-essence as well, and quantities of tomatoes and onions; in short, all that a gourmet could deserve. This sight I often remembered later when we spent weeks together in the trenches on a rigid allowance of bread, washy soup, and thin jam.[68]

Later, near Cambrai, Jünger again bemoaned the food situation: 'Here, too, we were miserably fed. For a long while there was nothing for supper but gherkins, which the men very drily and aptly named "gardener's sausage".'[69]. German troops plundered captured British supply dumps and delayed their advance to eat and drink. They also took whatever they could find from the bodies of dead British soldiers. Georg Maier of the 1st Bavarian Infantry Regiment wrote: 'We found hundreds of cigarettes in the dead soldiers' knapsacks, along with chocolate, fine biscuits and lots of good things we didn't know any more.'[70] In addition to the shortages of food and drink for the soldiers there was a lack of other necessities – oil, grease, tyres, fuel and spare parts for lorries and fodder for the horses. Michael and Georgette petered out as both troops and supplies became exhausted. German morale was beginning to deteriorate.

A second factor behind both the survival of the BEF in March–April and the advances of August–November was the appointment of General Foch as supreme commander on the Western Front. Haig had instigated the Doullens Conference and he had given his full support to Foch's role as co-ordinator of the Allied forces and, later, as commander-in-chief. Haig's action had averted the potential disaster of separating the French and the British forces as indicated by Petain at the time of the Amiens crisis of 25 March. Foch immediately cancelled Petain's proposal, moved French reinforcements to defend Amiens and ordered that there should be no further retreat. The contrast between Petain's apparent defeatism and Foch's energy and confidence was a much needed boost to Allied morale.

Lloyd George had seen Foch's appointment as a way of controlling Haig. In one sense it did. Foch may have provided reinforcements at Amiens, but he refused to do so during the German Georgette advance in the second week of April. Foch was intent on building up his reserves for an offensive against the Amiens salient and, as things turned out, he was justified in his belief that the British would hold the line. In another sense, Foch's appointment resulted in Haig having a greater freedom of action than he had previously enjoyed under the prying interventions of Lloyd George. Haig's relationship with Foch was established following the BEF success on 8 August. Foch wanted to continue to push forward, but Haig's generals, particularly Rawlinson, considered that the German resistance was hardening and a further attack over the difficult area of the old Somme battlefield would only result in heavy casualties. When, on 10 August, Haig ordered the continuation of the attack, Rawlinson asked: 'Are you commanding the British Army or is Marshal Foch?' It was far from usual for a subordinate to question his superior officer in this challenging and defiant way, especially when the superior officer was also the commander-in-chief. It was a sign of Rawlinson's confidence in his assessment of the situation and also of Haig's readiness to put the implied criticism to one side, and to listen and re-think as the circumstances required. On 14 August Rawlinson showed Haig aerial photographs of the German defences and added that the Canadian commander, Lieutenant General Currie, also thought that a further advance would be too costly. On this basis Haig cancelled the proposed advance and informed Foch. The two generals met at Sarcus the following day and had a difficult conversation. Both Haig and Foch explained their positions. Haig wrote in his diary:

> I spoke to Foch quite straightly, and let him understand that I was responsible for the handling of the British Forces. Foch's attitude at once changed and he said all he wanted was early information of my intentions, so that he might coordinate the operations of the other Armies, and that he thought I was quite correct in my decision not to attack the Enemy in his prepared position.[71]

The meeting at Sarcus determined the Foch-Haig relationship for the rest of the war. Both men had genuine respect for each other and Foch was ready to be influenced by Haig, who was thereafter allowed considerable freedom in planning and carrying out the BEF's successful pursuit of the German army.

The battle tactics employed by the BEF during the Hundred Days had developed to become efficient and highly professional. Infantry, artillery, tanks and aircraft worked together and the BEF emerged, during this period of mobile warfare, as a powerful and effective fighting force. An example of this integrated approach was the attack at Hamel, near Villers-Brettoneux, on 4 July. The attack was carried out by the Australian Corps and four US Army companies under the Australian commander Lieutenant General Sir John Monash. Secrecy and surprise were of paramount importance. The infantry, purposely spread to avoid casualties, was supported by artillery, machine guns, the new Mark V tank and the RAF. A short opening bombardment concentrated on destroying German artillery placements and the infantry then followed a creeping barrage. Over 600 guns of various calibres were employed as part of Monash's effort to reduce the emphasis on infantry and make maximum use of artillery. Apart from some confusion amongst the tanks, the attack was a complete success. The village of Hamel and the surrounding area was taken within ninety minutes. Australian and US casualties were fewer than 1,000 and 1,470 German prisoners were taken. The performance of Monash's troops was so impressive that the Fourth Army Staff circulated a study, published as SS128, of the attack and the reasons for its success. It was a prelude to the 'all-arms' attack at Amiens a month later. General Monash wrote:

> a modern battle plan is like nothing so much as a score for a musical composition, where the various arms and units are the instruments, and the tasks they perform are their respective musical phrases. Each individual unit must make its entry precisely at the proper moment, and play its phrase in the general harmony.[72]

Not all future battle plans, nor their implementation, followed exactly this orchestral analogy, but the principles expressed formed the basis of BEF attacks during the remainder of the war. The context of the attack had also changed from the massive offensives of 1916 and 1917 and, indeed, from the large-scale operations of Michael and Georgette in 1918. During the Hundred Days the BEF carried out no major offensives. There was no major breakthrough. Instead there was constant pressure on various parts of the enemy line which gradually pushed the German army, now at a numerical disadvantage and lacking Reserves, into defeat.

In 1918 the main contribution made by the United States to the war on the Western Front was the fear generated in the minds of the German leaders as they anticipated the arrival of vast quantities of men and material. The very presence of US troops, increasing in numbers by the month, affected German morale adversely. To the dismay of the Allies, however, the contribution of the United States to the fighting in France turned out to be much less than expected. The problem was that when America entered the war in April 1917 their army was small, ill-equipped, inexperienced and inadequately structured. By the end of 1917 only 175,000 men had arrived in France. Conscription was to boost the size of the American army to 3 million, but the recruits had to undergo a lengthy period of training before they were ready for front-line service. In February 1918, immediately before the German Spring Offensives, there was just one American division at the front. It was not until September 1918, at St Mihiel, that American forces fought their first independent operation. Even by the end of the war there were only eighteen divisions on the front line. The total number of American troops in France reached 2 million by November 1918, but of these 1.5 million had arrived during the last six months of the war when the Allies were already gaining the ascendant. The US army also lacked armaments. At St Mihiel it used 3,000 artillery pieces, but not one was made in America. Only fifteen tanks were built in America and the first one arrived in France in October 1918. The American Air Force, largely dependent on the French from whom they received 2,676 aircraft, was only really operational in the final weeks of the war.[73]

There was a further problem. When America entered the war it did so not as one of the Allies but as an 'Associate Power'. Pershing was instructed to co-operate with, but not to amalgamate with, the French or the British units. The rationale was that a distinctive American contribution would give a stronger bargaining position when negotiations took place after the war. Pershing accepted Foch as overall commander, but insisted that the AEF should be treated as an independent army. When Foch and Pershing disagreed about the American role at St Mihiel, Foch was driven to ask: 'Do you wish to take part in the battle?' to which Pershing replied: 'Most assuredly, but as an American Army and no other way'[74] The altercation ended in compromise, though St Mihiel was definitely an American battle. On the other hand there were many occasions, for example at Catigny in May and at Hamel in July, when Pershing relaxed his protest against amalgamation. Around a third of American troops took part in operations alongside French, British and Belgian forces during their time in France.

The Americans understandably lacked the battle experience hard-won by the French and the British and, while fighting with great enthusiasm and courage, learnt tactical lessons the hard way. Pershing still persisted with frontal attacks, as at Belleau Wood in June, and consequently the AEF suffered disproportionately heavy casualties. In total the US army had 320,000 casualties in the war. In October 1918 Haig gave his comments on the US forces to the British War Council: 'The American Army is disorganised, ill-equipped and ill trained. Good officers and NCOs are lacking'.[75] American forces certainly made a contribution to the war effort on the Western Front in 1918, but it fell short of what was anticipated – either by the Allies or the Germans. Had the war continued into 1919, the Americans would have grown in numbers, experience and armaments and the power of the AEF would by then have been irresistible.

At the 18 October meeting Haig also commented about the French and British armies. About the French army he said: 'worn out, and has not been fighting latterly. It has been freely said that "war is over" and "we don't want to lose our lives now that peace is in sight".' About the British army his comment was: 'never more efficient but has fought hard, and it lacks reinforcements. With diminishing effectives, morale is bound to suffer.'[76] In the event, it was the German morale that broke as the BEF pressed forward to victory.

# Conclusion: BEF Development and Victory

*'The unarmed and untrained island nation, who ... had faced unquestioningly the strongest manifestation of military power in human record, had completed its task'.*

*Winston Churchill*[1]

The innumerable changes that shaped the BEF during four and a quarter years of war on the Western Front enabled it to take a leading role in the final victory of November 1918. The BEF of 1918 bore little resemblance to the small force that crossed the Channel in August 1914. In terms of size, there had been a fifteen-fold increase from 125,000 to 1.8 million men, among whom were troops from the Dominions, America, Portugal and Italy. Organizationally, the BEF had grown from a single army made up of two army corps and one cavalry division to five armies made up of nineteen army corps and one cavalry corps. Within the BEF the technical corps (the Artillery, the RFC, the Tank Corps, the Engineers, the Medical Services) had increased in numbers and proportionately. The social composition had changed from a small force of professional volunteers, mainly drawn from the unskilled of the cities, to a combination of volunteers and conscripts from a cross-section of society. The BEF of 1914 was short of equipment of all kinds and, crucially, of guns and munitions. By 1918 all these items were in plentiful supply. British industry had become geared to the demands of war and had made startling advances technically and in quality standards and overall production levels.

The fledgling RFC benefited from improved aircraft design, armaments and tactics so that by 1918 its role had expanded from reconnaissance to strategic bombing. Both the RAF and the Independent Air Force were formed in April 1918 thus emphasizing the importance of supremacy in the air. Between 1916 and 1918 tanks had developed from little more than adapted farm equipment to the fearsome (if not wholly reliable) Mark IV and Mark V machines of Cambrai and the Allied advances of 1918. Artillery had become a war-winning force with dramatically increased fire-power and improved techniques of applying that power. Infantry tactics had moved from massive offensives aimed at making a 'breakthrough' to 'bite and hold' attacks which combined infantry, artillery, aircraft and tanks. By 1918 the BEF had become a formidable 'all-arms' fighting unit.

As the size of the BEF grew it took over increasing stretches of trench line from the French, ending the war with a front of 100 miles extending from Ypres to the Oise, south of the Somme. From being a minor appendage of the French army in 1914 it had become the key element in the victories of 1918. The generals of all the belligerent countries faced challenges that were completely outside their experience, with the BEF generals at a disadvantage in having to deal not only with a new form of warfare but also with the problems of managing a massively expanding army. British generals certainly made mistakes for which they have been castigated mercilessly over the years, particularly for the high casualty figures. It is therefore important, when judging their performance, to compare the death counts of the opposing armies. The British losses were proportionately fewer than those of both Germany and France.[2] And when all is said and done it was the Germans, not the French and British, who were on the losing side in November 1918.

* * *

Of all the factors that determined the development of the BEF between 1914 and 1918 by far the most important was the personal contribution of talented, determined and committed individuals. Lord Haldane created the BEF, the Territorial Force, the Officer Training Corps and also established a General Staff and the role of Chief of the Imperial General Staff. Brigadier General Sir Henry Wilson took Haldane's work a stage further. Working with General Ferdinand Foch, he reached an understanding with the French which determined the opening movements and destination of the BEF. Maurice Hankey produced the War Book which enabled the mobilization of the BEF to take place efficiently and speedily. Lord Kitchener grasped the implications of a European war. His view was that the war would be both long and bloody and that Britain would need to raise and supply an army of millions. Regardless of the later decline in his influence, Kitchener's determination and charisma in the early months of the war made possible a British army that by 1916 had become a significant continental force.

The British aircraft industry owed its origin to the imagination, skill and persistence of enthusiasts such as Roe, de Havilland, Handley Page, Sopwith and the Short brothers. They had scant assistance from the War Office. The work of Sir David Henderson, who commanded the RFC in France at the beginning of the war, was continued by Sir Hugh Trenchard who set the tone and operating ethos of the RFC. His leadership was outstanding and his insistence on constant offensive in the air denied German aircraft access to British air space. His policy may have resulted in heavy RFC casualties, but it saved thousands of lives on the ground and it earned much praise from Haig.

The development of the tank could not have taken place without the efforts of numerous committed individuals. Ernest Swinton, Thomas Tulloch, Maurice Hankey, William Tritton, Walter Wilson and Winston Churchill, among others, played their parts in developing the tank. General Hugh Elles and Lieutenant Colonel John Fuller confirmed its operational potential. It was a long, complicated and hard won process. Although tanks never quite reached the performance they promised, they were nevertheless a formidable weapon in the armoury of the BEF.

The technical and tactical development of artillery was also the result of the ideas and efforts of many gifted gunners and engineers. Brigadier General H.H. Tudor, Major B.F.E. Keeling, Lieutenant A.G. Bates, Major E.M. Jack and Captain H.H.J. Winterbotham were closely involved in developing accurate mapping for use in predicted firing. Captain Harold Hemming, Sir Lawrence Bragg, Charles Darwin, Corporal William Tucker, Lieutenant Lloyd Owen and J.A. Gray were among those who made sound ranging and flash spotting possible and Captain B.T. James, Lieutenant D.S. Lewis and Major W.G.H. Salmond were pioneers of aerial observation.

The growth and critical importance of the Ministry of Munitions cannot be over-emphasized. Lloyd George became Minister of Munitions in May 1915 and gathered around him entrepreneurs and experienced men from industry. These included Eric Geddes, Wilfred Stokes, Chaim Weizman, James Stevenson, Lord Moulton, Lord Chetwynd and the three heads of the Ministry who succeeded Lloyd George – Edwin Montagu, Christopher Addison and Winston Churchill. Without the organizational and motivational skills of these men and the efforts of the thousands who worked for them the BEF could not have developed as it did. The home manufacture of war materials was the prime example of state control and direct civilian involvement in the total war effort.

* * *

The development of the BEF was complex. In terms of a BEF 'learning curve' there was clearly not one curve, but many. Each of the various tactical and technical developments on the Western Front in the infantry, artillery, RFC, tanks, trench warfare and trench weapons – not to mention the developments in industrial inventiveness and performance on the home front – had its own curve. Moreover, these various curves had their own characteristics. Some started later than others; some were steeper than others; some faltered when progress was reversed; and some remained incomplete when the war ended. Nevertheless, the readily identifiable changes that took place in the BEF between 1914 and 1918 indicate a massive and sustained learning effort. Given the fact that Britain was unprepared for a continental war in 1914 and that it soon became clear that Germany might well overpower the French and British forces, it was essential that practical developments should take place. Learning was not optional; it was absolutely essential to survival and victory.

The following putative examples illustrate the different types of learning curve. The BEF generals themselves experienced a somewhat faltering curve in regard to the tactics they employed. For example, in 1915 at Neuve Chapelle and Aubers Ridge they experimented with short opening artillery bombardments to gain surprise. This approach gave way to the longer bombardments at Festubert, Loos and through 1916 and 1917 on the Somme and at Passchendaele which aimed at obliterating the German front line. From mid-1918 there was a return to short surprise bombardments starting at Hamel in July. Even so, this generalized sequence was by no means uniform. Rawlinson opted for a hurricane bombardment on 14 July 1916 on the Somme and in 1917 at both Messines (Plumer) and Cambrai (Byng) short artillery bombardments were successful. Apart from varying the lengths of bombardments the BEF generals had by 1918 learnt to use their artillery more effectively and to combine it with more imaginative infantry tactics. When the 46th Division succeeded brilliantly in breaking the Hindenburg Line at Riqueval in September 1918, it employed the element of surprise, a tremendous concentration of shells (using more heavy guns than on the first day of the Somme on a much narrower frontage), and it devised a novel way of crossing the St Quentin Canal.

Haig's belief that a 'breakthrough' was possible was evident in the 1915 preparations for Neuve Chapelle, Aubers Ridge and Loos as well as in the major offensives of 1916 and 1917. But an alternative approach – 'bite and hold' – was also being discussed. Rawlinson raised the issue as early as Neuve Chapelle and also during the planning of the Somme, but was overruled by Haig. After the first day of the Somme, however, the battle effectively became a series of 'bite and hold' operations. Vimy Ridge and Messines, in 1917, were 'bite and hold' attacks and so were the continual thrusts during the Hundred Days, by which time Haig had become a convert to the 'step by step' approach.[3]

Trench fighting had its own learning curve. Trench raids developed from ad hoc stunts carried out by daredevil volunteers to large, well-planned operations with artillery support. Trench weapons, particularly grenades and mortars, were developed. The Lewis machine gun was introduced in 1915 and the number per battalion increased from eight in 1915, to sixteen in 1916 and to thirty in 1918. The first machine-gun school opened in late 1914 and the Machine Gun Corps, using the heavier Vickers guns, was formed in October 1915. Sniping grew in importance and specialist schools were set up under Major Hesketh-Pritchard.

The defence of the British line had generally relied on a strongly held front trench system. This had also been the German policy under Falkenhayn, but Ludendorff, in late 1916, working from captured French papers, instructed that a defence in depth system should be constructed. Towards the end of 1917, the British, anticipating a German offensive, decided to copy the new

German method of defence. The British effort was a failure. The three-zone configuration and the role of the reserves, as used by the Germans, were misunderstood by GHQ and this gave rise to varied interpretations or plain disregard by British commanders along the front. This situation was far from helpful when the German Spring Offensive began. The nature of this particular learning curve was clearly short and negative.

On the other hand, the tactics for the British infantry attack developed more successfully from the in-line method used widely on the Somme to the adoption of a platoon-centred concept as set out in SS 143 at the end of December 1916. The effectiveness of this approach was not seen fully until late 1917 at Cambrai and during the Hundred Days. By this time the 'all-arms' approach had evolved which included a creeping barrage, predicted artillery bombardments and the use of the RFC and tanks. As might be expected, this formula was not always applied uniformly – some units in the Third Army, for example, used an 'all-arms' approach consistently in the second half of 1918 while other units continued to rely primarily on their artillery.[4] Nevertheless, it was a learning curve that was distinctly positive.

The curves associated with the RFC and with the tanks were of quite different shapes. The RFC curve pursued a generally upward trend. New technology such as wireless, photography, mapping and the Constantinesco gear together with better aircraft, improved training practices and flying tactics brought periods of air superiority. But any curve would have to take account of the pendulum swings of air supremacy in favour of the Germans as they gained the initiative during the Fokker Scourge, the Jagdstaffel squadrons and the Richthofen Circus. The curve may have been upward, but it was very uneven. The tank curve was also positive as the technology developed from the Holt Tractor to Little Willie to Big Willie and to the relatively sophisticated Mark V of 1918. While trending upward, however, the tank curve remained stubbornly shallow. The tank was never a reliable weapon even in 1918.

Probably the most important developments were associated with the technical advances in the artillery. From the traditional practice of gun registration used in 1914, the use of sound-ranging, flash spotting, calibration and improved mapping had made counter-battery work an essential part of any BEF attack and gave the British artillery a distinct advantage by 1918. As the war progressed the 106-model fuse was introduced and a greater range of guns, particularly mortars, and a greater supply of shells, mainly HE and gas, became available. The artillery was eventually supreme on the battlefield and, when integrated with the other arms, it made possible the successes of 1918. Its learning curve was incremental and consistently upwards.

The BEF was in a constant state of change throughout the war. It relied on new ideas for its survival and while most of these ideas originated within the BEF, many were the work of civilians or copied from the French or the Germans. As Lieutenant General Sir Charles Fergusson, commander of III Corps, said in May 1915: 'We cannot win the war unless we kill or incapacitate more of our enemies than they do of us, and if this can only be done by our copying the enemy in his choice of weapons, we must not refuse to do so'.[5] The British use of gas was in response to the German gas initiative at Ypres in 1915. The BEF also borrowed ideas from the French. Artillery sound-ranging was first investigated by the French in October 1914 and was eventually taken up and modified by the British in time for use on the Somme in 1916.

The War Office was not always supportive of technical developments, for example the development of the aeroplane, the tank and the Stokes mortar suffered from War Office delay and parsimony. The same cannot be said of the generals at the front. Far from being technophobes with closed minds, the leaders of the BEF incorporated new developments and new thinking into operating practices. It was obviously in their interests to do so. Practical ideas for improved operating performance were enthusiastically embraced throughout the war. A First Army document of November 1915 was headed 'Some Artillery Lessons to be Learnt'.[6] In March 1915 General Robertson received a report from Major General du Cane, the artillery adviser at GHQ, with the title 'Tactical Lessons of the Battle of Neuve Chapelle and Their Bearing on the Strategic Problem That Confronts Us'.[7] A list of General Staff publications, issued in December 1915, included twenty-four development reports on Military Engineering and Trench Warfare, eighteen on Artillery, ten on Tactics, seven on Machine Guns and six on Aeronautics.[8]

There was no magic date from which a blueprint for the 1918 victories emerged. The 1914 *Field Service Regulations*, anticipating the combined arms attacks of late 1917 and 1918, stated that: 'The full power of an army can be exerted only when all its parts act in close combination'.[9] The Vickers gun was already in use in 1914 and the Lewis gun was at the prototype stage in 1913. A translation of a French document emphasizing the importance of the creeping barrage was publicized throughout the BEF in June 1915.[10] The RFC policy of strategic offensive arose from a joint Anglo-French discussion between General Trenchard and his opposite number, Commandant de Peuty, in autumn 1915. The tank had not been heard of in 1914 and only became operational in September 1916. In July 1918 a BEF experiment took place to improve the delivery of poison gas. The wagons of a train, loaded with 5,000 gas cylinders, were driven to the end of the track and then man-handled as near to the front as possible before the gas was released.[11] It was considered a successful initiative. This list of BEF developments could be extended almost indefinitely. It serves to show how change and innovation were part of an ongoing process aimed at survival and eventual victory. The military competence of the BEF developed as an uneven continuum and was made up of many different learning curves.

Circumstances on the Western Front were constantly changing and new circumstances gave rise to new challenges. The use of gas by the Germans brought about the development, by the British, of the box respirator – a form of protection – which was quickly followed by the French and the Germans. The frequency and severity of battlefield injuries and wounds resulted in many medical advances.[12] The introduction of the Thomas Splint in 1917 stabilized leg fractures and reduced the previously high incidence of death from loss of blood. More sophisticated amputation procedures replaced the 'guillotine' method and this made prosthesis fitting considerably more successful. For the first time in war, a vaccination programme was introduced by the RAMC to combat typhoid, tetanus, diphtheria and meningitis. There was considerable development in plastic surgery. The size of the RAMC grew from fewer than 20,000 in 1914 to over 140,000 by November 1918.

The need for improved communications at the front gave rise to advances in wireless telegraphy and radio telephony with jamming and radio interception coming into use. The technology of wireless communication was never entirely successful during the war, but significant improvements were made. Towards the end of 1915 Captain A.C. Fuller came up with the Fullerphone which scrambled signals and prevented the enemy from intercepting messages. The British Field Trench Set of 1916 developed into the Loop Set and then into the Continuous Wave Set of 1917. In the air, any technical advance by one side had to be offset or superseded by the other. The pendulum of fighter aircraft superiority swung between the belligerents from the Vickers FB5 'Gunbus' to the Fokker 'Eindecker' to the FE2b and Nieuport Scout to the 'D' type Albatros and Halberstadt to the SE5 and Sopwith Camel. The Germans also had to counter the technical advances of the Allies. Improved artillery performance by the British and the French was an important factor in the development of defence in depth by the Germans.

* * *

While Britain was far from prepared for war in 1914, Germany was equipped and ready to take part in a large-scale European conflict. Economically, Germany had neither the world-wide trading connections nor the powerful creditor position of Great Britain. However, its industrial expansion since unification in 1870 had been remarkable. The German economy had moved from being essentially agricultural and rural in the 1870s to become industrial and urban forty years later. Coal production increased from 30 million tons in 1871 to 190 million tons in 1913. In the 1880s Germany doubled its output of steel and almost doubled that of iron. The German railway system was highly developed. Its navy was strong. During the years 1890–1914 the population increased by some 21 million.[13] By 1914 Germany with its large and well-trained army was well positioned to fight a war.

The German army had strong leaders. Falkenhayn, Hindenburg and Ludendorff were all able commanders who introduced new methods and were prepared to take significant risks. During the war they were supported by a series of experienced generals including Kluck, Hutier, Below, Marwitz, and Crown Prince Rupprecht. Colonel Bruchmüller was the foremost artillery commander of the war. Colonel Fritz von Lossberg, Colonel Max Bauer and Captain Hermann Geyer were instrumental in devising the German in depth defence system. Captain Wilhelm Rohr refined the ideas of the French Captain Laffargue and by October 1916 had trained eighteen Stormtrooper battalions. The Germans, like the British and French, circulated instruction manuals based on operational experience – for example, 'Basic Principles for the Conduct of the Defensive Battle in Position Warfare' was issued in December 1916; 'Orders Concerning the Training of Infantry during the Current War', giving increased freedom of action to NCOs, was circulated in January 1917; and 'The Attack in Position Warfare' was issued in January 1918. In terms of technical innovation, the German air service benefitted from the work of the Dutchman Anthony Fokker. Fritz Haber developed the chemical warfare programme which was always in advance of that of the Allies. The flamethrower, primarily a German weapon, was developed by Richard Fiedler before the war. Nor was the courage of the German aviator or soldier in doubt. For every Mannock, McCudden and Ball there was a Richthofen, Boelcke and Immelmann. The British awarded the Victoria Cross and the Germans awarded the Pour Le Merite. With amazingly few exceptions the rank and file in the opposing armies showed fortitude and considerable bravery.

From 1914 until mid-1918 the Allies had been unable to make any significant territorial progress in France or Belgium. In every month from August 1914 until July 1918 the British and French lost more men than the Germans. In every year of the war the Germans killed or captured more officers in the British sector than they lost. The British policy of attrition had only limited success. In 1918 Germany had more men becoming available for military service than the total of their dead in that year and in 1919 the number of available men was even higher than in 1918.[14] In spring 1918 Germany came very close to outright victory on the Western Front. And yet, despite this general situation, four months after the last major German attack of 1918 – that of 15 July in the Rheims area – the war was over. The Allies under Foch performed with great vigour during the Hundred Days and the series of stunning BEF victories, from the Battle of Amiens through to the Battle of the Sambre, brought the fighting to an end and obliged Germany to sue for peace. How did this remarkable achievement come about?

Many factors working together brought about the success of the BEF and the demise of the German army on the Western Front. The most important factor was the deterioration of German morale. This deterioration was caused by the costly failure of the Spring Offensives in 1918 when Germany lost almost a million of its best troops and also by the longer term effects of the 'wearing out' battles of 1916 and 1917 when the German army lost a high proportion of its experienced soldiers and NCOs. In 1918 the replacement soldiers from the rear units were frequently found to be poorly trained and with low morale. The history of the 9th Bavarian Infantry Regiment noted that 'the meagre replacements who trickled slowly from the Home Front were in no way sufficient to fill the holes. Moreover they were up to standard in neither soldierly nor moral qualities and frequently only contaminated the healthy core of soldiers facing the enemy'. Similarly, the GOC of the German 23rd Infantry Division observed in September that as a result of a new draft 'discontent and despondency seem to have been introduced into the Division'.[15] The high expectations held by the German army in March 1918 were unfulfilled. By the summer of 1918 it was clear that Germany could not win the war. In October, Edwin Kuhns, a German soldier, noted in his diary: 'our days were up. We were in retreat'.[16]

The growth of the American Expeditionary Force which, by the end of the war, was larger in size than the BEF, was a further demoralizing factor as the German army realized that the numerical advantage that they had enjoyed in early 1918 no longer applied. The spectre of hundreds of thousands of fresh American troops arriving on the Western Front was indeed a major concern of the German commanders. As Hindenburg observed: 'Thanks to the arrival of the American reinforcements, time was working not for us but against us'.[17] American troops may have fought with enthusiasm and courage, for example at Belleau Wood, Château-Thierry and St Mihiel, but in 1918 they were not war-winners. They lacked equipment and they were short of battle experience. Their contribution to the defeat of the German army was psychological rather than military. From August 1918 the involvement of the Americans meant that things could only improve for the Allies and get worse for the Germans.

For the Germans, neither the problem of numerical strength nor the problem of morale was helped by the influenza pandemic. The pandemic started in May 1918. It affected all the belligerent armies, but it reached the German forces on the Western Front some three weeks earlier than it did the Allied troops. Although the statistics are incomplete, it is likely that German soldiers suffered more than either the British or French with around 580,000 troops affected, to some degree or other, in July.[18]

A generally accepted measure of an army's state of morale is the number of soldiers who surrender. Only from August 1918 did German soldiers give themselves up as prisoners in large numbers. The number of prisoners taken by the British in France was 6,367 in 1914; 6,372 in 1915; 41,200 in 1916; 73,000 in 1917 and 201,600 in 1918.[19] In total some 363,000 Germans surrendered to the Allied forces during the Hundred Days. Of these, the British took 186,000 prisoners, the French 120,000, the Americans 43,000 and the Belgians 14,000. During the same period the Germans surrendered 6,400 guns.[20]

The effect of the British naval blockade was an important element in Germany's defeat, but was not of itself the deciding factor.[21] The blockade caused shortages of much-needed war supplies and of food and other provisions both in Germany and at the front. In March 1918 the meagre rations of the German soldier were in stark contrast to the well-stocked British supply dumps that they captured. In Germany, general rationing had been introduced in 1916 and bread quotas were reduced on a number of occasions. Fertilisers, especially nitrates, were made scarce because of the blockade and crop yields suffered. However, although the average German diet was not particularly balanced (there were around 11,000 Ersatz products) and many went hungry, there was no widespread starvation. One study shows that the per capita consumption of potatoes and fish was higher in 1918 than in 1912–13.[22] The problem was not so much the lack of food. With the interaction between German soldiers back from the front, many of them wounded, and civilians, it was, by autumn 1918, the debilitating knowledge that Germany was losing the war that brought about the food strikes and demonstrations at home. When hopes of victory disappeared, both military and civilian morale began to disintegrate. It is also the case that while certain items important to the conduct of the war were scarce as a result of the blockade – oil, grease, rubber, nitrates and cotton, for example – the German army was never short of guns or ammunition during the Hundred Days.

A key factor in the success of the BEF was its technical and tactical proficiency. It had developed a formidable weapons system. In particular, the artillery operated at peak performance. Guns and shells were readily available and used with a technical skill that enabled it to neutralize enemy guns and support the British infantry as never before. This technical superiority could also be seen in the increasingly important role of other specialist equipment such as the aeroplane, the tank and the extensive use of gas shells. The BEF 'all-arms' tactics did not merely coincide with the resumption of mobile warfare; after years of trench warfare mobile warfare made the employment of such tactics possible.

The successful implementation of the BEF attacks during the Hundred Days was considerably helped by the improved effectiveness of the BEF command, which benefited from the co-ordination of the Entente troops by Marshal Foch following his appointment as Supreme Allied Commander. Haig was given greater freedom of action in deciding BEF priorities and he in turn gave greater freedom to his subordinates. Haig, Rawlinson, Byng, Plumer, Horne, Monash and Currie had gained invaluable experience during the gruelling battles of 1915–17, as had the corps and division commanders, and they were now able to lead their troops during the Hundred Days with increasing confidence. The British Third Army carried out eighteen separate attacks between 21 August and 11 November, each lasting from one to seven days.[23] This freedom of action was not confined to the senior officers. As the XI Corps Commander Lieutenant General Haking wrote to his subordinates in August 1918:

> It is therefore of the highest importance for troops in the front line, first to ascertain immediately any withdrawal, and secondly, to follow-up with the greatest vigour, acting on a pre-arranged plan, and without waiting for any further orders … It is essential that every Battalion and Company Commander should have definite schemes of advance, with definite objective to gain without waiting for orders from anyone … They will not wait for orders but will act on their own initiative directly that they discover the enemy is withdrawing.[24]

The same general made the following statement at his Corps Conference on 28 September: 'the fact that Commanders of all units and formations must realize is the importance of initiative on their part, as it will help enormously in the whole operation if we can get Platoon and Company Commanders to use initiative and go on and take small localities one after another'.[25]

The commanders at various levels responded well and on 24 October Haking acknowledged the example of the 25th Battalion King's (Liverpool) Regiment: 'This Battalion advanced a distance of 30 miles, forced a crossing over the River Scheldt and engaged the enemy on the Eastern banks all within a space of 33 hours, a feat which could not have been surpassed'.[26] It was as though, after the constraints of three and a half years of trench warfare, a great energy had been released within the BEF.

It should be noted that the victories of the Hundred Days were not achieved without considerable losses among the BEF troops. The total number of BEF casualties between 8 August and 11 November was 350,000 – more than during the German offensives earlier in 1918 (240,000) and more than at Passchendaele in 1917 (244,000).[27] Despite the growing realization that the war could not be won, the bulk of the retreating German troops put up a fierce resistance. Victory was not achieved without much bloodshed.

The application of the BEF combined arms tactics coincided with a further factor that hastened the defeat of the German army in the second half of 1918. This was the significant change that had taken place in the extent and nature of the German front line following their advances March–July. The length of front that the Germans were now obliged to defend had much increased. At the beginning of March 1918 the German army had held a front of 250 miles, but by July it had been extended to 370 miles including three major salients at Noyon, Amiens and Merville – areas vulnerable to any determined Allied counter-attack. The heavily fortified defence system used by the Germans so effectively during the previous three and a half years had been abandoned. By summer 1918 German troops along much of their front were defending hastily constructed trenches. Ernst Jünger wrote that his company 'was without support in a front line that was both shallow and narrow, and we were separated from the 76th Infantry Regiment on our right by a large unoccupied gap'.[28] The British Official History described the German defences in front of the British First Army as: 'poor shallow trenches and shell holes … the dugouts were only rough weatherproof shelters, and the wire was salved British material, badly erected, with none in the hedges or ditches'.[29] Hindenburg noted in August 1918 that 'in comparison with 1917, our present defence lines had many defects. In the sector east of Amiens, as on other parts of the front, too much had been said about continuing our offensive and too little about the requirements of defence'. Hindenburg also described how, in September, the German troops 'had now to be thrown from one battle to another ... We had not the men to form a continuous line ... [the enemy] gradually slipped through the many gaps'.[30] As Corporal Elmer Sherwood of the AEF remarked in his diary on 12 September: 'the Boche are surrendering in droves. Surely they must regret giving up these luxurious dugouts and trenches which they have lived in for four years'.[31] Von Lossberg, the German defence expert, had suggested to Ludendorff on 19 July that there should be a withdrawal to the Hindenberg Line, but Ludendorff ignored the advice.[32]

The Germans gradually fell back on their old defence lines, but by then the damage had been done. As German morale collapsed, morale among the BEF troops strengthened. In September the 46th Division broke the strongest German defence position, the Hindenburg Line, with few losses. The Germans in March 1918 had broken the stalemate that had lasted since October 1914. It was the Allies, however, who took the opportunities presented by the changed military circumstances and forced the Germans in Belgium and France to retreat.[33]

A further important factor in Germany's defeat was its failure to harness the full strength of the country's industrial power. Germany had the Hindenburg programme and the Amerikaprogram, but did not develop the equivalent of the all-encompassing British Ministry of Munitions – nor did they have a Lloyd George or a Winston Churchill to push reforms and provide a strong national lead. As Hindenburg himself wrote: 'It was vital to create a common central authority ... some such authority alone would have been able to take far-seeing economic and military decisions ... There was no such authority'.[34] German targets for aircraft production and steel production, for example, were never met. So much steel was used in the construction of new shell factories that there was insufficient steel left to manufacture shells.[35] From July 1918 the monthly output of shells was half that of 1917. The railway system fell into disrepair because of lack of maintenance and coal failed to reach factories in adequate quantities.

A failure of German technical development was its neglect of mechanised transport and tanks. Aircraft development was given priority and the new Fokker all-metal monoplane would have been in a class of its own had not the war ended before that particular project came to fruition. The manufacture of engines was mainly directed at the aircraft industry. Lorries became desperately scarce. Tanks were taken seriously only when it was too late, mainly because the defensive role adopted by the Germans on the Western Front made such a development less necessary. After Cambrai there was a move to build tanks, but only twenty of the lumbering A7Vs were produced – fewer than the sixty-three British tanks which were captured at Cambrai and used by the Germans. Lightweight German tanks in large numbers could well have turned the 1918 Spring Offensive into an outright victory.

It had always been the contention off the Allied military leaders, French, Haig, Joffre and Foch that the war could only be won on the Western Front and they had been proved correct. The main forces of France, Britain, Germany and, latterly, America were concentrated in France and Flanders and it was there that victory was achieved in 1918. With the series of German defeats on the Western Front during the Hundred Days came the collapse of the Central Powers. Bulgaria sought an armistice on 28 September. Turkey followed on 30 October and Austria-Hungary on 3 November. On the night of 7/8 November a German armistice delegation arrived in the Forest of Compiègne. The armistice was finally signed at 5.15 on the morning of 11 November and the news was communicated to all the combatants on the Western Front. At 11 am the war ceased. The German army, defeated but not broken, marched back across the Rhine in good order. Soldiers were greeted with flowers on their return home. On 10 December *The Times* reported that the German Guards Cavalry Division marched down Unter den Linden in Berlin to the sound of the band playing 'Deutchland, Deutchland Uber Alles'. The actual Peace Treaty was agreed at Versailles on 28 June 1919. Marshal Foch was heard to say: 'It is not a peace, it is an armistice for twenty years'.[36] In twenty years another BEF, equally as unprepared as that of 1914, was again in France.

*Appendix*

# Main Events in the First World War 1914–1918

| | *Western Front* | *Other Fronts – Air and Sea* |
|---|---|---|
| **1914** | | |
| June: | | Archduke Franz Ferdinand of Austria assasinated in Sarajevo by Serbian Nationalist, Gavrilo Princip. |
| July: | | Germany promises to support Austria-Hungary in any action it takes against Serbia.<br>Serbia appeals to Russia for help.<br>Russia orders mobilization when Austria-Hungary declares war on Serbia. |
| August: | German troops cross French border.<br>Germany declares war on France and Belgium.<br>Britain declares war on Germany.<br>BEF lands in France.<br>France invades Alsace.<br>France and Britain declare war on Austria-Hungary.<br>German troops invade Belgium.<br>British troops meet Germans at Mons and Le Cateau.<br>British and French troops retreat to the Marne.<br>German advance halted. | Germany invades Poland.<br>German soldiers invade Cape Colony in Africa. British soldiers raid Dar-es-Salaam.<br>Russia invades East Prussia.<br>First RFC Squadrons arrive in France.<br>Britain blockades German ports<br>German troops defeat Russians at Battle of Tannenburg. |
| September: | 'Race to the Sea' begins.<br>French, British and German troops dig in.<br>Trench warfare begins.<br>Germans retreat to the River Aisne.<br>Fierce fighting around Albert. | Austria-Hungary lose 130,000 men at the Battle of Lemberg against Russia.<br>U-9 sinks three British cruisers.<br>HMS *Pathfinder* sunk by U-21. |

| | *Western Front* | *Other Fronts – Air and Sea* |
|---|---|---|
| October: | German troops attack Ypres. Antwerp and Ostend lost to the Germans.<br>British troops move from the Aisne to Flanders. First Battle of Ypres. | Joint German and Austria-Hungary attack against Russia.<br>Turkey joins Central Powers. |
| November: | Germans attack Ypres.<br>Fighting along the Western Front. | German troops invade along the Vistula in Poland.<br>At the Battle of Coronel a British naval squadron is defeated by Germans.<br>British and Indian forces invade Mesopotamia. |
| December: | French make major attack in Champagne.<br>Unofficial Christmas truces along the Western Front. | Hartlepool, Whitby and Scarborough bombarded by German ships. |

**1915**

| | | |
|---|---|---|
| January: | | Russians and Austrians fight in Carpathians.<br>Zeppelins bomb Great Yarmouth and King's Lynn. |
| February: | First Canadian soldiers arrive in France.<br>Heavy fighting around Verdun, Alsace and Arras. | Turks move towards the Suez Canal.<br>Russians driven out of East Prussia.<br>Germans use poison gas for the first time against Russian soldiers.<br>First US shipping loss – the *William P. Frye*.<br>Germany announces unrestricted submarine warfare. |
| March: | Battle of Neuve Chapelle. British attack German lines.<br>French forces attack in Champagne. | Austrians retreat in Carpathians.<br>SS *Falaba* sunk by a German U-boat. |
| April: | Australian government commits itself to the Allies.<br>Second Battle of Ypres. Poison gas used for first time on the Western Front by the Germans. | Turkey massacre some 800,000 Armenians.<br>Italy declares war on Austria. |

| | *Western Front* | *Other Fronts – Air and Sea* |
|---|---|---|
| | | British troops including Australians together with the French invade Gallipoli.<br>Zeppelins bomb East Anglia. |
| May: | Battle of Aubers Ridge when British troops support the French offensive in Artois.<br>Battle of Festubert. | Austrian and German troops gain a major victory at Gorlice-Tarnów in Galicia.<br>First Isonzo Battle in Italy.<br>British liner *Lusitania* sunk off the Irish coast with the loss of 1,195 lives, including 124 Americans.<br>Zeppelins raid London and Southend. |
| June: | | Fierce fighting on the Italian Front along the Isonzo River.<br>Some costly gains at Krithia in Gallipoli. |
| July: | The French make some advances in the Vosges.<br>Germans use flamethrowers at Hooge, Ypres. | German South-West Africa surrenders to British troops.<br>No. 11 Squadron of RFC arrives in France with new Vickers Gunbus.<br>In Mesopotamia British forces reach the River Euphrates.<br>Russia pulls back from Galicia. |
| August: | German attacks in the Vosges and Argonne. | Some German troops transferred from Eastern to Western Front.<br>The liner *Arabic* is torpedoed and sunk off the Irish coast.<br>Gallipoli campaign continues with heavy losses on both sides. Anzacs attack at Suvla Bay with heavy losses. |
| September: | Battle of Loos where British support the French attack in Artois. British use poison gas for the first time.<br>French successes in Champagne. | Germany suffer heavy losses at Pripet Marshes against Russia. |

| | *Western Front* | *Other Fronts – Air and Sea* |
|---|---|---|
| October: | Nurse Edith Cavel is shot by Germans for helping British prisoners to escape. | More fighting on the Isonzo.<br>British and French troops land in Salonica to support Serbia. |
| November: | Trench warfare continues. | Serbia routed by Austrian troops. |
| December: | FM French relieved of post and replaced by Sir Douglas Haig. | In Mesopotamia the Siege of Kut where British troops surrounded.<br>Gallipoli campaign abandoned. |
| **1916** | | |
| January: | Conscription introduced in Britain. | Several attempts made to relieve Kut.<br>German troops in the Cameroons surrender to Allied forces. |
| February: | Battle of Verdun begins and lasts for ten months. | Fighting continues on the Italian Front on the Isonzo. |
| March: | Heavy fighting at Verdun. | The French cross-Channel steamer *Sussex* is torpedoed. |
| April: | Easter Rising in Ireland.<br>Kitchener asks US to send troops to Europe. | British troops at Kut surrender.<br>America demands cessation of unlimited submarine warfare. Germany conforms. |
| May: | Leaders of Easter Rising executed. | Battle of Jutland takes place. German Fleet remains in harbour for rest of war. |
| June: | Lord Kitchener dies when HMS *Hampshire* is sunk by a mine. | Bruslov offensive begins in Galicia.<br>Arabs revolt against the Turks supported by British. |
| July: | Battle of the Somme begins.<br>Attack at Fromelles. | Middle East Brigade of RFC formed. |
| August: | Fierce fighting on the Somme.<br>Falkenhayn replaced by Hindenburg and Ludendorff. | Italians victorious at Battle of Gorizia.<br>Romania enters war on the side of the Allies. |

| | *Western Front* | *Other Fronts – Air and Sea* |
|---|---|---|
| September: | British tanks used for the first time at Flers on the Somme. | Dar es Salaam surrenders to the British. T.E. Lawrence leads Arab troops against the Turks.<br>First German airship shot down over Britain. |
| October: | | Romanians severely defeated by Austro-German attacks.<br>Germany resumes U-boat attacks. |
| November: | Battle of the Somme ends. | First German aeroplane raid on Britain. |
| December: | Lloyd George succeeds Asquith as Prime Minister.<br>Battle of Verdun ends. | |

**1917**

| | | |
|---|---|---|
| January: | | The German Zimmerman Telegram is intercepted. |
| February: | German troops fall back to the Hindenburg Line. | Kut is evacuated by Turks and occupied by the British. |
| March: | | Revolution in Russia. Tsarist regime overthrown. |
| April: | Offensive of Gen Nivelle begins on Chemin des Dames.<br>Vimy Ridge taken by Canadians.<br>French offensive fails and mutinies in French army. | America declares war on Germany.<br>General Pershing to command American troops.<br>Lenin arrives in Petrograd.<br>Germany declares unrestricted submarine warfare. |
| May: | | Britain introduces convoy system to protect merchant ships. |
| June: | General Pershing and Staff arrive in England. | Heavy fighting in Italy where Italian troops forced back from Gorizia. |

| | *Western Front* | *Other Fronts – Air and Sea* |
|---|---|---|
| | Battle of Messines begins with explosion of 19 mines.<br>First US troops land in France. | Germany bomb London using Gotha aircraft. |
| July: | British Royal Family changes name to Windsor.<br>Third Battle of Ypres (Passchendaele) begins. | Russian offensive in Galicia fails.<br>Gothas raid London.<br>Arabs with T. E. Lawrence capture Aqaba. |
| August: | French regain all land lost to the Germans in 1916 at Verdun. | In Italy the eleventh Battle of Isonzo begins. |
| September: | British make some gains at Zonnebeke and Polygon Wood. | Russia defeated at Riga. |
| October: | Mata Hari, accused of spying for Germany, is shot.<br>Fighting continues towards Passchendaele Ridge. | Italian troops routed at Caporetto.<br>Fall back to Piave River.<br>Eleven Zeppelins carry out last airship raid on Britain.<br>Revolution in Russia.<br>Bolshevik Government formed. |
| November: | Passchendaele captured by Canadians.<br>Battle of Cambrai. | Gaza captured by General Allenby. |
| December: | | Jerusalem surrenders to General Allenby.<br>Bolshevik government arranges armistice with Germany. |

**1918**

| | | |
|---|---|---|
| January: | Germans transfer troops from the Eastern Front to the West. | The US President Wilson puts forward his 'Fourteen Points' for peace.<br>Austro-Hungarian Navy mutinies. |
| February: | Sir Henry Wilson replaces Sir William Robertson as British CIGS. | British forces take Jericho. |
| March: | Germany starts its Spring Offensive with Operation Michael.<br>First British 'Whippet' tanks used. | Treaty of Brest-Litovsk signed between Germany and Russia. |

| | *Western Front* | *Other Fronts – Air and Sea* |
|---|---|---|
| April: | Germany continues its offensive with Georgette.<br>General Foch appointed commander-in-chief of Allied forces on Western Front. | Royal Air Force founded.<br>Richthofen, the Red Barron, shot down and killed. |
| May: | Germans launch 'Blucher' attack.<br>US troops take part for first time in battle. | Germany makes last air raids on Britain. |
| June: | US troops suffer heavy losses but hold Germans at Château-Thierry and Belleau Wood. | British Independent Air Force formed to carry out strategic bombing. |
| July: | German Friedensturm attack fails.<br>Battle of Le Hamel.<br>Allied counter-attack begins. | In Italy an Austrian offensive defeated by joint Italian, French and British forces.<br>Tsar Nicholas II and family shot by Bolsheviks. |
| August: | Battle of Amiens. Germans pushed back.<br>'Black Day' for German army.<br>French troops drive Germans from Aisne. | Allied troops assist anti-Bolsheviks at Vladivostok. |
| September: | Germans fall back to Hindenburg Line.<br>Battle of St Mihiel – first major US offensive.<br>Hindenburg Line broken at St Quentin. | Bulgaria surrenders.<br>British and Arab troops take Damasus.<br>RAF aircraft in Palestine destroy Turkish Seventh Army. |
| October: | German army continues to retreat along length of Western Front.<br>British troops reach River Scheldt.<br>General Ludendorff resigns. | Italians have success at Vittorio Veneto.<br>Italy freed of invaders.<br>German sailors of the High Seas Fleet refuse to engage British Fleet.<br>Turkey signs armistice. |
| November: | Central Powers collapse.<br>Austria-Hungary signs armistice.<br>Kaiser Wilhelm II abdicates.<br>Armistice signed by Germans. | The German forces in East Africa surrender.<br>German Fleet mutinies at Kiel.<br>The High Seas Fleet surrenders. |

# Notes

**Introduction**

1. For example, John Laffin, *British Butchers and Bunglers of World War One*, Alan Sutton, Stroud, 1992 and Alan Clark, *The Donkeys*, Pimlico edn, London, 1993. Useful comment on the vast amount of literature condemning British generals can be found in: Alex Danchev, 'Bunking and Debunking. The Controversies of the 1960s', in Brian Bond, ed., *The First World War and British Military History*, Clarendon Press, Oxford, 1991, pp. 263–288; John Terraine, 'Understanding', *Stand To!* No. 34, 1992, pp. 7–12; Gary Sheffield, *Forgotten Victory*, Headline Books, London, 2001; Ian Beckett, *The Great War, 1914–1918*, Longman, 2001, pp. 462–65.
2. Winston S. Churchill, *World Crisis 1916–1918*, Thornton Butterworth, London, 1927, Part I, p. 62.
3. Len Thomas, Letter in *Stand To!*, Summer 1983, No. 8, p. 26.
4. Lloyd George, *War Memoirs*, Odhams Press Limited, London, 1936, Vol. II, p. 1366.
5. Winston S. Churchill, *The World Crisis 1916–1918*, Part II, p. 564.
6. Lloyd George, *War Memoirs*, Vol. II, p. 1588.
7. For example, Trevor Wilson, *The Myriad Faces of War*, Polity Press, Cambridge, 1986: Tim Travers, *The Killing Ground*, Pen & Sword Military Classics, Barnsley, 2003: Tim Travers, *How the War was Won*, Routledge, London, 1994: Gary Sheffield, *Forgotten Victory. The First World War: Myths and Realities*, Headline Books, London, 2001: Simon Robbins, *British Generalship on the Western Front 1914–1918*, Routledge, London, 2005.
8. Paddy Griffith, *Battle Tactics of the Western Front. The British Army's Art of Attack 1916–1918*, Yale University Press, New Haven, 1994, p. 199.
9. Gary Sheffield, *Forgotten Victory*, p. 237.
10. Paddy Griffith, *Battle Tactics of the Western Front*, p. 200.
11. For example, Tim Travers, *How the War was Won*, pp. 175–183 and G.C. Wynne (on defensive tactics), *If Germany Attacks: The Battle in Depth in the West*. Tom Donovan Editions, Brighton, 2008, p. 240.

**Chapter 1**

1. *Mr Punch's History of the Great War*, Cassell and Co. Ltd, London, 191, p. 6.
2. The figures relating to the size of the German and French forces are variously stated by John Terraine, *White Heat: The New Warfare 1914–18*, BCA, London, 1982, p. 21; Niall Ferguson, *The Pity of War*, Penguin Books, London, 1998, pp. 91–2; Philip J. Haythornethwaite, *The World War One Source Book*, Arms and Armour Press, London, 1992, pp. 173, 193.
3. These periods of service applied to the Infantry. The artillery periods of service were – six with the colours and six in reserve; the Household Cavalry – eight and four; and the Foot Guards – three and nine.
4. Matthew Richardson, 'Tigers at Bay? The Leicestershire Regiment at Armentières', in *Stand To!*, No. 69, January 2004, p. 9, The Western Front Association.
5. See Philip J. Haythornethwaite, *The World War One Source Book*, Arms and Armour Press, London, 1992, p. 219.
6. Colonel H.C.B. Rogers, *Artillery Through the Ages*, Seely Service and Co., London, 1971, p. 156.
7. Trevor Wilson, *The Myriad Faces of War*, p. 22.

8. General Sir Percy Radcliffe, 'With France', in *Stand To!* Spring 1984 No. 10, pp. 6–12.
9. Robin Neillands, *The Old Contemptibles*, John Murray, London, 2004, pp. 72–3.
10. FM Lord Carver, *Britain's Army in the Twentieth Century*, Pan Books/IWM, London, 1999 edn, p. 29.
11. Peter Simkins, 'The Four Armies', in *The Oxford History of the British Army*, eds D.G. Chandler and Ian Beckett, OUP, 2003 edn, p. 236.
12. Quoted in Philip Magnus, *Kitchener: Portrait of an Imperialist*, Penguin Books, Harmondsworth, 1968 edn, p. 339.
13. See Martin Middlebrook, *Your Country Needs You*, Pen & Sword Books, Barnsley, 2000.
14. FM Lord Carver, *Britain's Army in the Twentieth Century*, p. 40.
15. Ian F.W. Beckett, *The Great War: 1914–1918*, p. 213.
16. Quoted in *The First World War*, ed. Jon E. Lewis, Constable and Robinson Ltd, London, 2014 edn, p. 84.
17. Ian F.W. Beckett, *The Great War: 1914–1918*, p. 212.
18. Harry Fellows, '1914 The Memoirs of a Volunteer', in *Stand To!,* Summer 1984, No. 10, p. 34.
19. Quoted in Paul Cobb, 'William Maslin's Four Years with the British Army – Part I' in *Stand To!* January 2015, No. 102, p. 27, The Western Front Association.
20. Joe Beard, 'One Man's War', in *Stand To!* Spring 1992, No. 34, p. 33, The Western Front Association.
21. *Bucks Herald*, 7 November 1914.
22. Martin Middlebrook, *The First Day of the Somme*, Penguin Books, Harmondsworth, 1971, p. 13.
23. FM Sir John French, *1914*, Constable & Co., London, 1919, p. 294.
24. For a complete Order of Battle of British Infantry units on the Somme on 1 July 1916 listing the corps, divisions, brigades and battalions involved, see Martin Middlebrook, *The First Day on the Somme*, Appendix 1.
25. Roni Wilkinson, *Pals on the Somme*, Pen & Sword Books, Barnsley, 2008 edn, p. 62.
26. FM Lord Carver, *Britain's Army in the Twentieth Century*, p. 40.
27. Ray Westlake, *Kitchener's Army*, Spellmount, Stroud, 1989, pp. 30 and 32.
28. To Egypt in December 1915 as part of the 31st Division. See Richard Holmes, *The Western Front*, BBC Books, London, 1999, p. 54.
29. See Lietenant Colonel G. Christie-Miller DSO, MC, *The Second Bucks Battalion 1914–1918: An Unofficial Record*, Bucks Centre for Local Studies, Aylesbury.
30. Richard Holmes, *Soldiers*, Harper Press, London, 2011, p. 195.
31. Martin Middlebrook, *Your Country Needs You*, p. 45.
32. See Stephen Cooper, *The Final Whistle*, Spellmount, Stroud, 2013, pp. 21–23. Also, Anthony Seldon and David Walsh, *Public Schools and The Great War*, Pen & Sword Military, Barnsley, 2013.
33. Peter Parker, *The Old Lie*, Constable, London, 1987, p. 159, fn 1.
34. Robert Graves, *Goodbye to All That*, Penguin Books, Harmondsworth, p. 70.
35. Michael Senior, *Fromelles 1916*, Pen & Sword Books, Barnsley, 2011, Ch 3.
36. TNA, CAB 45/120.
37. This was a problem that faced all the major combatants. 180 French generals were dismissed by December 1914; 217 Italian generals were 'torpedoed' (silurato) by General Cardona before his own dismissal in 1917; and thirty-three German generals were dismissed following the failure of their 1914 campaign in France. See Ian F.W. Beckett, *The Great War 1914–1918*, p. 162.
38. Simon Robbins, *British Generalship on the Western Front 1914–1918*, Routledge, Abingdon, 2005, pp. 51–67.
39. TNA, WO 256/4. Diary of Sir Douglas Haig.
40. FM Sir John French, *1914*, Constable & Co., London, 1919, p. 272.
41. Charles Messenger, *Call to Arms*, Cassell, London, 2006, p. 305.
42. G. Goold Walker, *The Honourable Artillery Company 1537–1987*, Armoury House, London, 1986 edn, p. 268.

43. Simon Robbins, *British Generalship on the Western Front 1914–1918*, p. 85.
44. Lietenant Colonel G. Christie-Miller, *The Second Bucks Battalion 1914–1918.*
45. Hew Strachan, *The First World War*, Vol. 1, OUP, Oxford, 2001, p. 277.
46. Niall Ferguson, *The Pity of War*, p. 531, fn 125.
47. Ibid., p. 103.
48. Named after Lord Derby who, in October 1915, had been appointed Director-General of Recruiting.
49. Ilana R. Bet-El, *Conscripts: The Lost Legions of the Great War*, Sutton Publishing, Stroud, 1999, pp. 9–11.
50. Peter Simkins, 'The Four Armies' in *The Oxford History of the British Army*, eds D.G. Chandler and Ian Beckett, OUP, Oxford, 2003 edn, p. 252.
51. Ian F.W. Beckett, *The Great War: 1914–1918*, p. 218.
52. *Dictionary of National Biography* (DOB), OUP, 2004. Vol. 24, p. 518.
53. Charles Messenger, *The Call to Arms*, p. 16.
54. Trevor Wilson, *The Myriad Faces of War*, p. 198.
55. DNB, OUP, Vol. 59, p. 561.
56. Idem, p. 561.
57. Robin Neillands, *The Old Contemptibles*, p. 51.
58. FM Sir Henry Wilson, *Military Correspondence 1918–22*, ed. Keith Jeffery, Army Records Society. Bodley Head, London, 1985, p. 120.
59. David Lloyd George, *Memoirs*, pp. 75–6.
60. G. Sheffield and J. Bourne, *Douglas Haig: War Diaries and Letters 1914–18*, Weidenfeld & Nicolson, London, 2008, p. 55.
61. A.V. Sellwood, *The Saturday Night Soldiers*, Woolfe Publishing, London, 1974, p. 19.
62. Report of the Committee on the *Lessons of the Great War*, War Office, London, 1932, p. 39.
63. John Keegan and Andrew Wheatcroft, *Who's Who in Military History*, Routledge, London, 2007 edn, p. 154.
64. *Speaking for Themselves: Letters between Clementine and Winston Churchill*, ed. Mary Soames, Black Swan Books, London, 1999, p. 144.
65. Quoted in Richard Holmes, *Soldiers*, p. 49.

**Chapter 2**

1. Francis Quarles 1592–1644.
2. See Ian Beckett and Steven J. Corvi (eds), *Haig's Generals*, Pen & Sword Military Books, Barnsley, 2006.
3. Simon Robbins, *British Generalship on the Western Front 1914–18*, Appendix 2, p. 204.
4. J.P. Lethbridge, *Like Father, Like Son*, in *Stand To!* , No. 68, September 2003, p. 13.
5. See 'The Territorial Force on the Western Front in Early 1915', Bill Mitchison, in the Western Front Association *Bulletin*, July 2015, No. 102, p. 9.
6. See Robbins, *British Generalship on the Western Front 1914–1918*, pp. 4–6.
7. Robbins, *British Generalship on the Western Front 1914–1918*, Appendices 4, 7 and 9.
8. Sir Edward Llewellyn Woodward, *Great Britain and the War of 1914–1918*, Methuen, London, 1967, pp. xvii–xx.
9. *Douglas Haig: The Preparatory Prologue Diaries & Letters 1861–1914*, ed. Douglas Scott, Pen & Sword Militay, Barnsley, 2006, p. 60.
10. Sheffield and Bourne, *Haig's Diaries and Letters*, p. 218.
11. Ibid., pp. 165–66.
12. Richard Holmes, *The Little Field Marshal*, p. 1.
13. Quoted in Robbins, *British Generalship on the Western Front 1914–1918*, p. 13.
14. John Terraine, *The Smoke and Fire*, Book Club Associates, London, 1981 edn, p. 74.
15. Ian W. Beckett, *The Great War 1914–1918*, p. 162.
16. *British Infantry Tactics and the Attack Formation* by an Adjutant of Militia, Mitchel & Co., Charing Cross, 1880, p. 14.

17. Forbes, Macgahen, et al. 'The War Correspondent of the Daily News', 3rd edn, London, 1878, p. 368. Quoted in Paddy Griffiths, *Forward to Battle*, Anthony Bird publications, Chichester, 1981, p. 64.
18. Notebook of H.C. Potter held at the RMA Sandhurst.
19. Colonel G.F.R. Henderson, *The Science of War*, Longmans, Green & Co., London, 1908, p. 73.
20. *Field Service Regulations*, War Office, London, 1905.
21. A.E. Altham, *The Priciples of War Historiclly Illustrated*, London, 1914, p. 195. Quoted in Michael Howard, 'Men against Fire: The Doctrine of the Offensive 1914' in Peter Paret (ed.) *Makers of Modern Strategy*, Clarendon Press, Oxford, 1986, p. 510.
22. TNA WO 279/496. Report on a Conference of General Staff Officers at the Staff College, 17–20 January 1910.
23. *Field Service Regulations 1909*, War Office, London, Sections 99, 100 and 105.
24. Brigadier General R.C.B. Haking, *Company Training*, Hugh Rees Ltd, London, 1913, ch. II.
25. *Field Service Regulations 1909*, Part I Operations, War Office, London, 1914 edn.
26. See Tim Travers, 'Technology, Tactics and Morale, Jean Bloch, the Boer War and British Military Theory 1900–1914' in the *Journal of Modern History*, 51, 1979, p. 275.
27. Ian Hamilton, *A Staff Officer's Scrapbook*, 2 Vols, Edward Arnold, London, 1907, Vol. II, p. 48.
28. Tim Travers, 'Technology, Tactics and Morale', pp. 264–286.
29. Idem, p. 275.
30. General F. von Bernhardi, *On War Today*, 2 Vols, London 1912, Vol. II, p. 53. See Michael Howard, Makers of Modern strategy.
31. *The Memoirs of Marshal Joffre*, Geoffrey Bles, London, 1932, p. 32.
32. F.N. Maude, *The Evolution of Military Tactics*, London, 1905. Quoted in Michael Howard, 'Men Against Fire', p. 521.
33. TNA WO 279/25.
34. FM Viscount French of Ypres, *1914*, pp. 13–15.
35. See Trevor Wilson, *The Myriad Faces of War*, p. 44.
36. FM Viscount French of Ypres, *1914*, pp. 13–15.
37. Hew Strachan, *The First World War*, Simon & Schuster, London, 2003, pp. 135–7.
38. Major B.T. Wilson, *Studies of German Defences Near Lille*, Chatham, 1919. Quoted in a Report on Fromelles carried out by Peter Barton in 2007 for the Australian Army History Unit (unpublished).
39. Idem, Endnote 38, p. 43. Endnote 39, p. 45. Refers to the Barton Report.
40. BOH, *Military Operations France and Belgium 1915*, Vol. I, Compiled by Edmonds and Wynne, MacMillan & Co., London, 1927, p. 66.
41. Winston S. Churchill, *The World Crisis 1916–1918*, Pt I, p. 65.
42. BOH, *France and Belgium*, *1915*, Vol. I, p. 61.
43. BOH, *France and Belgium*, *1915*, Vol. I, p. 60.
44. This body, made up from members of the Cabinet together with military advisers, changed its name several times during the war. It became the Dardanelles Committee, then the War Committee and, under Lloyd George, the War Cabinet. Its function, to direct the war, remained the same.
45. David Lloyd George, *War Memoirs*, p. 222.
46. Idem, p. 248.
47. BOH, *Military Operations France and Belgium 1915*, Vol. I, p. 65.
48. FM Viscount French of Ypres, *1914*, p. 317.
49. Haig's Diary 28 March 1915. Quoted in John Terraine, *Douglas Haig: The Educated Soldier*, Leo Cooper, London, 1990 edn, p. 135.
50. *The Military Correspondence of FM Sir William Robertson*, ed. David R. Woodward, Army Records Society, The Bodley Head Ltd, London, 1989, p. 25.
51. Sheffield and Bourne, *Haig's Diaries and Letters*, p. 339.
52. Niall Ferguson, *The Pity of War*, pp. 300–1.
53. See Winston S. Churchill, *The World Crisis 1916–18*, pp. 36–62.

54. David Lloyd George, *War Memoirs*, Vol. II, p. 1405.
55. See William Philpot, *Bloody Victory*, Abacus, London, 2010, p. 596.
56. FM von Hindenburg, *The Great War*, ed. Charles Messenger, Greenhill Books, London, 2006, p. 100.
57. Quoted in William Philpot, *Bloody Victory*, p. 599.
58. Idem, p. 453.
59. Quoted in Robert Neillands, *The Great War Generals on the Western Front 1914–18*, Robinson, London, 1999, p. 297.
60. *War Diaries and Letters*, ed. Jon E. Lewis, Robinson Publishing, London, 1998, p. 319.
61. See Trevor Wilson, *The Myriad Faces of War*, pp. 348–52.
62. John Terraine, *Douglas Haig: The Educated Soldier*, Leo Cooper, London, 1990 edn, p. 183.
63. See John Terraine, *The Smoke and the Fire*, p. 57.
64. Winston S. Churchill, *The World Crisis 1916–1918*, Pt I, pp. 36–62.
65. Niall Feguson, *The Pity of War*, p. 299.
66. David Lloyd George, *War Memoirs*, Vol. II, p. 2014.
67. See Richard Holmes, *The Western Front*, BBC Books, London, 1999, p. 141.
68. Quoted in 'Haig and the Government' in *Haig: A Re-appraisal 80 Years On*, eds Brian Bond and Nigel Cave, Pen & Sword Books, Barnsley, 2009 edn, p. 111.
69. Lloyd George, *WarMemoirs*, Vol. II, p. 2016.

**Chapter 3**

1. Lloyd George, *War Memoirs*, Vol. II, p. 1588.
2. The numbers are, approximately; BEF –160,000; RAF – 300,000. (All theatres).
3. The Wright brothers were very reluctant to give information about their invention, but, nevertheless, Lieutenant Colonel John Capper, who visited the Wrights, recommended the machine to the British army.
4. Sir Peter Thompson, *The Royal Flying Corps*, Hamish Hamilton, London, 1968, p. 20.
5. Ian Mackersey, *No Empty Chairs*, Hachette UK, London, 2012, p. 9.
6. See Ferguson, *The Pity of War*, p. 164.
7. See Bernard Bergonzi, *Heroes' Twilight*, Macmillan Press, London, 1980, p. 27.
8. J.M. Bruce, *The Aeroplanes of the Royal Flying Corps*, MacDonald & Co., London, 1970, p. xiii.
9. Idem, p. xiii.
10. Quoted in John Terraine, 'World War One and the Royal Air Force' in *Royal Air Force Historical Society Proceedings*, 12 September 1994, p. 12.
11. France was in much the same state. Holland became a major supplier of these items.
12. Maurice Baring, *Flying Corps Headquarters 1914–1918*, Buchan and Enright, London, 1985, p. 198.
13. Christopher Campbell, *Aces and Aircraft of World War I*, Treasure Press, London, 1984, p. 9.
14. Thompson, *The Royal Flying Corps*, p. 27.
15. M. Prevost on a Deperdussin at 126mph; A. Seguin in a Henri Farman over 634 miles; and G. Legagneux in a Nieuport at 20,000ft.
16. Baring, *Flying Corps Headquarters*, p. 28.
17. Idem, p. 192.
18. Derived from Appendix XXVII of *The War in the Air*. Due to a series of accidents in 1912 the monoplane fell into disrepute.
19. IWM, 73/235/1. Papers of Lt Y.E.S. Kirkpatrick.
20. IWM, 80671. P.E. Butcher, *Skill and Devotion*.
21. IWM, 86/48/1. Papers of Captain C.A. Brown.
22. The Maurice Farman Longhorn was so-called because it had a forward elevator between long skids at the front of the plane. The Shorthorn was without this characteristic.
23. IWM, 87/55/1. Papers of Captain F.C. Ransley.
24. IWM, 90/32/1. Papers of Lieutenant C.A. Box.
25. IWM, 84/31/1. Papers of Lieutenant A.J. Robinson.

26. Denis Winter, *The First of the Few*, Penguin Books, Harmondsworth, 1983, p. 36.
27. IWM, 79/25/1. Papers of Lieutenant C.E. Young.
28. Mackersey, *No Empty Chairs*, p. 71.
29. Winter, *The First of the Few*, p. 37.
30. Lord French, *The Complete Despatches 1914–1916*, p. 12.
31. Edmonds, *Military Operations France and Belgium 1914*, Vol. I, p. 420.
32. Nicholas C. Watkis, *The Western Front from the Air*, Wrens Park Publishing, Stroud, 2000, p. 10.
33. Idem, p. 12.
34. TNA, AIR 1/724/91/6/1. J. Jefford, *Corps Reconnaissance 1914–18*, in the RAF Historical Journal 54 (2013), Windrush Group. I am indebted to Air Marshal Sir Michael Simmons for this reference. The numbers of prints were: 1915 estimate 80,000; 1916 – 552,453; 1917 – 3,925,169; 1918 – 5,946,096.
35. Michael Ashcroft, 'Inside the First World War', *The Telegraph*, 1 December 1913, p. 10.
36. Thompson, *The Royal Flying Corps*, p. 44.
37. Idem, p.65.
38. Idem, p. 65.
39. Analysis derived from Appendix XXXIII of Jones, *The War in the Air*, Clarendon Press, Oxford, 1922.
40. IWM, Papers of Lieutenant H.G. Holman.
41. IWM, Acc 15726/18 (410 249/3. Illingworth and Robson, *History of No. 24 Squadron*, p. 28.
42. Cecil Lewis, *Sagittarius Rising*, Penguin Books, Harmondsworth, 1983, p. 59.
43. IWM, 52054. Verses from C.H. Ward Jackson and Leighton Lucas, *The Airman's Song Book*, p. 14.
44. Thompson, *The Royal Flying Corps*, p. 46.
45. See Nigel Steel and Peter Hart, *Tumult in the Clouds*, Hodder ad Stroughton, London, 1997, pp. 26, 58–9.
46. See Campbell, *Aces and Aircraft of World War I*, pp. 140–41.
47. Thompson, *The Royal Flying Corps*, p. 60.
48. Idem, p. 71.
49. Idem, p. 106.
50. Developed by a Rumanian mining engineer named Georges Constantinesco in partnership with a British artillery officer Major G.C. Colley.
51. Cecil Lewis, *Sagittarius Rising*, p. 156.
52. Idem, p. 125.
53. Jones, *The War in the Air*, Vol. 4, p. 316.
54. Trevor Wilson, *The Myriad Faces of War*, p. 608.
55. Baring, *Flying Corps Headquarters 1914–1918*, p. 45.
56. Idem, p. 115.
57. Bruce Lewis, *A Few of the First*, p. 24. I am indebted to Francis Hanford for this reference.
58. Trenchard, 'Future Policy in the Air', September 1916. Quoted in Thompson, *The Royal Flying Corps*, p. 133.
59. Trenchard, 'The Employment of the Royal Flying Corps in Defence', January 1918. Quoted in Thompson, *The Royal Flying Corps*, p. 140.
60. Sheffield and Bourne, *Haig's Diaries and Letters 1914–1918*, p. 212.
61. Idem, p. 232.
62. Cecil Lewis, *Sagittarius Rising*, p. 88.
63. Quoted in Baring, *Flying Corps Headquarters*, p. 264.
64. Quoted in Duff Cooper, *Haig*, Vol. II, p. 213.
65. Trevor Wilson, *The Myriad Faces of War*, p. 609.
66. William van der Kloot, *World War One Fact Book*, Amberley Publishing, Stroud, 2010, p.62.
67. Cecil Lewis, *Sagittarius Rising*, p. 48.
68. David Jordan, 'The Battle for the Skies. Sir Hugh Trenchard as Commander of the Royal Flying Corps', in Hughes and Seligman, *Leadership in Conflict 1914–1918*, p. 72.
69. See Nigel Steel and Peter Hart, *Tumult in the Clouds*, pp. 133 and 397.

70. Of these 'aces', only Bishop survived the war. The German 'aces' Boelcke, Immelmann and Richthofen were all killed in the war.
71. Beckett, *The Great War 1914–1918*, p. 257.
72. See Jordan, 'The Battle of the Skies. Sir Hugh Trenchard as Commander of the Royal Flying Corps', pp. 79–87.

**Chapter 4**

1. Miles and Edmonds, *Military Operations France and Belgium 1916*, Vol. II (IWM/Battery Press, Nashville, 1992 edn), p. 248, fn 3.
2. John Glanfield, *Devil's Chariots*, (Sutton Publishing, Stroud, 2001), Chapter One.
3. Idem, p. 6.
4. Miles and Edmonds, *Military Operations in France and Belgium 1916*, Vol. II, p. 245.
5. Glanfield, *Devil's Chariots*, p. 22.
6. TNA, MUN 5/210/1940/13.
7. Bod MS, Asquith 14, Fols 7–10, Churchill to Asquith, 2.1.15.
8. TNA, MUN 5/210/1940/13
9. See Trevor Wilson, *The Myriad Faces of War*, (Polity Press, Cambridge, 1988 edn), p. 341.
10. See Miles and Edmonds, *Military Operations France and Belgium*, *191*6, Vol. II, p. 249.
11. See Trevor Wilson, *The Myriad Faces of War*, p. 343.
12. Winston S. Churchill, *The World Crisis 1916–1918*, Part I, p. 186.
13. Miles and Edmonds, *Military Operations in France and Belgium 1916*, Vol. II. p. 233.
14. Idem, p. 300.
15. Quoted in Richard Holmes, *The Western Front*, p. 137.
16. Quoted in David Fletcher, *Tanks and Trenches*, (Sutton Publishing, Stroud, 1998 edn), p. 12.
17. Idem, p. 12.
18. See Glanfield, *Devil's Chariots*, p. 157.
19. Sheffield and Bourne, *Douglas Haig: War Diaries and Letters 1914–1918*, p. 230.
20. LHCMA, Robertson Mss, I/14/90, 17 .9.16.
21. Idem, p. 231.
22. Quoted in Lyn Macdonald, *The Somme*, (Papermac, London, 1985 edn), p. 275.
23. Macdonald, *The Somme*, p. 277.
24. William Philpott, *Bloody Victory: The Sacrifice of the Somme*, (Abacus, London, 2010 edn), p. 369.
25. Quoted in John Terraine, *The Smoke and the Fire*, p. 149.
26. TNA, CAB 23/2, War Cabinet No. 102.
27. *The Military Correspondence of Field Marshal Sir William Robertson*, ed. David R. Woodward. (Army Records Society, Vol. 5, Bodley Head, London, 1989), p. 101.
28. See John Terraine, *The Smoke and the Fire*, pp. 152–3.
29. See Winston S. Churchill, *The World Crisis 1916–1918*, Part I, p. 312.
30. P.H. Arscott, 'Gunfight at St Julien', in *Stand To!*, Spring 1993, No. 37, p. 22. The Western Front Association.
31. Major J.A. Coughlan, 'Cambrai Day-A Memoir' in *Stand To!*, Winter 1987, No. 21, p. 16.
32. Quoted in Jon E. Lewis, *The First World War*, p. 362.
33. Major General J.F.C. Fuller, *The Conduct of War 1789–1961*, (Eyre and Spottiswoode, London, 1961), p. 176.
34. See Richard Holmes, *The Western Front*, p. 201.
35. Quoted in Jon E. Lewi (ed.) *The First World War*, p. 404.
36. David Stevenson, *With Our Backs to the Wall: Victory and Defeat in 1918*, (Allen Lane, Penguin Books, London, 2011), p. 217.
37. Idem, p. 218.
38. *Stand To!*, April 2003, No. 67, p. 30. The Western Front Association.
39. See I.W.F. Beckett, *The Great War 1914–1918*, pp. 176–8.

40. Quoted from a XV Corps report in David Fletcher, *Tanks and Trenches*, Sutton Publishing, Stroud, 1998, p. 17.
41. See Robin Prior and Trevor Wilson, *Passchendaele: The Untold Story*, (Yale, 2002 edn), p. 106.
42. Quoted in Glanfield, *Devil's Chariots*, p. 253.
43. Miles and Edmonds, *Military Operations France and Belgium 1916*, Vol. II. p. 245.
44. Miles and Edmonds, *Military Operations France and Belgium 1916*, Vol. II, pp. 245–9.
45. Quoted in J.P. Harris, *Douglas Haig and the First World War*, (CUP Cambridge, 2008), p. 261.
46. Simon Robbins, *British Generalship on the Western Front 1914–18*, p. 113.
47. Idem, p. 112.
48. Miles and Edmonds, *Military Operations France and Belgium 1916*, Vol. II, p. 367.
49. *Military Correspondence of FM Sir William Robertson*, p. 83.
50. Idem, p. 223.
51. Idem, p. 255.
52. Quoted in Bidwell and Graham, *Fire-Power*, (Pen & Sword Military Classics, Barnsley, 2004 edn), p. 130.
53. TNA, WO 95/168, SS1226/14.
54. Beckett, *The Great War 1914–1918*, p. 177.
55. See Stevenson, *With Our Backs to the Wall*, pp. 212–13.
56. Quoted on Miles and Edmonds, *Military Operations in France and Belgium 1916* Vol. II, p. 366, ft 4.

**Chapter 5**

1. General Sir William Robertson to Field Marshal Sir Douglas Haig, 15 September 1917, *The Military Correspondence of Field Marshal Sir William Robertson December 1915–February 1918*, p. 223.
2. *Statistics of the Military Effort of the British Empire during the Great War 1914–1920*, The Naval and Military Press, London, 1999, pp. 158–60, 162.
3. Sir Martin Farndale, *History of the Royal Regiment of Artillery. Western Front 1914–18*, Henry Ling Ltd, Dorchester, 1986, p. 341.
4. John Terraine, *The Smoke and the Fire: Myths and Anti-Myths of War, 1861–1945*, p. 127.
5. See Ian V. Hogg, *The Guns 1914–18*, The Pan/Ballantyne Illustrated History of the First World war, Book No. 5, London, 1971, pp. 32–47.
6. The Krupp 42cm howitzer was known as 'Dicke Bertha' (Big Bertha) after the wife of the manufacturer, Gustav Krupp. The heavy Skodas were 'Schlenke Emmas' (Slim Emmas) simply because they were anything but slim.
7. French, *1914*, p. 358.
8. Hogg, *The Guns 1914–18*, p. 32.
9. BOH, 1915 Vol. I, p. 123
10. Robin Neilland, *The Death of Glory: The Western Front 1915*, John Murray, London, 2006, p. 80.
11. Richard Holmes, *The Western Front*, p. 60.
12. Quoted in Richard Holmes, *The Little Field Marshal*, p. 286.
13. BOH 1915 Vol. II, p. 41.
14. BOH1915 Vol. I, p. 28.
15. French, *1914*, p. 355.
16. Idem, p. 355.
17. In turn, Kitchener claimed that he had been told by Sir John French that there was adequate ammunition.
18. BOH 1915 Vol. II, p. 78.
19. French, *1914*, p. 357.
20. Richard Holmes, *The Western Front*, p. 63.
21. Lloyd George, *Memoirs Vol. I*, pp. 112–14.

22. Idem, Vol. I, p. 123.
23. Harold Nicolson, *King George V: His Life and Reign*, Constable & Co. Ltd, London, 1953, p. 261. Fn 1.
24. Lloyd George, *Memoirs* Vol. I, p. 115.
25. Idem, p. 82.
26. Idem, p. 155.
27. Idem, pp. 190–91.
28. Nicolson, *King George V*, pp. 261–62.
29. James Bishop, *A Social History of the First World War*, Illustrated London News, Angus and Robertson Co. Ltd, London, 1982, p. 80.
30. Paul Strong and Sanders Marble, *Artillery in the Great War*, Pen & Sword Military, Barnsley, 2013, p. 91.
31. Idem, p. 92.
32. Simkins, Jukes and Hickey, *The First World War, The War to End all Wars*, Osprey Publishing, Oxford, 2003, p. 109.
33. Terraine, *White Heat*, p. 214.
34. Quoted in Strong and Marble, *Artillery in the Great War*, p. 136.
35. TNA WO95/3066.
36. IWM, Lieutenant Colonel G. Christie-Miller, *The Second Bucks Battalion 1914–18*, p. 183.
37. A Report in the *North German Gazette*, 3 August 1916.
38. Strong and Marble, *Artillery in the Great War*, p. 86.
39. Terraine, *White Heat*, p. 216.
40. Beckett, *The Great War 1914–1918*, p. 176.
41. Gordon Corrigan, *Mud, Blood and Poppycock*, Cassell & Co., London, 2003, p. 173.
42. Haythornethwaite, *The World War One Source Book*, p. 90.
43. BOH 1915 Vol. I, p. 152.
44. Lloyd George, *Memoirs*, p. 164.
45. Simkins, Jukes and Hickey, *The First World War, The War to End All Wars*, p. 98.
46. Ian F.W. Beckett, *The Making of the First World War*, p. 83.
47. Lloyd George, *Memoirs*, p. 171.
48. Idem, p. 380.
49. See John Grigg, *Lloyd George: From Peace to War 1912–1916*, Harper Collins, London, 1991 edn, p. 258.
50. Beckett, *The Great War 1914–18*, p. 262.
51. Wilson, *The Myriad Faces of War*, p. 221.
52. Lloyd George, *Memoirs*, pp. 386–90.
53. Strong and Marble, *Artillery in the Great War*, p. 90.
54. Peter Simkins, 'The Four Armies 1914–1918', in *The Oxford History of the British Army*, eds David G. Chandler and Ian Beckett, OUP, 2003 edn, p. 249.
55. Winston S. Churchill, *The World Crisis 1916–1918*, Part II, p. 301.
56. See David Stevenson, *With Our Backs to The Wall, Victory and Defeat in 1918*, pp. 117–25.
57. Beckett, *The Great War 1914–1918*, pp. 257–8.
58. See Sheldon and Bidwell, *Fire Power*, pp. 71, 82, 104.
59. IWM Documents Dept No. 7197. I am indebted to Prof Andrew Rice for this reference.
60. Major General P.R.F. Bonnet, *A Short History of the Royal Regiment of Artillery*, Royal Artillery Historical Trust, 1994, p. 27.

**Chapter 6**

1. Baron Antoine Henri de Jomini, *The Art of War*, J.B. Lippincot, Philadelphia, 1862, pp. 69–71.
2. Captain C.C. Esson, *Battalion Drill Illustrated*, Harrison & Sons, London, 1915, p. 26: Captain Esson acknowledged that his comments are based on 'Infantry Training 1914' as practised at 'the School of Instruction, Chelsea Barracks, London.'

3. Adrian Gilbert, *The Challenge of Battle*, Osprey Publishing, Oxford, 2013, p. 60.
4. Journal of the Royal United Services Institute, Vol. 52, 1908, p. 331.
5. BOH, 1915 Vol. I, p. 26, Ft 3.
6. Adrian Gilbert, *The Challenge of Battle*, p. 248.
7. Michael Glover, *Warfare from Waterloo to Mons*, B.C.A., 1980, p. 248.
8. Quoted in Jon E. Lewis, *The First World War*, p. 32.
9. Adrian Gilbert, *The Challenge of Battle*, p. 218.
10. A. Laffargue, *Attack in Trench Warfare, Impressions and Reflections of a Company Commander*, Infantry Journal, Washington, The US Infantry Association, 1916.
11. Edward Spears, *Liaison 1914*, Cassell & Co., London, 2000 edn, p. 36.
12. BOH, 1915 Vol. I, Macmillan & Co. Ltd, London, 1927, p. 65.
13. Captain G.C. Wynne, *If Germany Attacks*, pp. 2–3.
14. David Stevenson, *Cataclysm*, Basic Books, New York, 2004, p. 147.
15. Herbert Salzbach, *With the German Guns. Four Years on the Western Front*, Leo Cooper, Barnsley, 1973, pp. 36–7.
16. Sheffield and Bourne, *Douglas Haig: War Diaries and Letters 1914–18*, p. 109, 10 March 1915.
17. See the letter from Colonel F.G. Robson in *Stand To!*, Winter 1991. No. 33, p. 34. The Western Front Association.
18. Captain Cyril Falls, 'Contacts With Troops: Commanders and Staffs in the First World War'. In *The Army Quarterly*, Vol. 88, 1964.
19. F. Davies and G. Maddocks, *Bloody Red Tabs*, Leo Cooper, London, 1995. The total number of dead and wounded is related to all theatres.
20. TNA WO 9158/18, 2 December 1915, General Staff Note on the Situation.
21. TNA WO 158/17, 15 June 1915.
22. TNA, WO 158/17, 'Memorandum on the Possibility of Undertaking Offensive Operations' 8 February 1915. Quoted in Paul Harris and Sanders Marble, 'The 'Step by Step' Approach: British Military Thought and Operational Method on the Western Front, 1915–1917, in *War in History*, 2008 15 (1), pp. 17–42.
23. *The Times*, 29 September 1915.
24. TNA WO 158/17, 19 June 1915.
25. Sheffield and Bourne, *Douglas Haig: War Diaries and Letters 1914–18*, p. 107.
26. Idem, p. 114–15.
27. Idem, p. 144.
28. Idem, p. 229.
29. Idem, p. 108.
30. William Philpott, *Bloody Victory*, particularly Ch. V, pp. 172–208.
31. Quoted in Jon E. Lewis, *The First World War*, p. 222.
32. Tony Ball, 'Over the Top: British Infantry Battle Tactics on the First Day of the Somme – 1 July 1916', in *Stand To!*, No. 103, May 2015, pp. 23–32. The Western Front Association.
33. Wilson, *The Myriad Faces of War*, p. 325.
34. BOH, 1916, Vol. II, p. 572.
35. Sir Douglas Haig's Final Despatch, *London Gazette*, 8 April 1919.
36. BOH 1915, Vol. I, p. 358, Note I.
37. TNA WO 95/590.
38. BOH 1915, Vol. I, pp. 32–3.
39. BOH 1915, Vol. I, pp. 32–3.
40. TNA WO 95/195 OAM French to Army Commanders, 28 October 1915.
41. Duff Cooper, *Haig*, 2 Vols, Faber and Faber, London, Vol. I, p. 298.
42. TNA WO 95/161 OA 336. Kiggell to First Army.
43. TNA WO 95/161.
44. BOH 1916 Vol. II, p. 544, footnote I.
45. TNA WO 95/881.
46. TNA WO 95/164.
47. TNA WO 95/168.

48. Laurence Hopkinson, *Stand To!*, No. 102, January 2015, p. 3. The Western Front Association.
49. TNA WO 95/3065. 184th Brigade War Diary.
50. See Trevor Yorke, *The Trench*, Countryside Books, Newbury, 2014.
51. Jon E. Lewis, *The First World War*, p. 189.
52. Tony Ashworth, *Trench Warfare 1914–1918: The Live and Let Live System*, Pan Books, London, 2000, p. 57.
53. See John Ellis, *Eye-Deep in Hell*, Croom Helm Ltd, London, 1976, pp. 69–70 and T. Ashcroft, *Trench Warfare 1914–1918: The Live and Let Live System*. Also, Bill Harriman, 'Snipers and Sporting guns in the First World War', *Shooting*, March 2014, pp. 35–37.
54. Philip Stevens, *The Great War Explained*, Pen & Sword, Barnsley, 2014, p. 190.
55. Lieutenant Colonel C. Headlam, *The Guards Division in the Great War*, J. Murray, London, 1924, p. 106.
56. A.F. Barnes, *The Story of the 2/5th Gloucester Regiment 1914–18*, The Crypt House Press, Gloucester, 1930, p. 40.
57. James Roberts, 'Making the Butterflies Kill', in *Stand To!*, No. 68, September 2003, pp. 38–44. The Western Front Association.
58. Einar Eklof, 'My War Memoirs', in *Stand To!*, No. 20, August 1987, p. 28. The Western Front Association.
59. Michael Senior, *Haking: A Dutiful Soldier*, Pen & Sword Books, Barnsley, 2012, p. 254.
60. For example, Mark Connelly, *Steady the Buffs!*, OUP, Oxford, 2006, pp. 77–92.
61. Kirke Committee, Report on *Lessons of the Great War*, War Office, London, 1932, p. 23.
62. See William Philpott, *Bloody Victory*, p. 152.
63. FM von Hindenburg, *The Great War*, ed. Charles Messinger, Greenhill Books, London, 2006, pp. 140–1.
64. BOH 1917 Vol. II, p. 144.
65. See Ian Passingham, *All the Kaiser's Men*, Sutton Publishing, Stroud, 2003, pp. 138–144.
66. For a full discussion of the BEF defence tactics see Captain G.C. Wynne, *If Germany Attacks*. Also, Travers, *How the War was Won*, pp. 50–65 and Ian Beckett, 'Gough Malcolm and Command on the Western Front' in Brian Bond ed., *Look to Your Front*, Spellmount, Stroud, 1999, pp. 1–12.
67. TNA WO 95/881 RHS 726.
68. Ian Beckett, 'Gough, Malcolm and Command on the Western Front', p. 9.
69. TNA CAB 45/123 F 21 August 1931.
70. TNA CAB 45/123 F 25 August 1931.
71. BOH 1917 Vol. II, pp. 294–5.
72. SS143, February 1917. Issued by the General Staff.
73. Griffith, *Battle Tactics of the Western Front*, pp. 75–9.
74. But see A.J.P. Taylor, *The First World War*, Penguin Books, Harmondsworth, 1996 edn, p. 34.

**Chapter 7**

1. John Lewis (ed.), *The First World War*, p. 389.
2. Georg Bucher, *In The Line 1914–1918*, Jonathan Cape, London, 1932, p. 203.
3. Quoted in John Terraine, 'The U-Boat Wars, 1916-1945', in *Stand To!* Spring 1990, No. 28, p. 7. The Western Front Association.
4. Compared to 55 in the Royal Navy and 77 in the French navy. Germany was late in developing this relatively new weapon of war.
5. Gerd Hardach, *The First World War 1914–1918*, Allen Lane, London, 1977 translation, p. 39.
6. G.M. Trevelyan, *Grey of Fallodon*, Longmans, London, 1937, p 321.
7. Winston S. Churchill, *The World Crisis 1916–1918*, Part II, p. 351.
8. Idem, p. 218.
9. Idem, p. 218.
10. Martin Gilbert, *First World War*, Weidenfeld & Nicolson, London, 1994, p. 237.
11. Wilson, *The Myriad Faces of War*, p. 304.
12. FM von Hindenburg, *The Great War*, p. 138.

13. Winston S. Churchill, *The World Crisis 1914–1918*, Part II, p. 221.
14. Hardach, *The First World War 1914–1918*, p. 39.
15. B.H. Liddell Hart, *History of the First World War*, Cassell & Co., London, 1979, p. 401.
16. *The Military Correspondence of Field Marshal Sir William Robertson*, p. 177.
17. Marc Fero, *The Great War*, Routledge, London, 2002, p. 121.
18. Winson S. Churchill, *The World Crisis*, Part II, p. 230.
19. Alan Palmer, *Victory 1918*, Weidenfeld & Nicolson, London, 1998, p. 92.
20. C.R.M.F. Cruttwell, *A History of the Great War 1914–1918*, Clarendon Press, Oxford, 1934, p. 199.
21. Alan Palmer, *Victory 1918*, pp. 93–4.
22. J.M. Roberts. *The Twentieth Century*, Allen Lane, Penguin Books, London, 1999, p. 255.
23. Hardach, *The First World War*, p. 98.
24. Gary Sheffield, *Forgotten Victory*, Review edn, London, 2002, p. 55.
25. Hardach, p. 137.
26. Quoted in Andrew Roberts, *A History of the English Speaking Peoples Since 1900*, Weidenfeld & Nicolson, London, 2006, p. 90.
27. Quoted in Wilson, *The Myriad Faces of War*, p. 92.
28. For a full account see Barbara Tuchman, *The Zimmerman Telegram*, Papermac, London, 1981.
29. I.F.W. Beckett, *The Making of the First World War*, Yale UniversityPress, New Haven, 2012, p. 365.
30. Russia used the Julian calendar which was thirteen days behind the Gregorian calendar used in the West. The Julian calendar is here used for dates in February and March 1917 and the Gregorian calendar is used thereafter.
31. Quoted in J. Winter and B. Baggett, *1914–18: The Great War and the Shaping of the 20th Century*, BBC Books, London, 1996, p. 259.
32. Lloyd George, *War Memoirs*, Vol. I, pp. 969–70.
33. Idem, p. 395.
34. Hew Strachan, *The First World War*, p. 261.
35. John Terraine, *The Great War*, Wordsworth Editions, London, 1998, p. 369.
36. Sir William Robertson, *The Military Correspondence*, p. 223.
37. John Terraine, *To Win A War*, p. 37.
38. FM von Hindeburg.*The Great War*, p. 170
39. Idem, pp. 163–4.
40. John Terraine, *To Win A War*, pp. 20–6.
41. On the background to the fighting in 1918 see: Martin Kitchen, *The German Offensives of 1918*, Tempus, Stroud, 2001; Gregory Blaxland, *Amiens 1918*, W.H. Allen & Co. Ltd, London, 1981; John Terraine, *To Win A War*, Papermac, London, 1986; J.H. Johnson, *The Unexpected Victory*, Arms and Armour, London, 1997; Chris Barker, *The Battle for Flanders*, Pen & Sword Military, Barnsley, 2011; Barry Pitt, *1918 The Last Act*, Cassell & Co. Ltd, London, 1962; Alan Palmer, *Victory 1918*, Weidenfeld & Nicolson, London, 1998; David Stevenson, *With Our Backs to The Wall, Victory and Defeat in 1918*, Allan Lane, London, 2011; Nick Lloyd, *Hundred Days: The End of the Great War*, Penguin Books, 2014.
42. John Terraine, *To Win A War*, p. 65.
43. Brigadier General John Charteris, *Field Marshal Earl Haig*, Cassell & Co., London, 1929, p. 333. Interestingly, Haig does not record this Order in his Diary.
44. Alan Palmer, *Victory 1918*, p. 198.
45. Sheffield and Bourne, *Douglas Haig: War Diaries and Letters 1914–1918*, p. 440.
46. John Terraine, *The Great War*, p. 354.
47. Correlli Barnett, *The Great War*, Penguin Books, Harmondsworth, 2000 edn, p. 162.
48. Sheffield and Bourne, *Douglas Haig, War Diaries and Letters*, p. 370.
49. Niall Ferguson, *The Pity of War*, p. 313.
50. Idem, p. 434.
51. Winston S. Churchill, *The World Crisis*, Pt II, p. 484.
52. Sheffield and Bourne, *Douglas Haig, Diaries and Letters*, p. 469.

53. Idem, p. 489.
54. Niall Ferguson, *The Pity of War*, p. 313.
55. Winston S. Churchill, *The World Crisis*, Pt II, p. 496.
56. Quoted in Cyril Falls, *Marshal Foch*, Blackie & Son, London, 1939, p. 153.
57. Foch to Allied commanders in chief, 30 August 1918. *BOH France and Belgium 1918*, Vol. III, p. 588.
58. Jonathan Boff, *Winning and Losing on the Western Front*, p. 50.
59. Idem, pp. 24–34.
60. TNA, WO 95/522, S.G. 436/23.
61. Sheffield and Bourne, *Douglas Haig: Diaries and Letters*, p. 447.
62. Quoted in *Voices and Images of the Great War*, Lyn MacDonald (ed.), Michael Joseph Ltd, London, 1988, p. 304.
63. Sheffield and Bourne, *Douglas Haig: Diaries and Letters*, p. 486.
64. Idem, p. 488.
65. John Terraine, *To Win A War*, p. 258.
66. FM von Hindenburg, *The Great War*, p. 178.
67. Quoted in Ian Passingham, *All the Kaiser's Men*, p. 209.
68. Ernst Jünger, *The Storm of Steel*, Constable & Co. Ltd, London, 1994 edn, pp. 267–68.
69. Idem, p. 301.
70. Richard Baumgartner, 'A Bavarian Returns', in *Stand To!*, Winter 1982, No. 6, p. 5. The Western Front Association.
71. Sheffield and Bourne, *Douglas Haig: War Diaries and Letters 1914–1918*, p. 446.
72. Quoted in Gary Sheffield, *Forgotten Victory*, pp. 235–6.
73. See I.W.F. Beckett, *The Great War*, p. 208; John Terraine, *The Smoke and the Fire*, p. 275.
74. John Terraine, *To Win A War*, p. 133.
75. Sheffield and Bourne, *Douglas Haig: War Diaries and Letters 1914–1918*, p. 475.
76. Idem.

**Conclusion**

1. Winston S. Churchill, *The World Crisis 1916–1918*, Part II, p. 541.
2. Niall Ferguson, *The Pity of War*, p. 299.
3. See Paul Harris and Sanders Marble, 'The 'Step by Step' Approach: British Military Thought and Operational Method on the Western Front, 1915–1917', *War in History*, 2008 15 (1), pp. 17–42.
4. See Jonathan Boff, *Winning and Losing on the Western Front: The British Third Army and the Defeat of Germany in 1918*, CUP, Cambridge, 2012, p. 245.
5. Quoted by Simon Jones, 'Gas Warfare', in *Stand To!*, Summer 1985, No. 14, p. 15. The Western Front Association.
6. TNA, WO 95/160, 7 November 1915.
7. TNA, WO 158/17, 15 March 1915.
8. IWM, CDS 58, December 1915.
9. IWM, *Field Service Regulations*, Pt I, 1909 (1914 reprint).
10. IWM, SS 24, Object and Conditions of Combined Offensive Action, London, HMSO, June 1915.
11. Martin Gilbert, *The First World War*, p. 439.
12. I am indebted to Prof Andrew Rice and Dr Emily Mayhew for their contribution.
13. See John Terraine, *The Great War*, p. x.
14. See Niall Ferguson, *The Pity of War*, pp. 294–301.
15. Quoted in Jonathan Boff, *Winning and Losing on the Western Front*, p. 51.
16. Quoted in Ian Passingham, *All the Kaiser's Men*, p. 238.
17. Hindenburg, *The Great War*, p. 188.
18. Ian Beckett, *The Great War*, p. 387.
19. *Statistics of the Military Effort of the British Empire During the Great War*, p. 632.
20. See Martin Gilbert, *The First World War*, p. 499.

21. However, B.H. Liddell Hart claims that, of all the causes of the Allied victory 'the blockade ranks first …'. B.H. Liddell Hart, *History of the First World War*, Cassell, London, 1979 edn, p. 592.
22. Niall Ferguson, *The Pity of War*, p. 276.
23. Jonathan Boff, *Winning and Losing on the Western Front*, p. 36.
24. TNA, WO 95/884, S.S. No. 24/7.
25. TNA, WO 95/884 V.S. 6/11.
26. TNA, WO 95/884 G.S. 68/22.
27. John Terraine, *The Smoke and the Fire*, p. 46.
28. Ernst Junger, *The Storm of Steel*, Constable, London, 1994 edn, p. 283.
29. BOH 1918, Vol. III, p. 196.
30. Hindenburg, pp. 202 and 217.
31. Jon E. Lewis, (ed.), *The First World War*, p. 424.
32. Jonathan Boff, *Winning and Losing on the Western Front*, p. 23.
33. See Michael Senior, 'Learning Curves and Opportunity Curves on the Western Front', in *Stand To!*, No. 93, pp. 11–14. The Western Front Association.
34. Hindenburg, *The Great War*, p. 132.
35. Robin Prior and Trevor Wilson, *The First World War*, Cassell & Co., London, 2000, p. 182.
36. Jon E. Lewis (ed.), *A Brief History of the First World War: Eyewitness Accounts of the War to End All Wars, 1914–18*, Robinson, London, 2014, p. 497.

# Bibliography


**Unpublished Primary Sources**

Butcher P.E. *Skill and Devotion*
CAB, MUN, SS and WO Series
Captain C.A. Brown Papers
Captain F.C. Ransley Papers
Centre for Buckinghamshire Studies:
Illingworth and Robson, *History of No. 24 Squadron*
Imperial War Museum:
LHCMA:
Lieutenant C.A. Box Papers
Lieutenant C.E. Young Papers
Lieutenant Colonel G. Christie-Miller, Typescript. *The Second Bucks Battalion 1914–1918*
Lieutenant H.G. Holman Papers
Lieutenant Y.E.S. Kirkpatrick Papers
Lieutenant A.J. Robinson Papers
Notebook of H.C. Potter
Robertson Manuscripts
Royal Military Academy, Sandhurst:
The National Archives, Kew:
Ward Jackson C.H. and Leighton Lucas, *The Airman's Song Book*

**Published Primary Sources**

An Adjutant of Militia, *British Infantry Tactics and the Attack Formation* (Mitchel and Co., Charing Cross, 1880).
Barton, Peter, *Report on Fromelles* for Australian Army History Unit, 2007.
*Bucks Herals*
Dictionary of National Biography
Edmonds, Brig Gen Sir James, *History of the Great War: Military Operations France and Belgium 1914–1918*, XIV Vols (IWM and the Battery Press, Nashvilee, 1995 edn).
Esson, Captain C.C., *Battalion Drill Illustrated* (Harrison & Sons, London, 1915).
General Staff, War Office, *Field Service Regulations* and SS Publications.
Haking, Brigadier General RCB, *Company Training* (Hugh Rees Ltd, London, 1913).
Hamilton. Gen Sir Ian, *A Staff Officer's Scrapbook*, Vols 1 and 2 (Edward Arnold, London, 1907).
Jones H.A. Raleigh, Sir Walter, *The War in the Air*, 6 Vols (Clarendon Press, Oxford, 1922).
Keegan, J. and Wheatcroft, A., *Who's Who in History* (Routledge, London, 2007 edn).
Kirke Committee Report on *Lessons of the Great War* (War Office, London, 1932).
Lewis, Jon E. (ed.), *War Diaries and Letters* (Robinson Publishing, London, 1998).
Sheffield, Gary and Bourne, John, *Douglas Haig: War Diaries and Letters 1914–1918* (Weidenfeld & Nicolson, London, 2008).
Soames, Mary (ed.), *Speaking for Themselves: Letters Between Clementine and Winston Churchill* (Black Swan Books, London, 1999).
—— *Statistics of the Military Effort of the British Empire During the Great War 1914–1920*
(The Naval and Military Press, London, 1999 edn).
*The Daily Telegraph*
*The Times*

**Published Secondary Sources**

***Memoirs and Biographies***

Charteris, Brigadier General John, *Field Marshal Earl Haig* (Cassell, London, 1929).

Churchill, Winston S., *The World Crisis 1916–1918*, Parts I and II (Thornton Butterworth, London, 1927).

Duff Cooper, *Haig*, 2 Vols (Faber and Faber, London,1935).

Falls, Cyril, *Marshal Foch* (Blackie & Son, London, 1939).

French, FM Sir John, *1914* (Constable & Co., London, 1919).

—— *Complete Despatches 1914–1916* (Naval and Military Press, London, 2001 edn).

Graves, Robert, *Goodbye to All That* (Penguin Books, Harmondsworth, 1960 edn).

Jeffery, Keith (ed.), *Military Correspondence of Sir Henry Wilson 1918–1922* (Army Records Society, Bodley Head, 1985).

Jünger, Ernst, *The Storm of Steel* (Constable and Co. Ltd, London, 1994 edn).

Lloyd George, *War Memoirs*, Vols I and II (Odhams Press, London, 1936).

—— *The Memoirs of General Joffre* (Geoffrey Bles, London, 1932).

Messenger, Charles (ed.), *FM von Hindenberg, The Great War* (Greenhill Books, London, 2006).

Scott, Douglas (ed.), *Douglas Haig: The Preparatory Prologue Diaries & Letters 1861–1914* (Pen & Sword Military, Barnsley, 2006).

Terraine, John (ed.), *General Jack's Diary* (Cassell Military Paperbacks, London, 2000).

Trevelyan, G.M. *Grey of Fallodon* (Longmans, London, 1937).

Woodward, David R. (ed.), *The Military Correspondence of FM Sir William Robertson* (Army Records Society, Bodley Head Ltd, London, 1989).

***Monographs***

Adams, R.J.Q., *Arms and the Wizard: Lloyd George and the Ministry of Munitions 1915–16* (Cassell, London, 1978).

Ashworth, Tony, *Trench Warfare 1914–1918: The Live and Let Live System* (Pan Books, London, 2000).

Baring, Maurice, *Flying Corps Headquarters 1914–1918* (Buchan and Enright, London, 1985).

Barker, Chris, *The Battle for Flanders* (Pen & Sword Books, Barnsley, 2011).

Barnes, A.F., *The Story of the 2/5 Gloucester, 1914–1918* (The Crypt House Press, Gloucester, 1930).

Barnett, Correlli, *The Great War* (Penguin Books, Harmondsworth, 2000 edn).

Beckett, Ian F.W., *The Great War 1914–1918* (Longmans, Harlow, 2001).

—— *The Making of the First World War* (Yale University Press, New Haven, 2012).

Beckett, Ian F.W. and Corvi, Steven J., *Haig's Generals* (Pen & Sword Military Books, Barnsley, 2005).

Bet-El, Ilana R., *Conscripts: The Lost Legions of the Great War* (Sutton Publishing, Stroud, 1999).

Bergonzi, Bernard, *Heroes' Twilight* (Macmillan Press, London, 1980).

Bernhardi, Gen. F. von, *On War Today*, Vols 1 and 2, (London, 1912).

Bidwell and Graham, *Fire-Power: The British Army Weapons & Theories of War 1904–1945* (Pen & Sword Military Classics, Barnsley, 2004 edn).

Bishop, James, *A Social History of the First World War* (Illustrated London News, Angus and Robertson Co. Ltd, London, 1982).

Blaxland, Gregory, *Amiens 1918* (WH Allen, London, 1981).

Boff, Jonathan, *Winning and Losing on the Western Front: The British Third Army and the Defeat of Germany in 1918* (CUP, Cambridge, 2014 edn).

Bond, Brian, (ed.), *The First World War and Military History* (Clarendon Press, Oxford, 1991).

Bond, Brian and Cave, Nigel, (eds), *Haig: A Re-Appraisal 80 Years On* (Pen & Sword, Barnsley, 2009 edn).

Bruce, J.M., *The Aeroplanes of the Royal Flying Corps* (Macdonald & Co., London, 1970).

Bucher, George, *In The Line: 1914–1918* (Jonathan Cape, London, 1932).

Campbell, Colin, *Aces and Aircraft of World War I* (Treasure Press, London, 1984).

Carver, FM Lord, *Britain's Army in the Twentieth Century* (Pan Books/IWM, London, 2004).
Clark, Alan, *The Donkeys* (Pimlico edn, London, 1993).
Connelly, Mark, *Steady the Buffs!* (OUP, Oxford, 2006).
Cooper, Stephen, *The Final Whistle* (Spellmount, Stroud, 2013).
Corrigan Gordon, *Mud, Blood and Poppycock* (Cassell, London, 2003).
Cruttwell, C.R.M.F., *A History of the Great War 1914–1918* (Clarendon Press, Oxford, 1934).
Davies, F. and Maddocks, G., *Bloody Red Tabs* (Leo Cooper, Barnsley, 1995).
Ellis, John, *Eye-Deep in Hell: Life in the Trenches 1914–1918* (Croom Helm Ltd, London, 1976).
Farndale, Sir Martin, *History of the Royal Regiment of Artillery: Western Front 1914–18* (Henry Ling Ltd, Dorchester, 1986).
Ferguson, Neill, *The Pity of War* (Penguin Books, Harmondsworth, 1998).
Fero, Marc, *The Great War* (Routledge, London, 2002).
Fletcher, David, *Tanks and Trenches* (Sutton Publishing, Stroud, 1998).
Fuller, Major General J.F.C., *The Conduct of War 1789–1961* (Eyre and Spottiswoode, London, 1961).
Gilbert, Adrian, *The Challenge of Battle* (Osprey Publishing, Oxford, 2013).
Gilbert, Martin, *The First World War* (Weidenfeld & Nicolson, London, 1994).
Glanfield, John, *Devil's Chariots* (Sutton Publishing, Stroud, 2001).
Glover, Michael, *Warfare from Waterloo to Mons* (BCA, London, 1980).
Griffith, Paddy, *Battle Tactics on the Western Front: The British Army's Art of Attack 1916–1918* (Yale University Press, New Haven, 1994).
—— *Forward To Battle: Fighting Tactics from Waterloo to the Near Future* (Anthony Bird Publications, Chichester, 1981).
Grigg, John, *Lloyd George: From Peace to War 1912–1916* (Harper Collins, London, 1991 edn).
Harris, J.P., *Men, Ideas and Tanks: British Military Thought and Armoured Forces 1903–1939* (Manchester University Press, Manchester, 1995).
Hardach, Gerd, *The First World War 1914–1918* (Allen Lane, London, 1977 translation).
Haythornthwaite, Philip J., *The World War One Source Book* (Arms and Armour, London, 1992).
Headlam, Lieutenant Colonel C., *The Guards Division in the Great War*, 2 Vols, (John Murray, London, 1924).
Henderson, Col G.F.R., *The Science of War* (Longmans, Green & Co., London, 1908).
Hogg, Ian V., *The Guns 1914–18* (Pan/Ballantyne Illustrated History of the First World War, London, 1971).
Holmes, Richard, *The Western Front* (BBC Books, London, 1999),
—— *The Little Field Marshal* (Cassell, London, 2005 edn).
Johnson, J.H., *The Unexpected Victory* (Arms and Armour, London, 1997).
Jomini, Baron Antoine-Henri de, *The Art of War* (JB Lippincot, Philadelphia, 1862).
Kitchen, Martin, *The German Offensives of 1918* (Tempus, Stroud, 2001).
Kloot, William van der, *World War One Fact Book* (Amberley Publishing, Stroud, 2010).
Laffin, John, *British Butchers and Bunglers of World War One* (Alan Sutton, Stroud, 1992).
Lewis, Bruce, *A Few of the First* (Pen & Sword Books, Barnsley, 1996).
Lewis, Cecil, *Sagittarius Rising* (Penguin Books, Harmondsworth, 1983).
Liddell Hart, B.H., *History of the First World War* (Cassell, London, 1979 edn).
Lloyd, Nick, *Hundred Days: The End of the Great War* (Penguin Books, London, 2014).
MacDonald, Lyn, *Somme* (Papermac, London, 1985 edn).
—— *1914–1918: Voices and Images of the Great War* (Michael Joseph Ltd, London, 1988).
Mackersey, Ian, *No Empty Chairs* (Hachette, London, 2012).
Magnus, Philip, *Kitchener: Portrait of an Imperialist* (Penguin Books, Harmondsworth, 1968 edn).
Messenger, Charles, *Call to Arms: The British Army 1914–18* (Cassell, London, 2005).
Middlebrook, Martin, *Your Country Needs You* (Pen & Sword Books, Barnsley, 2000).
—— *The First Day of the Somme* (Penguin Books, Harmondsworth, 1971).
Mr Punch's *History of the Great War* (Cassell and Co. Ltd, London, 1919).
Neillands, Robin, *The Old Contemptibles* (John Murray, London, 2004).

—— *The Great War Generals on the Western Front* (Robinson, London, 1999).
—— *The Death of Glory: The Western Front 1915* (John Murray, London, 2006).
Nicolson, Harold, *King George V: His Life and Reign* (Constable, London, 1953).
Palmer, Alan, *Victory 1918* (Weidenfeld & Nicolson, London, 1998).
Parker, Peter, *The Old Lie* (Constable, London, 1987).
Passingham, Ian, *All the Kaiser's Men* (Sutton Publishing, Stroud, 2003).
Philpot, William, *Bloody Victory: Sacrifice on the Somme* (Abacus, London, 2010).
Prior, Robin and Wilson, Trevor, *Passchendaele. The Untold Story* (Yale, 2002 edn).
—— *The First World War* (Cassell, London, 2000).
Robbins, Simon, *British Generalship on the Western Front 1914–1918* (Routledge, London, 2005).
Roberts, Andrew, *A History of the English Speaking Peoples Since 1900* (Weidenfeld & Nicolson, London, 2006).
Roberts, J.M., *The Twentieth Century* (Allen Lane, London, 1999).
Rogers, H.C.B., *Artillery Through the Ages* (Seely Service & Co., London, 1971).
Salzbach, Herbert, *With the German Guns: Four Years on the Western Front* (Leo Cooper, Barnsley, 1973).
Seldon, Anthony and Walsh, David, *Public Schools and the Great War* (Pen & Sword Military, Barnsley, 2013).
Sellwood, A.V., *The Saturday Night Soldiers* (Woolfe Publishing, London, 1966).
Senior, Michael, *Fromelles 1916* (Pen & Sword Books, Barnsley, 2011).
—— *Haking: A Dutiful Soldier* (Pen & Sword Books, Barnsley, 2012).
Sheffield, Gary, *Forgotten Victory: The First World War, Myths and Realities* (Headline Books, London, 2001).
Simkins, Jukes and Hickey, *The First World War: The War to End All Wars* (Osprey Publishing, Oxford, 2003).
Spears, Edward, *Liaison 1914* (Cassell, London, 2000 edn).
Steel, Nigel and Hart, Peter, *Tumult in the Clouds* (Hodder and Stroughton, London, 1997).
Stevens, Philip, *The Great War Explained* (Pen & Sword Books, Barnsley, 2014).
Stevenson, David, *With Our Backs to The Wall: Victory and Defeat in 1918* (Allen Lane, London, 2011).
—— *Cataclysm: The First World War as Political Tragedy* (Basic Books, New York, 2004).
Strachan, Hew, *The First World War* (Simon & Schuster, London, 2003).
Strong, Paul and Marble, Sanders, *Artillery in the Great War* (Pen & Sword Books, Barnsley, 2013).
Terraine, John, *White Heat: The New Warfare 1914–18* (BCA, London, 1982).
—— *The Smoke and the Fire: Myths and Anti-Myths of War 1861–1945* (BCA, London, 1981 edn).
—— *Douglas Haig: The Educated Soldier* (Leo Cooper, London, 1990).
—— *The First World War* (Wordsworth Editions, London, 1998).
—— *To Win a War: 1918, The Year of Victory* (Papermac, London, 1986).
Thompson, Sir Peter, *The Royal Flying Corps* (Hamish Hamilton, London, 1968).
Travers, Tim, *The Killing Ground* (Pen & Sword Military Classics, Barnsley, 2003).
—— *How the War Was Won* (Routledge, London, 1994).
Tuchman, Barbara, *The Zimmerman Telegram* (Papermac, London, 1981).
Watkis, N.C., *The Western Front from the Air* (Wrens Park Publishing, Stroud, 2000).
Westlake, Ray, *Kitchener's Army* (Spellmount, Stroud, 1989).
Wilkinson, Roni, *Pals on the Somme* (Pen & Sword Books, Barnsley, 2008 edn).
Wilson, Trevor, *The Myriad Faces of War* (Polity Press, Cambridge, 1986).
Winter, Denis, *The First of the Few* (Penguin Books, Harmondsworth, 1983).
Winter, J. and Baggett, B., *1914–18: The Great War and the Shaping of the 20th Century* (BBC Books, London, 1996).
Woodward, Sir Edward Llewellyn, *Great Britain and the War of 1914–1918* (Methuen, London, 1967).

Wynne, Captain G.C., *If Germany Attacks* (Tom Donovan, Brighton, 2008).
Yorke, Trevor, *The Trench* (Countryside Books, Newbury, 2014).

*Articles*

Ashcroft, Michael, 'Inside the First World War' in *The Telegraph*, 2015.
Beckett, Ian, 'Gough, Malcolm and Command on the Western Front' in Bond, Brian (ed.), *Look To Your Front* (Spellmount, Stroud, 1999).
Howard, Michael, 'Men Against Fire: The Doctrine of the Offensive 1914' in Paret, Peter (ed.), *Makers of Modern Strategy* (Clarendon Press, Oxford, 1986).
Jordan, David, 'The Battle for the Skies. Sir Hugh Trenchard as a Commander of the Royal Flying Corps' in Hughes and Seligman, *Leadership in Conflict 1914–1918* (Pen & Sword Books, Barnsley, 2000).
Simkins, Peter, 'The Four Armies' in the *Oxford History of the British Army*, D.G. Chandler and Ian Beckett (eds) (OUP, Oxford, 2003 edn).

*Journals*

Arscott, P.H., 'Gunfight at St Julian' in *Stand To!*, No. 37, 1993, The Western Front Association.
Baumgartner, Richard, 'A Bavarian Returns' in *Stand To!*, No. 6, 1982, The Western Front Association.
Beard, Joe 'One Man's War', in *Stand To!*, No. 34, 1992, The Western Front Association.
Coughlan, Major J.A., 'Cambrai Day – A Memoir' in *Stand To!*, No. 21, 1987, The Western Front Association.
Einar Eklof, 'My War Memoirs' in *Stand To!*, No. 20, 1987, The Western Front Association.
Fellows, Harry, '1914 The Memoirs of a Volunteer', in *Stand To!*, No. 10, 1984, The Western Front Association.
Harriman, Bill, 'Snipers and Shooting Guns in the First World War' in *Shooting*, March 2014.
Harris, Paul and Marble Sanders, 'The Step by Step Approach: Military Thought and Operational Method on the Western Front, 1915–1917' in *War in History*, 2008, 15(1).
Jefford, J., 'Corps Reconnaissance' in the *RAF Historical Journal* 54, 2013.
Jones, Simon, 'Gas Warfare' in *Stand To!*, No. 14, 1985, The Western Front Association.
Lethbridge, J.P., 'Like Father, Like Son', in *Stand To!*, No. 68, 2003, The Western Front Association.
Mitchison, Bill, 'The Territorial Force on The Western Front in Early 1915', *Bulletin*, No. 102, 2015, The Western Front Association.
Robson, Colonel F.G., Letter in *Stand To!*, No. 33, 1991, The Western Front Association.
Radcliffe, Gen Sir Percy, 'With France' in *Stand To!*, No. 10, 1984, The Western Front Association.
Roberts, James, 'Making the Butterflie Kill' in *Stand To!*, No. 68, 2003, Western Front Association.
Robson, Colonel F.G., Letter in *Stand To!*, No. 33, 1991, The Western Front Association.
Senior, Michael, 'Learning Curves and Opportunity Curves' in *Stand To!*, No. 93, 2012, The Western Front Association.
Terraine, John, 'Understanding' in *Stand To!*, No. 34, 1992, The Western Front Association.
—— 'The U-Boat Wars 1916–1945' in *Stand To!*, No. 28, 1990, The Western Front Association.
—— 'World War One and The Royal Air Force' in *Royal Air Force Society Proceedings* 12, 1990.
Thomas, Len, Letter in *Stand To!*, No. 8, 1983, The Western Front Association.

# Index

**GENERAL INDEX**